Roy Cheville

The Graceland College Years

A Biography by

Malcolm L. Ritchie

1995

Roy Cheville
The Graceland College Years

A Biography by
Malcolm L. Ritchie
1995

Center for Christian Leadership
Graceland College
Lamoni, Iowa 50140

Copyright © 1995
Malcolm L. Ritchie
Dayton, Ohio

Printed in the United States of America

Ritchie, Malcolm
Roy Cheville: The Graceland College Years
Malcolm L. Ritchie
     p.   cm.

Published by
   Center for Christian Leadership
   Graceland College
   Lamoni, Iowa 50140

ISBN 0-9636457-1-4

Table of Contents

APPENDICES

List of Pictures

Preface

In this biography Malcolm Ritchie recounts a story that has long needed telling. One of those rare individuals who seems larger than life, Roy Cheville exerted a significant transforming influence on hundreds of individuals and on the institutions to which he devoted himself. Dr. Ritchie performs a very valuable service in refreshing our individual and institutional memories of the man in his prime. His account will also introduce Roy Cheville to those who did not know him.

The writing of biography is in its essence an impossible task. No human being can fully know another person, but the effort of discovering brings many rewards. Cheville's life and thought can instruct the reader in significant ways. Whether or not the reader knew him personally, we meet in these pages a person with highly developed gifts generously shared, and a person who displayed the defects of his qualities. Not only will the thoughtful reader gain a better understanding of an important era in the Reorganized Church of Jesus Christ of Latter Day Saints but may also achieve a greater degree of knowledge of self as he or she recognizes similar characteristics and resulting behavior.

Dr. Ritchie has chosen to let "Doc" speak for himself as often as possible. Rather than footnote each quotation as it occurs, references are identified by date. When no letter follows the date, only one publication appeared during that year. Single letters through 26 and double letters when more than 26 publications appeared during the year are listed sequencially. The dated references are spread across the first four Appendices—A for books, B for hymns, C for pamphlets, D for articles. The author also spoke with a number of people who knew the Chevilles personally. That this method of recovery of information will not end with this book, the Center for Christian Leadership invites readers to contribute memories of their own interaction with Roy Cheville during both the Graceland and the Patriarchal years. Send them to the Center for Christian Leadership, Graceland College, 700 College Avenue, Lamoni, Iowa 50140. The Center also looks forward to a companion volume describing Cheville as Presiding Patriarch.

Dr. Ritchie has spent nine years of intensive research in order to tell this story. The Center for Christian Leadership is honored to recommend this scholarly and thoughtful biography.

Barbara Higdon, Director

BOOK I.

Overview

BOOK I. OVERVIEW
Foreword

Biography presents a picture of a mind, a soul, a heart, of an environment; of successes and failures that make or seek to make, the subject immortal. [Quotation from "Collins" by Roy Cheville, 1938C]

I first met Roy Cheville on a Sunday in the summer of 1937 at a reunion at Elgin, Illinois. I was 17 and he was 39. I was newly graduated from high school in Texas and had come to Chicago to find a job. I had been a member of the RLDS church for six years and had read some of his writings. He was attending the second summer session at the University of Chicago as a candidate for the Ph. D. in the Divinity School. On this Sunday I was in a class he taught, and I was intrigued. After the class I was introduced to him and we visited for a few minutes.

The next time we met was in January of 1946. I had arrived in Lamoni to become a Graceland College student after four and a half years in the Army Air Forces. "Doc" Cheville was assigned to be my advisor. Frequently I stopped by his office to ask a question or two. He always understood the background of my questions and left me with some additional ideas to consider. Through such discussions I began to learn that we do not need to assume that God is supernatural—instead we can presume that he works through natural principles we do not yet understand. That was an exciting idea which greatly expanded the range of ideas I now began to consider. I began to understand that the Christian message centers on personal development which includes spirituality.

There emerged a larger view of what my life might become. I had arrived at Graceland with the objective of earning the Associate in Arts degree. Before that semester was over I had decided that I should continue going to school until I had earned a Doctor of Philosophy degree— an idea which was very new to me. It certainly changed my life.

On the day in 1947 when I was graduated from Graceland, Roberta Ann Gossadge and I were married in the Graceland chapel. "Doc" performed the ceremony. "Bobbie" and I went immediately to Berkeley where we both earned bachelors degrees at the University of California, hers in sociology and mine in psychology, and I completed the course requirements for the masters' degree in social institutions in August 1949.

From 1949 until 1951 I was Dean of Students at Graceland, and "Doc" was Dean of Faculty. We were on 12 faculty committees together. I taught psychology courses and one section of Introduction to Christianity each year under his guidance.

In June of 1951 "Bobbie" and I moved to Urbana, Illinois, where I resumed graduate study in experimental psychology. In 1953 I earned the doctorate which I had never even dreamed about before 1946. In 1955 we moved to Dayton, Ohio, where Roy Cheville was a frequent visitor in our home until he moved into Resthaven in 1980. I visited him frequently there, as I had at other places he lived. When he died in 1986 we had been friends for 40 years. Much of what I have appreciated most about my adult life would probably not have occurred without his radiant influence.

About 1975 there arose a tacit understanding between us that I would write his biography. Toward that end we made some oral history tapes during one week together in 1980. Before he moved from his apartment in Wayne Zion's home into Resthaven, he brought me a car trunk full of his papers and books. Much more material has been consulted, mostly in Independence, Lamoni, and Chicago. He was a very private person, and it was not until his death that I felt free to research material he had not volunteered to give me. He wrote so much and did so much that I have had to read very carefully, to ponder, and to experiment. It has taken me a long while to get ready to write his story.

For years I have been encouraged in this project by Bill and Barbara Higdon, Dick and Lila Cheville, Bob and Charlotte Cheville Farrand, Ed and Charlene Gleazer, and Wayne and Ruth Zion. Bob Brackenbury's professional and personal opinions have been most helpful, as has the counsel of Roger Yarrington. Orville Hiles has spent many hours gathering material for me, and Norma Derry Hiles has provided help and counsel. Orville introduced me to Dave Allen, who made the fragile Lamoni Chronicle archives available, along with his encouraging counsel. The personnel of the libraries and archives of Graceland College and the RLDS Church have been most helpful and enthusiastic. Special thanks go to Dick Howard, Jean Reiff, Patricia Struble, and Sara Hallier, and to Enid DeBarthe, Lamoni Stake Historian. Les Gardner and Velma Ruch have gladly shared their significant personal files. Jacquie Fondy, Connie Galbraith, and Wilson Ritchie have been helpful as critics and knowledgeable supporters all along the way. June Fellows arranged to have some significant research done in the University of Chicago library. Judy Closson, Enid DeBarthe, and Katie Condit helped greatly to recreate the personality of Nell Cheville. Charlotte Gould, Elmo Hope, Ina Crossan, Joe and Iris Sage, Lily Castings, Priscilla Boeckman Siler, Myrtle Boeckman, Ed McGuire, and many others have been of great help. Roberta Ritchie, my companion, historian and archivist has put in long hours of constructive help, and has given steady understanding

15

support. Our three children, Karen Ritchie, Jennie Bowen, and Bill Ritchie have provided warm support and challenging interest, as has Floy Ritchie Parsons.

I am especially grateful to Barbara Higdon for her wise, perceptive, and diligent editorial guidance. She has greatly enhanced the organization and writing. Our son, her former student, warned me that as an editor she would pull no punches, and, thankfully, he was right. She has brought this book into being.

As I have written I have had two objectives in mind: 1) to tell Roy Cheville's story as best I can, making judgments where it appeared appropriate, and 2) to give as much of the flavor of the original documents as feasible. For the second purpose I have quoted liberally so others can use the material to make their own judgments. I have tried to give a balanced view of Roy Cheville, but have met some limitations. I have leaned heavily on written records and have found few written descriptions of his personal shortcomings.

This volume deals with Roy Cheville's life through the period of his interaction with Graceland College. The College and the RLDS Church changed Roy Cheville and he in turn changed both. I have ended this interpretive description of his life at the time he moved to Independence as Presiding Patriarch and no longer had regular functions on the campus. The rest of his life remains to be described in another volume. There are so many dimensions to the life and work of Roy Cheville that this volume must be considered an introduction.

Roy and I spent one day together during Christmas week in 1985, which was the last time I saw him. Characteristically he said, "Malcolm, I hope the work I and others have done will help you to go further than we did."

Malcolm L. Ritchie, August 1995

Introduction

Entitled "Roy A. Cheville—A Friend of the Young," an
ticle describing Roy Cheville appeared in the *Saints
erald* during the RLDS General Conference of 1930. It
id in part,

> A young man of mild manner and friendly face walks up to the
> microphone and takes charge. With the encouragement of his voice
> and the motion of the baton he proceeds to lead the people in the
> singing of their sacred songs, and out of the noise and disorder he
> gradually brings a spirit of reverence and comparative quiet.
>
> Roy A. Cheville is by this time a familiar figure to everyone who
> attends the business sessions. Those who know him wonder at his
> versatility. They have seen him carry the heavy leading role in the
> Graceland College play at Memorial Hall . . . They have heard him
> sing a part in the beautiful performance of the A Capella Choir at
> the Graceland program in the Auditorium.
>
> As important as these major roles are, they are less important
> than some of his less conspicuous services. He is and has been for
> years a friend of young people, tirelessly providing social times of a
> wholesome character for their recreation, tirelessly participating in
> the strenuous round of activities that absorb their surging powers.
> As a counselor and adviser of young men he has an honorable record.
>
> It is significant that in all his work and leadership he has always
> exercised a constructive and affirmative influence. He is no devotee
> of "Don't;" he is a disciple of "Do!" To those who would like to fill
> their lives with friendship and usefulness, we point to him as a
> helpful and instructive example. [SH 14 April 30][1]

Those words suggest that the life of Roy Arthur
heville is worth examining in some depth. As teacher,
uthor, musician, minister, and counselor, he would live
nd work for another 56 years.

Many people have tried to describe him. Four years
after he joined the faculty of Graceland College, the 1927
Acacia[2] called him perhaps the most versatile man on
he campus. That yearbook went on to say,

17

He ranks with the best as an educator, enthusiastic and qualified. He is a fair minded and reverent religious leader. He can officiate at a dormitory stag party or give administrative advice when called upon. Above all, he is congenial, a social diplomat, friendly, dominant, yet inconspicuous. We regret that there is only one of him and that his day has only 24 hours.

A story about him and his contributions to the college was issued as a part of the celebration of the fiftieth anniversary of Graceland in 1945. It said,

> It is impossible to judge accurately the influence Roy Cheville has had on Graceland College. Since he came to the college faculty in 1923, he has exerted great influence in the lives of individual students. Hundreds think of him as the one who guided them to an understanding of their church, and he—more than any other person—represents "religion" and "the church" at Graceland. "He didn't tell me what to do, but he helped me to decide for myself," is the expression of many young people who, when puzzled, disillusioned, or awakened by a little learning, dropped in to "have a talk" with Cheville. [SH 16 Aug 47]

In 1950 Katherine Metz, editor of the *Lamoni Chronicle* wrote this description:

> Then there is our friend, R. A. Where he keeps such a super amount of energy stored we can't imagine but his exuberance is something which gives life to those about him and that is a gift few men possess, in or out of history.
>
> He makes religion come to life and he has the capacity of being interested in everything from the simple talk of children to the deep philosophy of the wisest. He can run the gamut of interests like a musician does the scales and pause on any note. [LC 9 Jan 50][3]

A story about him in the *Graceland Alumni Magazine* in 1950 was entitled "The Guiding Genius of Graceland:"

> For over 27 years Roy Arthur Cheville has been one of the key "stewards" on the Graceland campus. The "Spirit of Graceland" is the genius of Graceland and remains active today in inspiring and challenging men and women of the faculty, staff, and student body

to carry out the "laboratory experience in kingdom building on the campus."

However, through the life and ministry of Dr. Cheville has come what thousands of friends, students, and many colleagues recognize as the "guiding genius of Graceland." Whether in the classroom, in committee sessions, at the athletic contests, in formal and informal services, no matter where or when, Dr. Cheville has sensed and extended the possible prophetic mission of Graceland and has given of life completely that this mission might find fulfillment. . .

Many times we have heard that the highest calling to which any person may be called is to be a "Saint of God," according to Dr. Cheville. His successful demonstration has stood as a beacon light for over two decades on the hill.

Yes, through the life and ministry of Dr. Cheville has come what many thousands of friends, students, and many colleagues recognize as the "guiding genius of Graceland."

Despite the seeming diversity of his accomplishments, Roy Cheville's life and activities were integrated to a remarkable degree. He said in 1952, "I do good work when all of me is devoted to all of the divine endeavor." [1978D][4] From age 16 until his death at age 88, his activities followed directly from the baptismal commitment he made at 16. He became a full-time minister at age 20. Thereafter he served the church and its college for the rest of his life. Virtually all of the things he did expressed the ministerial function to which he was committed. Except during his student years, he never had to devote large blocks of his time to activities which made money. He earned his modest subsistence through the things he did directly to fulfill his commitment.

One thing agreed upon by all who knew him well was his prodigious ability to accomplish work. "I never knew a man who got as much work done as he does," was often said of him by his faculty colleagues. Graceland President Edmund J. Gleazer, Jr. said, "How does he do it? We work with him regularly and see him several times every day. We think we have all his hours accounted for. We see his tremendous output and marvel that he can do so much so well. Then, suddenly, there appears a new book written by him. How can it happen?"

When President Gleazer made that statement Cheville was Dean of Faculty and Director of Religious Activities. As Dean of Faculty he directed all the academic endeavors. He also represented his office on a dozen faculty committees. As Director, he planned and executed all the religious activities on campus. He also taught a full load of courses. The aforementioned 1945 article about him describes some of the activities which were normal to his schedule:

In the winter months, students can look out of the windows of Marietta Hall as they sleepily shut off the alarm clock and see the light burning in Cheville's office. "That's when I get my work done," he says, "when nobody is around to bother me." And students on the way to breakfast look in his window and see him bent over his desk, preparing for the day's classes, planning the student social program for the coming quarter, outlining the assembly program for the week, preparing for the student fellowship meeting Wednesday evening, writing a new quarterly for the general church, or answering a letter from a lonely, bewildered young person. He's the busiest man on the campus. During the day, there is a constant stream of students trickling into his office. When he isn't there, they poke their heads in the next door and ask, "Does Dr. Cheville have a class this hour? When will he be back?" Students with romantic problems, students confused about life in general, student committees wanting help, students just wanting to talk, students of former years returning for a visit, and a dozen faculty committees conspire to prevent him from doing very much personal work during the day. In spite of all this, his work production schedule continues to amaze all who know him. [SH 16 Aug 47]

The work that Roy Cheville accomplished at this pace and in these circumstances did not suffer in quality. He was an inspiring role model in the practice of religion as

20

well as a scholar in theology and in religion. He was well grounded in science. His doctoral dissertation was a social science study of his own church, and he taught social science over a number of years. He understood the study and writing of history. He taught philosophy for a number of years. Many of his students who went on to earn doctorates at universities across the country have said that he was the best teacher they ever had. Some who later became professors drew upon their memories of Cheville's methods to improve their own teaching.

How did he manage to do so much?

He did have considerable native intellectual ability, but a study of his high school, college, and university records does not suggest his native powers were significantly beyond the range of other intellectuals. He did have an ability to discipline himself and stay focused on current objectives. In that he was even further above the norm than in native intellect. But even these abilities together do not seem adequate to explain his accomplishments.

Some of the things that have been said about John Wesley, the founder of Methodism, could be said about Roy Cheville. Francis G. Ensley wrote that Wesley,

> put behind his endeavor a disciplined vitality. . . [his] achievement goes back to the fact that he conjoined drive and discipline. . . Wesley's vitality was more than physical; his wonderful bodily vigor flowed from a spiritual power quite as surprising. . . The curse of evangelism—a narrow, militant adherence to a fragment of the gospel, or a segment of human nature, or a solitary method—was completely foreign to him.[5]

How Cheville managed to do what he did may be explained by the development he made in understanding and working with the spirit of God. What he experienced seems to have followed the principles suggested by Fred-

21

erick Madison Smith, Graceland's first graduate and church president.[6] Smith believed that there are higher powers which humans can experience when they have fully exploited their normal abilities toward a worthy objective. In several of Cheville's writings, including his 1975 book, *Spiritual Resources Are Available Today* [1975A], he described his understanding of the aspects of divinity that involve human interaction. He said, "I have made contact."

Notes

1. The abbreviation SH will be used to refer to the *Saints' Herald*, a periodical of the RLDS Church.
2. The *Acacia* is the Graceland College yearbook.
3. The abbreviation LC will be used to refer to the *Lamoni Chronicle*, a newspaper published in Lamoni, Iowa.
4. References in this form are publications by Roy Cheville listed in the appendix. 1978D was his fourth publication in the year 1978.
5. Francis G. Ensley, *John Wesley, Evangelist* Methodist Evangelistic Materials, Nashville, Tennessee, 1958. Roy Cheville had a copy of Ensley's book in his library and the sentences quoted above were marked with Cheville's emphasis marks.
6. Frederick M. Smith, *The Higher Powers of Man* Independence, Mo. Herald House, 1918, reprinted 1968.

Roy Cheville and his siblings about 1909. Roy is in the center of the back row, with Mable on his right. In the front row are Fred, Mildred, and Cora.

BOOK II.

Beginnings

BOOK II. BEGINNINGS
Childhood

Roy Arthur Cheville was born on October 2, 1897, on a farm near Maxwell, Story County, Iowa, and went to high school in Rhodes, Iowa. He was the third of five children. Roy's parents were of English descent. His father, George Cheville, was born on 4 July 1867, near Guelph, Ontario, Canada, five months after his parents had migrated from Cambridgeshire, England. Roy's mother used to call George "her little Canadian firecracker." George's parents had been working people of English stock with a French name.

George had a younger brother Hezekiah and two sisters, Martha and Mary (later called Marie). They moved down near Iowa Center, Iowa, in Story County. The parents died when the children were young, and they were placed with different families. George located with the Angelo family who were very fine people and were members of the Christian Church. Roy described his father, "He wasn't a big man but he was energetic. One of the things he said was, 'Work, and work doing something. Put in an honest day's work, and plan to like your work.'" Roy said that he did not have a close personal relationship with his father, and he wished that he had been close enough to understand him. George Cheville died at Rhodes, Iowa, October 31, 1951, at age 84.

Charlotte Mary Backous Cheville, mother of Roy Arthur, was born in Yorkshire, England February 26, 1872. She died at State Center, Iowa November 13, 1966, at age 94.

The Backous family had migrated from the British Isles to central Iowa in 1884, where their older sons had preceded them. Charlotte lived with a farm family where she worked for her "board and keep." George Cheville lived on the farm of a relative of the family with whom Charlotte Backous resided.

Roy described his mother:

My Mother—a big heart! A sunshiny face. A worker in growing way. As far back as I can remember my mother sang as she went about her household and her gardening duties. Generally she sang songs that spoke good cheer and good hope. Much of the time she sang cheerful, conventional songs such as "Revive us again." "Fill our hearts with thy love." These were singing to Jesus. Sometimes, however, she would sing songs that would be suitable for her and God to sing together. This song made a marked impression on me in contrast to those that sang about sins and evils in the world and the urgent need for "getting saved." This was a stanza and refrain that spoke to me with impression that Jesus was going along with Mother, for she was trying to go along with him.

There is sunshine in my soul today,
  More glorious and bright,
Than glows in any earthly sky,
  For Jesus is my light.

Then came the refrain with its cheery, promising testimony of spiritual happiness.

O there's sunshine, blessed sunshine,
  While the peaceful, happy moments roll,
When Jesus shows his smiling face,
  There is sunshine in my soul. [notes found in 1986]

On February 25, 1891, George Cheville and Charlotte Backous drove to Nevada, Iowa, the county seat, and were married by a judge. Mable was born in 1892 and became Mrs. Sidney Atkinson. Cora was born in 1895 and became Mrs. Amasa Shimel. George did not approve of Amasa, and would not let him come to the family home. In May of 1897 the George Cheville family migrated to a farm near Maxwell, in Story County, Iowa.

There Roy Arthur Cheville was born October 2, 1897. Roy said that was a big event for his father because a boy would be a farmer. His father bought a farm the next day.

In 1902 Fred M. Cheville was born. Fred attended Graceland from 1925 to 1927, when he received an A.A. in the teacher training program. Into the 1990's he was living in Rhodes, Iowa. Mildred Cheville was born July 11, 1906. She entered Graceland in 1924, but did not complete the semester. Discovering after arriving on campus that she was pregnant, she tried, through an abortion procedure, to keep from bringing shame to herself and her family. She died of blood poisoning February 12, 1925, in the hospital in Leon, Iowa. Mabel Carlile Hyde said that her funeral was the only one ever held in the Graceland chapel. Roy said of Mildred only that she died in youth. Although he never discussed this tragedy, several of her college textbooks and a 1925 *Acacia* containing her picture were among his effects.

Roy remembered many of the childhood experiences and impressions which shaped him. He recalled living on a farm a mile from the town of Maxwell. He went to the one-room rural White Chapel school a mile away, so called because it had also been used for church meetings. There were several classes in the same room. While the class ahead was reciting, Roy would listen and learn from their recital. He reported that that was always fascinating: "The teachers always felt that I enjoyed going to school, and I did." He felt that his teachers were unusually good, and he remembered announcing that he was going to be a teacher when he got big.

At the end of one school day he walked part way home with a group as usual. The kids talked about Halley's comet, which was due to hit that night. The older ones

29

made such a big thing of the comet that Roy was frightened and that night tried to pray—his first attempt.

Roy remembered the 1903 funeral of his maternal grandfather. He concluded that everything about the funeral expressed sadness, thus showing respect for the dead.

Dark colored clothing was worn, black if possible. The hearse was black and was drawn by a team of black horses. A mixed chorus sang the songs with sad tones. Funeral hymns sang of death, of going to heaven. The tone was Weepy. When the minister said 'Ashes to ashes and dust to dust', two or more designated mourners picked up a handful of dark sod and tossed this into the open grave. Weeping was considered an expression of sadness. Genuine mourners would toss a handful of dark sod into the open grave. A small group sang "A Song of Sorrow." A few years later I stood alone by the tombstone and asked myself, "Is this the way God expects us to respond to death?"[1]

Roy was introduced to Japanese culture in 1906 when a great aunt came from Tokyo to spend a few days with the family. She had lived in Chicago and had served as housekeeper for a businessman. When his business took him to Tokyo, Aunt Mary went to Japan as his housekeeper. She was there two or three years. She had appreciated her years in Japan and had adopted several patterns from Japanese life. She brought with her two Japanese dogs, named Yukasan and Fukasan, which she kept in her room. Five-year-old Roy stood by Aunt Mary when she gave her two dogs a daily bath, and she caressed them affectionately. He enjoyed patting these dogs and calling them by name.

When Roy was ten to 14 years old, he attended Sunday school in a Christian (Disciples) church in Maxwell, Iowa. His teacher stressed the Bible and spoke with finality about its message. Among other things she emphasized the "chosen people" and "the temple" that stood in Jerusalem. She presented word pictures of this "sacred building" and the people who were to be with God. Roy said later, "I developed a more-than-ordinary interest in what a temple was supposed to be, but I learned very little."[2]

When Roy was eight, the Cheville family migrated from Maxwell to a small acreage called "Pleasant Hill Stock Farm" near Rhodes, Iowa. Ten acres of woods, Indian Creek, a natural spring, and a few hills added charm to the grain, cattle, and hog operation. Roy and his sister Cora chose to attend a small Methodist Church. They developed a circle of friends who believed in baptism by sprinkling with the possibility of immersion. Their hymns spoke of coming to Jesus, of getting saved through "believing" in Jesus. One song shouted confidently that "Jesus saves! Jesus saves!" Roy remembered wanting to get acquainted with this "saving Jesus," but he was not portrayed in adequate terms for him. "I did not respond to the invitation to come to the front and confess."[3]

Notes

1. Desk notes found in 1986.
2. Ibid.
3. Ibid.

The Covenant

My Main Birthday. January 14, 1914. When I got with, covenanted with Christ Jesus—a new birth, a real birthday. Paul—"If any man gets with Christ, he is a new *creation*." The new has come! Yes, My Major Birthday—January 14, 1914, 66 years ago. [Cheville notes 1980]

When Roy Cheville was in high school, he learned that religion could be viewed in functional terms—the principles which produced the religious experiences of biblical times will produce similar experiences today if the conditions are met. A small congregation in Rhodes not only believed these things about God, they organized their religious practices to learn together the conditions under which they could interact with divinity.

In due time the young Cheville decided that he must join this group to find out if these ideas and their practices were valid. If they were, his would be an enduring covenant. Thus Roy Cheville became a member of the Reorganized Church of Jesus Christ of Latter Day Saints in January of 1914, at age 16. His relation to that church shaped the rest of his life. It led him to become teacher, minister, college professor, and to write 26 published books, 48 published hymns, 36 published pamphlets, and 345 published articles. Along the way he helped to redefine and shape that small church.

He described his first encounter:

In the fall of 1912 I first met Reorganized Latter Day Saints. I was in my second year of high school. In this town to which my family had moved a little over a year before was a small group of Saints. They met in a home and little had been heard of them. That fall they made, for them, a daring adventure: they set up a small tent for two weeks of missionary meetings. Seats were planks set on tile. There were no backs to these improvised pews. On a small platform was a locally constructed pulpit, often referred to as 'the sacred desk,' and a borrowed reed organ. My sister two years older than I was asked to play the organ since their own accompanists were not much accomplished in techniques. I went along.

What the preacher talked about that first night, I do not recall. Neither that sermon nor those of following nights made much impression. The preachers did not appeal to me in method or in message. I did remember, however, my impression as I walked into the tent that first evening. There were not many in the congregation. The tent would have seated about a hundred. There were 30 to 40 present. Perhaps eight were nonmembers. But, oh, how those people were singing! Someone handed me a book and I started singing, too. At 14, I was halfway between tenor and bass and quite inexperienced in part singing, but I sang—everybody else was singing. The song was Number 100 in the *Zion's Praises*. How lustily they attacked the refrain! They sang "How beautiful to walk in the steps of the Savior . . Led in paths of light" as if they meant it, as if they were happy to be there. My first impression of Latter Day Saintism was that it was a joyous movement. [1955A]

About a year later Orman Salisbury, a Des Moines businessman who served as district president, contacted Roy Parker who was a church appointee. Salisbury wrote in his memoirs,

Brother Parker came to visit me on his way to this series. He was somewhat discouraged and remarked that this town of Rhodes was where I. N. White and his brothers had already preached enough to convert the trees, with no apparent results; but I assured him this would be the greatest series he had ever taken part in. . . Several were baptized during that series, and among them was a young musician, about 17 years old named Roy Cheville. [SH 2 May 60]

Roy remembered the experience in detail:

My sister was asked to play the piano, an instrument of confused pitch and marred cabinet. I was asked to sing in the choir. By this time I was singing tenor and doing quite well as to spirit and volume. There were ten or twelve in the choir. My sister and I were the only nonmembers. We accepted the invitation because a Latter Day Saint woman—a crippled little old lady, Mattie Hughes, who got about with a cane and a wheel chair—used to sing in the Methodist choir with us.

The meetings were scheduled for about two weeks. The first evening I went in response to the invitation. On succeeding nights I went because I wanted to. The missionary, J. L. Parker was friendly, fervent, forthright. His narration of the calling of Joseph Smith and of the restoring of the church made an appealing story. His interpretation of the Book of Mormon was completely new to me. Yet it was so strange, I asked myself, "Did this really happen? What stood out to me was the portrayal of God as doing things today. This man's God was revealing himself today, as man would listen. The Holy Spirit was available today as man would respond. The living Christ had ministered to a rural youth in western New York in the 1920's. This brought things up-to-date. The Book of Mormon pictured Jesus Christ as coming to the Western continent in ancient times. This made him the universal Christ.

I wrestled with the query, "Is all this valid?" As the meetings came toward the close I asked myself, "Should I take the risk?" I concluded that I would venture and give it a try. I realized that one could not explore a movement by sitting aside and looking on. I said to myself that I would give it a fair try and that if I found it to be a hoax, I would go out as honestly as I came in. And God knew that I meant it.

Roy Parker was to preach 10 nights. After he had been there probably 5 nights, one night he had an experience, a dream or vision, in which he saw me and heard a voice saying, "I have need of this young man in my church." But he never publicized that, and praise be, he never said anything to me about it. I didn't learn about this until several months after my baptism.

I had asked for confirming evidence to guide me. This kind of evidence did not come to me but to others. The district president had directed the missionaries to come to Rhodes as surely as Paul had been directed to go into Macedonia.

When it came Monday night, they announced that there would be a baptism next day. I think it was three that they were going to baptize. When I went to school that morning, I knew I had to make a decision. But this was a whopper. The two missionaries went down to see my folks—I think it was that morning—because this fellow had had that experience about me that he didn't publicize. Now; how was he going to get me in? They talked about it and they asked my father. He said, "I have nothing to say about that." He said I would have to make that decision. He never stood in my way, but I found

35

out after a while that he wasn't too happy about it. Teachers had always said that I had half a brain or something and ought to do something with it. He thought, if he gets mixed up with this ridiculous bunch of people, what's going to happen to his life. But he never said a word about that—this was my decision.

That morning around 11 o'clock the telephone rang. O, I was just suffering. It was Roy Parker. He said, "Could we see you outside the school at noon?" I said yes. In that hour I made my decision. And I walked out and met the two men and said, "I have decided to be baptized if that is all right with you." They were just so happy, but they didn't say anything about this experience at all.

I went home and told my folks. It was winter time, so they went down to the pond, cut a hole in the ice and put a stepladder down—that was the baptismal font. Some people have asked, "Weren't you afraid of the cold?" I wasn't concerned about the cold. My concern was, Was this thing what I think it is? A large crowd of townspeople had gathered on the bank above. Down closer to the ice stood the little group of Saints. Again they sang. This was their day of rejoicing. They sang "Nearer, My God, to Thee" with joy and thanksgiving, and with expectation of a new day. They sang from the overflow.

Something happened as I was going down there. Roy Parker stepped down in the water and baptized the one man. I never learned about this until two or three years later—Roy Parker said that it was the only time in his experience it happened to him—but when I was going out there and down there, he heard celestial music. He didn't tell about it until much later. [recorded 1 Nov. 1980 by M. Ritchie]

Roy was baptized and confirmed by J. L. Parker, and D. J. Williams. Five adults were baptized including his sister Cora. A year later Charlotte Cheville was baptized.

Just before Roy made his decision to affiliate with the church a friend advised him against it. She said that if he went with that little church it would change the whole course of his life. She noted that he was popular and said that if he was baptized by these Latter Day Saints he would lose all of his friends, and he would miss out on what he could make of his life. His friend's warning and prediction was partially true. His neighbors did not turn against him. Instead his life verified the counsel in his patriarchal blessing: "Be consistent and even in your life. . . and you will make friends among those who oppose the church and they will respect it because of your integrity." He did make many friends, including three presidents of the Mormon church, Roman Catholic priests, Jewish rabbis, Hindus and Moslems. In old age he could not recall one statement of a disparaging nature made to him about his church or faith. However, his decision to join did change his life forever. Of his life in the church he said,

> There has come to me in this Church of Jesus Christ a company of friends of precious quality. This circle reaches around the world. It includes those of every continent, of every race, of many languages. What a wealth of spiritual friendship has come to me. [notes written in 1970, found in 1986]

Roy participated in church activities with characteristic enthusiasm and soon was elected "chorister" of the branch. In that role he selected hymns and conducted their singing in branch meetings. In a testimony service he mentioned that he wanted to understand more and develop adequate foundations in his new endeavor. In that service a visiting elder directed him to read Section 9 of the Doctrine and Covenants[1] as if this message were addressed to him personally. The instruction to Oliver Cowdery was to "Study it out in your mind; then you must ask me if it be right; and if it is right, I will cause that your bosom shall burn within you." As Roy reflected on it, the counsel appeared to fit him as if it had been given directly to him. He began to understand the need of preparation for growing perception.

When Roy was ordained a Deacon at Rhodes January 24, 1915, Orman Salisbury spoke in counsel, "This is the first of the callings of this youth. He will be called to several other ordinations, but he will ever magnify this calling to be a deacon." Salisbury later recalled a testimony service in which Roy stood and said, "Friends, I want to be the first." He said wanting to be the first to testify was characteristic of Roy.

Not all of Roy's experiences with this small church group were beneficial and uplifting. When the congregation considered his call to the office of deacon, one conscientious brother did not vote in approval. He had scriptural support for his concern. The New Testament told him that the deacon should be the husband of one wife and Brother Roy was not married. On another occasion a brother in the small congregation set forth scriptural proof that he should vote for the candidate in the Democratic party since he believed that Jesus denounced the (Re)Publicans.

Notes

1. The Doctrine and Covenants is a publication of the RLDS Church.

The Country School Teacher

In the two years from 1916 to 1918 Roy Cheville was a country school teacher. He himself had been a good student. He had respect for his teachers and that led him to think about the possibility of becoming a teacher himself. He said,

> Somewhere in my high school days I picked up the thought that the two greatest teachers of our civilization were Jesus of Nazareth and Socrates of Athens . . These great teachers placed their students in the center. [1931B]
>
> The other field in which I got along with such good teachers was in the field of history. I had one course in Ancient History, one year; one course in Modern History; and one course in U.S. History. So Latin and history were pretty well done. Then I had two years of mathematics, a year of algebra, a year of plane geometry, and one semester of solid geometry. I just got along in math fine. [Recorded in 1980]

After he graduated from high school he received a scholarship for tuition from Drake University. A high school friend and his family had moved to Des Moines and now lived near Drake; they offered Roy housing. That combination enabled him to begin college work at Drake.

When he arrived in Des Moines he evaluated his purposes in being there. Early in his life he had resolved to be a teacher. Now he must consider what, where, and how he would teach. He had observed that his best teachers had taught with breadth, and he now concluded that he needed a broad foundation. So he enrolled in a liberal arts curriculum. He took English, German, solid geometry, inorganic chemistry, medieval history, and Bible. In chemistry he earned the grade of C, the only "not good" grade he remembered in his academic career.

The year in Des Moines at Drake brought him into fellowship with the Des Moines congregation. At that time the branch was meeting in a rather simple building a few blocks from the State Capitol. For the first time he was in an urban church. He came to know the administrators of the district and he met Apostle U. W. Green, Bishop E. L. Kelley, and Seventy J. J. Cornish.

An important event in Roy's development occurred in 1915 when he was at home in Rhodes for the week-end. After Roy had spoken testimonially about the many things he was wanting to find out about the Church and the Gospel, Fred Mussel stood and said,

> I do not know the name or the condition of this young man but God is prompting me to speak to him prophetically, You are advised to receive and follow the counsel that was spoken to Oliver Cowdery by Joseph Smith, Jr., "You must study it out in your own mind." Your searching is to continue through your life. God's spirit will guide and confirm. Clarity of perceptions will come to you as you proceed.

He paid for his room rent and breakfasts with checks he wrote on his father's bank account. Soon he began working part time at a home for the elderly. He did odd jobs such as cleaning and shoveling snow. His father cut his hair on his infrequent trips to Rhodes. His tuition included tickets to football, basketball and track events. He limited the number of cross-city trips to church to save streetcar fare. When it became clear that he would not be able to afford another year in the university, he inquired about obtaining a provisional teacher's certificate, then wrote the Superintendent of schools of Marshall County to see if he could teach the next year. Thus, in September of 1916, he began teaching in a one-room school on the outskirts of Rhodes, about three miles from his parents' home.

He commuted to school on horseback. Fourteen students from six to 11 years in age, most of them bare-foot, walked from half a mile to a mile and a half. They brought their lunch, their paper and pencil or slate and slate-pencil. Some also brought books that they or their brothers and sisters had used during the previous year. Roy decided that the focus should be on the three R's: Reading, wRiting, and aRithmetic. He also had them sing from time to time, remembering their renditions of "We're From Iowa."

One assignment for the students was to question their parents about the farm operation and equipment of their own farms. This included reports on the grains, the animals, the machinery of the farms. The results taught Roy the importance of students' starting from where they are—an insight he would employ throughout his teaching career.

After a month in that school, the county superintendent of schools came to visit. He liked what he saw and mentioned the possibility of Roy's moving some 30 miles away to a larger rural school. Roy moved for the winter and spring terms to a rural school near the small town of Green Mountain in Marshall County, Iowa. This school had a larger enrollment and a wider age range. Every Friday evening he returned to his parents' home in Rhodes. In the fall of 1917 Roy began teaching in the ten-grade school in Aredale, Iowa.

When Roy Cheville was ordained a priest October 7, 1916, the ordaining spokesman, Orman Salisbury, said in essence, "You shall lead forth in study, often alone. The saints will not always understand and approve." After the ordination, in private, he prepared Roy for the opposition he would face in his ministry and urged him to stand fast. [1962K]

41

In the summer of 1918 Roy attended Iowa State College in Cedar Falls, Iowa. He studied teacher education. During that summer session he met Mabel Carlile whose home was Lamoni. They became friends, but apparently did not date. They did not know that they belonged to the same church, and they were surprised when they met again on the Graceland College campus in 1919. Mabel later remarked that they must not have let their light shine very brightly.

The Commission

A place may become sacred because there men have made a decision that changed their lives. . . In my life certain spots stand out. The banks by a railroad reservoir near a little town in Iowa speak a personal message to me. There I was baptized. One time later I returned to that willow bank to make a life decision: It was there I decided to enter the ministry of this people. [1928H]

In the Fall of 1918 Roy Cheville made a new commitment. He would end his short career as a country school teacher and would become a full time minister for his church. The *Saints Herald* announced his appointment in Autumn of 1918. He was assigned to Des Moines District with specific responsibility for the Nevada, Iowa, Branch. On October 12, 1918, he was ordained an elder at Perry, Iowa, in the Conference of the Des Moines District, E. O. Clark and J. E. Laughlin officiating.

As one of his first assignments Roy spent three months working with Daniel Macgregor, a well-established minister who had published a book entitled *A Marvelous Work and a Wonder*. A close friendship developed between Cheville and Macgregor. The young man caught the mood, the method, and the message of Daniel Macgregor, but he observed that Macgregor made some of his points by moving historical events around to fit his thesis. Roy concluded that the use of "signs and seasons" by this man he admired so much was unsound in selection, interpretation, and in emphasis. He resolved that his own religious scholarship would be factually sound and intellectually honest.

In September of 1919 Roy was assigned to Graceland College for a year's training for ministry in a program begun by the church to increase the educational level of appointee ministers. Roy was designated to prepare for ministry in Scandinavia. He and E. Y. Hunker started a study of the Norwegian language. After two weeks of college Roy became ill with typhoid fever which terminated the year of college for him. His doctors feared he would not survive, but he slowly recovered. He returned to Rhodes for recuperation, then continued his ministry in the Des Moines District.

Roy had a significant experience in June of 1920, at the district conference in Runnells, Iowa. He received spiritual counsel through Orman Salisbury:

> You are going into new fields. You will explore alone. During these years just before you, multitudes of forces will be coming together to take you from the Church. Be not hasty in formulating conclusions. Hold to what is positive. So shall you come through. You are to be at home in the gift of charity with kindly heart toward peoples and toward persons. You will round out your life with the respect and with the affection of your brothers and sisters in the Church of Jesus Christ.

The first published item from the pen of Roy Cheville appeared in the *Saints' Herald* of September 1920 entitled "Letter to the First Presidency." He wrote,

> The month of August has been one of progress and spiritual uplift in the Des Moines District. Our reunion was marked by the spirit of devotion and consecration and the Saints caught a vision of the possibilities of the work and their personal application to it. It was the most spiritual we have ever enjoyed and its effects will be far-reaching. The missionary zeal and enthusiasm is spreading.

Roy Cheville's second publication was a hymn written for a pageant observing 100 years of Latter Day Saintism. It provides an early view of his poetry and of his theology:

SONG OF ENTREATY (Tune, "Admonition")

O my people, hear my pleadings;
  'Tis the call of God to you,
Unto high and noble service,
  To a task divine and true.
Hear ye, then, this solemn challenge;
  Note ye, too, the world's dismay
As it in its doubts and chaos
  Calls you, Saints, to lead the way.

Zion's plan has long been given
  Ages gone God's servants pled;
Bidding, come and build a city
  That God's glory would reflect.
But that call was long unheeded,
  God's celestial law untaught;
So today there comes the message,
  For his work cannot be fraught.

But my work can be accomplished
  Not by purpose men design;
Only by the laws celestial—
  Love and sacrifice are mine.
As my people oft have tasted
  Of the heavenly joys above,
Ye may, too, in Zion's fullness
  Drink in of your Father's love.

Bring ye, then, your tithes and of'rings
  Lay them at my servants' feet;
But e'en more than wealth is wanted—
  Yes, a life for glory meet.
Lives, undaunted, true and faithful,
  Charged with love and sacrifice;
This alone can build our Zion
  This alone will e'er suffice.

So, I beckon ye, my people,
  Give as I have given for you.
Lives, ambitions, talents, riches;
  Thus be my disciples true.
Thus with consecrated effort,
  Zion shall redeemed be,
And the world shall stand to witness
  God still lives and dwells with thee. [1921]

45

J. A. Dowker and Roy Cheville conducted tent meetings in Des Moines for most of the summer of 1920. Thirteen were baptized. Roy described an unusually rich experience which took place in a district reunion just before he returned to Graceland College as a student in the fall of 1920. District President Henry Castings spoke to the congregation in an unknown tongue, then gave the interpretation in English. To Roy he said, "My son, in your lifetime your voice will be heard across the water in many lands. You will go to meet those in other lands as a friend and as a brother." [recorded 1980]

BOOK III.

Foundations

BOOK III. FOUNDATIONS
Graceland College Student

Counsel through Orman Salisbury, "You are going into new fields. You will explore alone. . . Be not hasty in formulating conclusions. Hold to what is positive. So shall you come through."

Roy Cheville had attended three other colleges before he became a student at Graceland. He studied at Drake University in the year 1915–1916, at Iowa State Teachers College in the summer of 1916, and at Des Moines University in the summer of 1917. Just before Cheville enrolled, Graceland, founded in 1895, discontinued its bachelor's degree and became a junior college.

Having recovered from the illness that aborted his first year at Graceland, he returned to the campus in September of 1920, again assigned as a student in the church program to increase the educational level of church ministers. This time he was to study one year at Graceland and then serve two years in Spain or South America. He would be in training to teach those who would be ministering in Spanish-speaking countries.

The College Catalog listed George N. Briggs as President, J. A. Gunsolley as Business Manager, and Floyd M. McDowell as Dean of the College. Page 13 reads in part, "The school is non-sectarian and no attempt is made at compulsory instruction, but in chapel services and special lectures, an effort is made to consider the relation of science, philosophy, and religion to everyday life, and to secure widest possible development." 99 students were enrolled in the collegiate program and 38 in religious education.

All of the faculty members listed in the 1920–1921 catalog of Graceland College and Conservatory of Music became Roy's long-time friends, and most were colleagues when he returned to Graceland as a faculty member in 1923. The faculty included Gustav Platz, Cyril Wight, Lonzo Jones, Johannes Bergman, A. R. Gilbert, Paul N. Craig, Mabel Carlile, and Ray Whiting.

Two people became significant early contributors to his developing ideas. RLDS Church President Fred M. Smith was not a faculty member, but he was a frequent visitor to the campus, and he commanded attention in classes and in special services. We have a picture of his activities on the campus in an article entitled "President Smith at Graceland" in the *Saints' Herald* for January 21, 1920. The article noted that Fred M. spent four days in Lamoni speaking eight times. He addressed the missionary class, the college assembly, and the Lamoni Branch. To the college assembly he said,

> The highest inspiration comes in the course of intelligent development, and as a result of the most thorough preparation we can make; that it represents the highest manifestation of the powers of man. . . the highest inspiration does not come through making the mind vacant, and going into a sort of a trance, but that revelation comes when a man is concentrating his best intelligence on the solution of the problem before him, and the spirit of God reaches down and illuminates his intelligence.

This emphasis on the suitability of spiritual experience as a subject for scientific exploration reinforced the direction which Roy Cheville's concepts had already been moving. Fred M. had earned a master's degree in sociology and a doctorate in psychology. His doctoral dissertation, *The Higher Powers of Man*, was done under the direction of G. Stanley Hall of Clark University. It was published by Herald House in 1918. It implicitly questioned whether we know enough to draw a line between what is human and what is divine. Roy would later say that drawing such a line constitutes setting limits on God. The core of shared convictions between Fred M. and Roy would last as long as they lived.

The other person on the campus who had a significant role in the direction of Roy's developing theories was Floyd McDowell. Brother Mac had earned a bachelor's degree at the University of Iowa and then studied under G. Stanley Hall at Clark University for his master's degree. He served three years on the Graceland faculty and then left to earn a Ph.D. in education at the University of Iowa, with a dissertation on the junior college. He returned to Graceland to establish the junior college, becoming its dean. He recommended the study of the emerging science of psychology. It was now being demonstrated that psychological events, though fleeting in time and non-material, could nevertheless be identified, described, and even measured. The concept took an important position in the intellectual development of Roy Cheville.

In a 1920 [SH 3 Mar 20] article McDowell identified the church's mission in changing the lives of people and developing an improved society as a problem in education. He used the term "education" to mean the process of change, growth, and development by which lives are transformed. The means of this education include preaching, Sunday school, study, and recreation.

In a few years Brother Mac would become a member of the First Presidency. Still later he would be director of the Church's Department of Religious Education. Throughout his life he and Roy would maintain a position of mutual regard and respect. Roy would extend much further the implications of their shared convictions.

As a Graceland student Roy's literary flair manifested itself in a short story he wrote which apparently earned some kind of prize. It was published in *Autumn Leaves* with the title, "Pride and Porch Paint," (A Graceland College Contest Story). It was a study in the relations between two strong personalities:

> The Marsh family home, substantial, built in the sixties. Mostly painted white, except the front porch which was painted a bright barn red. No one knew just why. The Marshes were proud of the Scottish heritage and that "A Marsh never has to, and never does, change his mind." (To keep from painting that front porch white, while Luvina was gone Thomas put on a new front porch and painted it white, moving what had been the front porch to the back and repainting it a bright barn red. Both kept their word and the front porch got painted.) [1922]

Roy was graduated from Graceland College on June 8, 1921, with an A.A. degree in two fields, liberal arts and religious education. Roy's picture in the 1921 *Acacia* is accompanied by the statement, "They're only truly great who are truly good." He was Niketes president in the second semester, religious education class president, in debate, glee club, and Harmony Eight.

Roy began keeping a diary[1] as he was finishing his year at Graceland. He continued the diary for a year— the year of his undergraduate work at the University of Chicago. The first entry deals with finishing his work at Graceland:

> June 8, '21. Commencement Day. Supervised Class Day Exercises at Graceland. Was Cardinal of May Exercises. Ball Game— Graceland Vs. Leon. Graceland defeated. Tired as could be. Rained. Address by W. W. Smith. Received diplomas from Junior College and Religious Education Departments. Wedding of Bergman. Remained at Arbor Villa until very late.

In the middle of Roy's year at Graceland, President G. N. Briggs had advised him that plans of the general church were changing and that he would not be continuing in the specialization in Spanish. Promising financial aid, Briggs requested that Roy go on in advanced study and prepare to teach in the field of religion at Graceland College. Briggs believed that the outstanding place in the field of religion was the University of Chicago. (Briggs himself had been a graduate student in the University of Chicago in 1907.) Both Briggs and Cheville seem to have been comfortable with the idea that they were choosing the best university in the country for their purpose.

The second entry in Roy's diary deals with the manner in which he left home and Rhodes before going to Chicago:

> June 19. Spoke at Rhodes on Revelation. Good effort. Church decorated. Good dinner and pleasant day at home. Drove to State Center and took Northwestern to Chicago at night.

Notes

1. The diary of Roy Cheville for the academic year 1921–1922 is reproduced in part in Appendix E. The original is in the RLDS Church library.

Chicago Undergraduate

Aug. 1. Monday. Spent most of day digging into philosophy. Problems arise that I do not know how to meet. Have faith though.

Aug. 2. Classes. Am pondering over scriptural interpretation and criticism of Old Testament.

Sept. 2. Exams. Received philosophy paper back—on James' conception of truth—subject "What Is Truth?" Defined truth as in D.C. 90:4–5.—This subject as well as History of Hebrew Ethics caused me to wonder at many things as to origin and existence of the Universe. Will await fuller understanding before forming opinions.

Jan. 22. Am perplexed—yet have faith—as to many things of the Church. [Diary]

The University of Chicago played a very important role in the intellectual and scholarly growth of Roy Cheville. His career was facilitated by the knowledge, by the intellectual and professional tools, and by the confidence he acquired there. Through the University he grew a great deal. He was strongly influenced but was not put into a mold by his experiences there. Before he went to Chicago he had observed a number of facts relating to experience-based religion. He had begun to develop his own systematic interpretation of them, and he was convinced that any interpretation must agree with the body of accumulating scientific data.

Roy was 23 years old when he arrived in Chicago. It can be argued, as Graceland President Briggs had concluded, that the University of Chicago was the best school in the country for the assignment given to Roy to gain the background required to teach religion courses at Graceland. By the time Cheville had earned an undergraduate and two graduate degrees from Chicago, he had some assurance that he had measured up with the best. He did not talk about his academic prowess and accomplishments as a matter of principle. He felt that the results of academic preparation should show in his work.

He arrived on the Chicago campus in June of 1921 and was a resident student continuously until September of 1923. Thereafter he took courses at Chicago in the summers until he completed the Ph.D., except for the depression years of 1930 to 1934, and for the summer of 1926 when he studied at the University of California.

When President Briggs had made the plans for Cheville to study at the University, Graceland College was expected to provide the necessary funds. But the finances of the church and the college were strained at the time and he received little help. He stayed in school by working, by acquiring scholarships, and "by frugality."

In four quarters of what Roy described as "heavy schedule" he completed the baccalaureate degree. The degree he earned was the Ph. B.—Bachelor of Philosophy. Throughout he continued a very active schedule of church work. In his diary one can read of his joyful encounters, some agonizing doubts, his interest in sports, and adventures in music and art.

The diary begins just before he left Graceland in May of 1921 and continues until he was awarded the baccalaureate degree in June of 1922. He arrived in Chicago on June 20, enrolled in Elementary Greek, Introduction to Philosophy, and Religion of Israel Before Amos, and began meeting classes the next day. Although throughout his life he seldom commented on his own emotional state, on his first day on campus he noted "a little homesickness for Graceland." He also commented uncharacteristically after his first class session that "Greek appears hard." He would enroll in correspondence work in Greek at the end of the summer before leaving Chicago for a brief holiday. His second four week term consisted of a continuation of Greek, american philosophy and the Epistle to the Hebrews. He left Chicago on September 2 and returned to begin the fall term on October 3, enrolling in Greek 3, sociology, Beginnings of Christianity, Beginnings of Old Testament History, and Swimming. The second full semester, beginning on April 3, 1922, found him in social psychology, the Teachings of Jesus, and Old Testament History.

In addition to class attendance his intellectual curiosity took him to lectures, concerts, theater, and opera. He also swam frequently in Lake Michigan and in the University pool. He attended some athletic events. He described the Chicago-Purdue football game on October 9 as "thrilling—my first big game." Of the Ohio State-Chicago football game on November 5 he wrote, "Ohio won 7-0. Big game, over 30,000. Best game I ever saw. Fine bands."

He explored Chicago, going to Hull House, museums, and galleries and on field trips to businesses such as Sears Roebuck. His observations in the Chicago ghetto led him to make a mental connection between poverty and undisciplined habits. He wrote, "Impressed with big need of social work as never before at seeing dirt and filth of Maxwell St. market. . . Made new determinations for a clean life."

He did not use his "heavy" schedule at the university as an excuse to give his participation in the life of the Chicago congregations of the church a lower priority than his academic work. He preached frequently, taught classes, attended mid-week prayer and testimony meetings, and accepted the presidency of the local Religio. He also appears to have been a popular dinner guest with church families. His ministry to a black congregation stimulated a specific concern for the role of this minority in the mainstream of American life, a concern that would mature in his years of teaching Races and Minorities at Graceland.

His financial position was quite insecure during this period. When, on December 8, he received word that Graceland would be unable to provide its promised contribution, he responded to the news with a characteristically optimistic note, "Rather perplexed. All will turn out." To help it "turn out" he supplemented other sources of income with work in the Commons of the University. By April of 1922 he had added work in the School of Education cafeteria and the Divinity School Library. After a visit from President George Briggs on January 11, 1922, he expressed more anxiety about finances. They agreed he would stay on to complete a master's degree. He wrote, ". . don't know where finances are coming from." Shortly after that he spoke to the Dean of the Divinity School, Shailer Mathews, about a scholarship for the following year. He also mentions receiving a $200 loan from his father.

He gained a high degree of respect for Shailer Mathews. But he felt otherwise about Edgar Goodspeed. To his diary he said about a Goodspeed course on the Epistle to Hebrews, "Appeared to be a language course and didn't think much of the instructor so changed to Hebrew Ethics under Smith."

Cheville's exposure to scientists, philosophers, and some of the foremost thinkers of the day in theology and church history inspired re-evaluation and even doubt about some of his previously held beliefs. On February 5 he wrote, "Problems, perplexities, doubts as to the gospel, L.D.S. harass on every hand. I long for a solution— may I have faith." This experience undoubtedly gave him a personal basis for understanding the problems of countless young people and insight into the best ways to offer counsel to those going through the same experience. Always a private person, even to his diary which was almost totally an external narrative, he does not reveal the specific nature of his theological dilemma.

As the pressures of the academic year's closing weeks accumulated, he confessed to being tired and getting too little sleep. He even noted that he skipped a class in order to write a paper. His participation at church, however, seems to have been undiminished during these final days. He graduated with the Ph.B. in June 1922.

The Chicago School of Divinity

In the university I set out to select good teachers. The list includes outstanding scholars and teachers. There were J. M. Smith and Edgar Goodspeed in Bible, George Herbert Mead and James H. Tufts in philosophy, Charles Judd and Sir John Adams in education, Ernest Burgess and Robert Park in sociology, William W. Sweet in church history, and Shailer Mathews in theology. I pay tribute in a special way to Dean Mathews. He stirred me with the dynamic qualities of his theology and of his own self. He made me stretch my soul. He sent me out to explore. There was something in him that made him a gentleman and scholar in his own right. [1956E]

Having completed the baccalaureate degree, Roy was now ready to enter the Divinity School as a candidate for the degree of Master of Arts. Here he would get what he came for—preparation to teach religion courses at Graceland. And he would be prepared well because the Chicago Divinity School was outstanding. In 1921 the Divinity School not only ranked high among schools of religion in the country, it ranked high among the graduate schools in the University itself. The Divinity School was a shining light among the University of Chicago professional schools. That was partly a matter of its history. The Divinity School was born as part of the process that created the University. When John D. Rockefeller gave the money to create the University he had been for some time on the board of the Baptist Union Theological Seminary (founded in 1866). He made it a condition of his gift that the Seminary should become the Divinity School of the University. It became an integral part of the University, conducting its activities according to University standards.

While studying in the Divinity School, Cheville learned to distinguish between "human" and "person" in thinking about relations with divinity. He got the idea from Shailer Mathews, and he expanded his understanding of it in study under George Herbert Meade. We become human through biology, but we become persons through interacting with other persons. The most important person we can interact with is the person of God. It is in our capacity to become persons that we are created in the image of God. Cheville's most extended discussion of the concept is found in his 1975 book *Spiritual Resources Are Available Today*. [1975A]

Another shining light in 1921 was Chicago's Department of Sociology. Chicago was the leading center of sociology in the world at this period. The department's approach was one of broad, collective intellectual endeavor. That stance was aided by other strengths of the University: the Chicago School of Philosophy, founded by John Dewey, was at the height of its influence, the Chicago School of Political Science was gaining in influence and reputation, the Chicago School of Economics was still over the horizon. There was a blending of firsthand inquiry with general ideas, the integration of research and theory as part of an organized program.[1]

In 1921 both Ernest W. Burgess and Robert E. Park were on the sociology faculty. Robert Faris[2] wrote that their book, *Introduction to the Science of Sociology*, has been one of the most influential works ever written in sociology, setting the direction and content of American sociology after 1921. Both Park and Burgess were cross-listed as Divinity School faculty. A student could register for credit in the Divinity School for the following sociology courses, most of them taught by Park and Burgess: The Church and Society, The Family, Social Pathology, Races and Missions, The Rural Church, The Social Survey, and Crime and its Social Treatment.

In the summer of 1922 Roy began graduate study in the Divinity School, Department of Practical Theology, Subdepartment of Religious Education. In the summer of 1922 he took Ancient Church and earned the grade A-, Materials of Religious Education (B), and the Psychology of Religious Development (B). In the autumn quarter of 1922 Roy took Evolution, Genetics, and Eugenics (A), The Curriculum (A-), Development of Modern Christianity (A-), and Organization of Religious Education (A-). In the winter quarter of 1923 Roy took Advanced Social Psychology (B), Social and Political Philosophy (B), Principles of Religious Education (A-), and Introduction to Church Music (B).

He declared candidacy for the Master's degree on January 23, 1923, and the candidacy was approved by the faculty on February 10, 1923. In the spring quarter of 1923 he took Social Origins (B), Religious Education of the Adult (B), Systematic Theology III (A-), and Ear Training and Sight Reading (A-).

Roy Cheville passed the Final Examination for the A.M. in Divinity May 31, 1923, and the degree was conferred June 12, 1923. His thesis was "The Function of Music in Religious Education." Some representative statements in the thesis deal with the needs of children, with the poetry used in hymns, and with the potential for music to be uplifting or to be used in furthering an anti-religious life:

> Religion has to do with the values of life, with attitudes, purposes, and social ideals that challenge faith. It endeavors to enlist the child in those happy experiences that shall develop him as a "progressively socialized individual in a community of which God is the chief member...

> Our hymnology, great and inspiring as it is, has not served well the needs of religious education: it was not written for children.

The Poetry. Songs that are not worth reading are not worth singing... (1) There should be literary merit... (2) There should be richness of religious values... (3) There should be a true conception of God and our relationship to Him... (4) Songs should contain imagery that is wholesome to the singer and the hearer... (5) Music should be marked by healthy sentiment... (6) Hymns should be true to life and portray the desirable life....

Music is essentially a language of feeling and belongs to the things that are dearest in the soul. In it lie potentialities for the highest, noblest, and most uplifting in life; it also has possibilities that easily tend toward the anti-religious life. [1923]

As Roy completed the Masters' degree he was advised by Briggs to stay in school for the summer and begin work toward his next degree, the Bachelor of Divinity. In the summer of 1923 he took Sociology of Adolescence (A-), Problems of Missionary Expansion (B), General Speaking (B-), Statistical Methods and Educational Problems (B-), and Statistical Methods and Educational Problems 2 (B).

At this point Roy had completed nine quarters sequentially in residence at Chicago. The rest of his formal courses as a student would be accomplished in summer sessions. He would return to the University of Chicago each summer until he completed the Bachelor of Divinity degree in 1925. In the summer of 1926 he studied at the University of California in Berkeley. He resumed summer attendance at Chicago in 1927 and continued with some exceptions until 1942, when he finished the Ph. D.

Though he was a student with a "heavy schedule" while in residence at Chicago from 1921 to 1923, Roy maintained ministerial activities with the Chicago Saints. He held regular responsibilities in the Central Branch. In August of 1923 there were farewell parties for him. An article in the *Saints' Herald* in September noted,

On August 16 the Glee Club held a beach and farewell party in honor of Roy Cheville, who has been with this branch for the past two years and so ably assisted in various activities of the branch. In appreciation of his work and their regard, the club presented him with a gold watch. On August 18 the branch also held a farewell party in his honor at the home of Sister Faye McDonald, and presented him with a beautiful gold chain.

After he joined the Graceland faculty Roy Cheville continued his studies at the University of Chicago, but now he studied there only in the summers. In the summer of 1924 he took The Church and Society (A-), Introduction to Systematic Theology (A), Protestantism in Europe since the Reformation (A-), General Oratory (B), and Psychology of Elementary Education (B). On July 4, 1924 he declared candidacy for the D.B. degree in the Department of Practical Theology. His candidacy was approved on July 11, 1924.

In the summer of 1925 Cheville was again at Chicago. He took Christian Doctrine of Sin and Salvation (A), Person and Work of Christ (B), God in Reason and Experience (B), Problems and Measurement in Religious Education (A), Vocal Expression for the Minister (B), and Educational Psychology (B).

He passed the final examination for the D.B. in Practical Theology on August 18, 1925, and the degree was conferred September 4, 1925. His thesis title was "The Junior Church."

Noting that it was a new field of ministry, Cheville's thesis on the junior church argued that religion should be expressed meaningfully to boys and girls in language on their level. In research for the paper he had visited a number of congregations, exploring their approaches to the junior church. This research provided the material from which he wrote four articles for the *Saints' Herald* in 1926. [1926A, B, C, D]

Notes

1. Bulmer, Martin. *The Chicago School of Sociology*, The University of Chicago Press, 1984.
2. Faris, Robert E. L. *Chicago Sociology, 1920–1932*. University of Chicago Press, 1970, (originally published in 1967).

The Berkeley Interlude

The rough draft [of the Alma Mater Hymn] was made on a train west-bound through Colorado. The refinement was made under eucalyptus trees on the hills above the Berkeley campus looking out into the ocean. A great uncharted future lay before. [Cheville notes: Prophetic Songs]

For the summer of 1926, Cheville decided for a change to go to the University of California at Berkeley. Near the Berkeley campus on Haste Street while looking for a place to stay he saw a sign advertising a room to rent, and he signed up. Sometime later his landlord introduced himself as J. D. White, president of the Northern California District of the RLDS Church. White had recognized Roy's name on the travelers' checks with which he had paid for the room. Both he and Sister White had once lived in Rhodes, though Roy had not known them then.

He described that summer at the University of California as an extraordinary experience. He took Philosophy of Evolution from a Dr. Nelson, who was head of the department of philosophy at Harvard, Comparative Education from Sir John Adams of the University of London, and Anthropology from Dr. Bronislaw Malinowski who had just returned from field studies in the south Pacific islands.

Those courses had a lasting effect on him. In a 1935 quarterly Cheville discusses practicing a large view of the world. He introduces the phrase "Pisgah view," and tells a story about the term:

An instructor [Sir John Adams in a course in Education] once asked his class to get this kind of view of the subject being studied. Some returned to tell him they could find no reference book in the library written by any one named "Pisgah." Quite surprised at this weakness in their education, he told them the story of the aged Moses climbing Mt. Pisgah on the borders of Canaan and getting a panoramic view of the Promised Land. [1935C]

Cheville would Challenge his students to take a "Pisgah View" during the years of his teaching career. When he wrote an article about "radiant teachers" years later [1956E] he included Sir John Adams. In the funeral sermon he preached for Congressman Steven Carter [1960A], he talked about "the Pisgah View." He noted that he got the phrase from Sir John Adams, who "enriched my life."

During this summer venture to Berkeley he wrote the Graceland Alma Mater hymn. It was the oldest hymn in his folder labeled "Prophetic Songs," accompanied by a description of its writing, which emphasizes the role of Graceland in his personal mission:

> The Alma Mater hymn was stimulated by a year of student life and three years of faculty life at Graceland. The idea of Graceland of the living now, of the world of yesterday's memories, and of the dreams of tomorrow's mission took shape on the campus. The rough draft was made on a train west-bound through Colorado. . . A great uncharted future lay before. The simple campus of Graceland lay behind as the agency through which the ideals of the coming day might be realized. So all the sons of Graceland are summoned to the call of the Blue and Gold. [Cheville notes: Prophetic Songs]

The next to last sentence in that quotation probably represented a review of his mission. He had now experienced two major universities, he could see the direction he might take toward a prestigious career, and his contacts could start him on that path. But his course was set. As he looked over the great Berkeley campus, he chose the simple campus of Graceland "as the agency through which the ideals of the coming day might be realized."

Chicago Doctorate

As Roy Cheville was completing the Ph. D. in religion with a social science dissertation he received the following counsel by Fred M. Smith: "You are expected to continue in exploration that will stimulate the saints to move forward into the larger light."

In each of the summers of 1927, 1928, and 1929, Cheville took graduate courses at the University of Chicago. He took a number of church history courses including History of the Church in Russia, Rise of Catholicism, The Dark Ages, Christianity and the American People, and Social and Industrial History of the U.S. He took five courses in classical theology and one in practical theology. He was not yet a candidate for another degree. His course selections appear to have been generally in support of his teaching and ministerial functions at Graceland. He still loved to go to school.

Cheville was married late in 1929 and the Great Depression settled upon the campus shortly thereafter. There was no summer school for him in the years 1930, 1931, 1932, 1933, and 1934.

He resumed study at Chicago in the summer of 1935. Along with a course in practical theology and a sociology course, he took a course to prepare for the French proficiency requirement for the Doctor of Philosophy degree. He was now clearly heading for that degree. In the summer of 1936 he took a Bible course, a religious education curriculum course, and a sociology course on the family. In that summer he passed the examination for divinity preparation courses.

In the summer of 1937 (Second Term) he took two theology courses and passed the divinity examination on intermediate courses. On March 7, 1938, he passed the

French reading exam. In the summer of 1938 he took two theology courses and the German reading course. In that summer he also attended a young people's convention at Detroit, the Lamoni reunion, and the Colorado Springs reunion. In the summer of 1939 he continued the German reading course and other typical courses. He also worked on the Youth Conference Manual. On March 1, 1940, he passed the German exam. In the summer of 1940 he took two regular courses and registered for research problems. This registration probably signaled serious work on his dissertation. He also attended a youth rally in Detroit.

During this summer session Cheville had an opportunity to take advantage of his scholarly study of RLDS church history:

> While studying at the University of Chicago School of Divinity I was enrolled in a course in church history, "Religion on the Frontier in the United States 1820–1850." This was the period of the initiation of the Latter Day Saint movement. The instructor, Dr. W. W. Sweet, was considered an authority in this field. Each student was to write a "term paper." When I went to Dr. Sweet to confer about the paper, he asked, "Of what church are you a member?" When I told him he said at once, "Write on your own church. It is a story that has never yet been written." Then he asked, "What is your thinking about what happened in the field of plural marriage during those years of your church in Nauvoo?" I told him of the speculation about the hereafter, celestial marriage, and plural marriage. Immediately he asked another question: "What is your thinking about Joseph Smith himself? Did he get into plural marriage?"
>
> I said that I did not think Joseph was ever a polygamist. Thinking that I was defending the conventional viewpoint of my church the professor asked, "On what grounds do you base your opinion?" I said that I based my conclusion on two major fields of evidence. First, Emma Smith would never have sanctioned plural marriage for her husband. In the theory of the Mormons, the husband was required to procure the sanction of his wife before marrying another woman. If Joseph had made such a proposal, Emma would have replied as

negatively as she spoke up about the bar in the Mansion House. She would have told Joseph that if he brought home another woman, she, Emma, would leave. Second, if Joseph had had all the wives attributed to him, and had sex relations with them, in those days of limited contraception there would have been pregnancies and progeny. I added that if a child had been born to this presumed practice of plural marriage, when Joseph died this child would have been announced from the housetops. It would have been considered an honor to be the mother of a child sired by the prophet. Dr. Sweet listened attentively and then said, "Those are the soundest arguments I have heard." [1977A]

He was in Chicago in the summers of 1941 and 1942. He was registered in a thesis course. The school of divinity usually did not allow a student to do a dissertation on his own church because it might the student's objectivity more difficult. It was a compliment to Cheville that he was allowed to make this study of his church. He passed the Final Examination for the Ph. D. in the divinity school on August 22, 1942. The degree was conferred on September 11, 1942.

Roy Cheville's doctoral dissertation is a sociological study of the RLDS church. Its title is "The Role of Religious Education in the Accommodation of a Sect." It was done in the Department of Practical Theology, Sub Department of Religious Education.

The following excerpts give some of the flavor of the work:

This church claims the attention of the world for a number of distinctive features that give it a unique place and message. We feel that these features recommend it to the attention of thoughtful people because they offer solutions to the problems that have been particularly vexing in the late social and economic conditions of the world.

These distinctive features are: the restored and revitalized inspiration of the Christian message; a social philosophy and an economic program point the way to the creation of new conditions under which men can live and work happily and hopefully; an educational program which will indefinitely expand the outlook and possibilities of human life.

Dangers before the Group
1. A straddle-the-fence theory
2. An exultation of and devotion to institutionalism
3. Ecclesiastical control
4. The loss of creative thinkers
5. The lack of cultivation of non-priesthood men
6. Ambiguity in the role of women
7. Disregard of the nature of human nature
8. Loss of conviction in multiple types of experience
9. Misplacement of emphasis
10. Employment of programs and propaganda and mass controls

A sound system of religious education must be rooted in the spiritual foundations of the universe itself. With this goes an understanding of the way man can tap the spiritual resources inherent in his Universe for personal and social living. Latter Day Saints must interpret how this is to be done through their church. A theology for them must fall in line with historical Latter Day Saintism and accord with its genius, but must also square with the growing body of verifiable data about man and his environment. [1942A]

A short version of the dissertation was written as a pamphlet with the title, *The Latter Day Saints and Their Changing Relationship to the Social Order*. This pamphlet was published in 1942 by Herald House in "Church School Leadership Series," 75p. [1942B]

BOOK IV.

Life Patterns

BOOK IV. LIFE PATTERNS
Halo and Warts

. . let's look at the job designed for the church. It is not a museum of plaster saints nor an exhibit of angels. [1951C]

Roy Cheville was a real person. He was gifted but also flawed. His gifts and the use he made of them are so impressive that his life deserves to be studied. It is important, then, that he be understood as one who lived in our time and who confronted the same kind of choices we confront. He made many good choices and followed their implications. Those are the ones he is and will be remembered for—he may well deserve a halo. He made some less than good choices and we will recognize but not celebrate them—those warts will allow us to understand better the reality of his life.

There were many people who loved and respected Cheville, and some who grudgingly respected him but did not love him. In his prime years he had a great deal of self-confidence. This allowed him to teach, to write, and to preach effectively. But that characteristic turned off some of his students. Many of those met him when they were not yet established as persons and had insecurities about their own abilities. In that situation it was easy for some to resent a professor who appeared to have all the answers he needed. Some who lived through that kind of experience may appreciate reading in this volume of the struggles that student Cheville went through, especially in 1921 to 1923 at the University of Chicago. Some students may have considered him flamboyant, and others may have had different reasons not to relate well with him.

If Cheville had held himself back and assumed a more restrained style, he would not have accomplished as much as he did. He would not have generated as many fresh insights and as many sound ways of communicating them to enhance the lives of others. By the time he was 20 years old he was better educated and better informed than nearly all of the people he lived and worked with. He adjusted to working with that realization as a given. Once he was asked a rather profound question in class. He responded by saying "modestly," he did not know. Then he went on to say that "with less modesty I can say that nobody else knows the answer either."

He made it a habit not to criticize people who knew less than he. One of the ways he avoided "putting people down" was to ascribe immature ideas and behavior to fictitious characters. For that purpose he invented Brother and Sister DuBuzzy. They had all the painful characteristics he was teaching his students to overcome. He could hold the DuBuzzies up to ridicule without creating the problems that come from criticizing real people.

Certainly in his Graceland years Roy Cheville had reason to be self-confident. Velma Ruch said once that Cheville's mind seemed to work faster than that of many other people. In computer terms, he had a faster processor. It is not clear that such was the case in his earlier years. It probably speeded up in the first half of his faculty period, and was clearly up to speed in the last half. It was not just processor speed. By the time he had earned his doctorate, he had extensive knowledge of the Bible, the Book of Mormon, church history, much other history, much philosophy, and a great many other materials. Much of this knowledge was currently available to him. In computer terms, when he was at work this material was loaded into RAM (random access memory) and available to be applied instantly in support of the task at hand.

Cheville's degree of self-confidence sometimes translated into impatience. He could do so many things so rapidly himself that it was difficult for him to wait for others to get things done. If it was a matter of waiting for students to get some major concept, or if he was waiting for them to make some great personal commitment, he had a great deal of patience. But if he was waiting for something that had to be done before he could do the next important thing—then he could be impatient.

Some times he had a short fuse. He could get angry at a person very quickly without taking time to hear the other side. That anger usually did not last very long, and he would soon be again a sensitive colleague. Such anger erupted once in the late forties toward a student he respected. The reason for the anger was her participation in a demonstration aimed at getting black students on the Graceland campus. What she did not know was that Cheville had been working for 20 years to change the hearts of college and church people in such a way that there would be no opposition to the advent of blacks or people of any other color on campus. This is, of course, an arguable strategy. It was an approach that was completely consistent, however, with Cheville's theology.

Cheville took this long view in dealing with social problems. In a later section of this book, that approach will be seen in a program for world peace which he worked on relentlessly for more than 40 years. His approach was non-confrontational. He believed in achieving social justice through changing the hearts of people just as he believed Jesus had done. He had become convinced by the middle 1930's that he had to choose between the long view—nurturing the spiritual roots of quality decision-making—and the short view—urging action on specific problems. He always chose the long view.

Cheville took the long view in dealing also with the loss of human potential caused by the restrictive role the church allowed for women. He described the problem clearly in his 1942 dissertation. By 1945 he invited women to function in roles normally assigned to priesthood in Graceland's religious emphasis week. Throughout his career he presented clear reasons for analyzing the bases on which such discrimination had been supported. Focusing on the crux of the matter in 1974 (ten years before ordination for women was accepted by the church) he wrote,

> If this trend continues within a very few years the denial of the priesthood to women will seem as antiquated and irrational as the uncritical acceptance of the institution of slavery seems to us now. I have a hunch that an Old Testament prophet, looking at this development, would discern the hand of God in it. [1974A]

Along with his self-confidence was a rather definite need to be in control. He felt usually that he knew best how to deal with the problem at hand. He was often right, but frequently did not give colleagues much room to act. It was typical that he would have an extensive draft of a committee report by the second meeting of the committee. It was usually so good that the committee would vote his way rather than put in an equal amount of work to write a different report. That strong need to be in control lay behind some of his long hours of intensive and productive work.

Psychiatrist Karen Ritchie has suggested that many very productive people like Roy Cheville have some manic characteristics. They produce enormous amounts of work, need little sleep, are outgoing and talkative, and have lots of energy. These characteristics may last over much of a life-time. The combination of a brilliant mind and great drive can put one in exclusive company.

Being a team member with "Doc" was always rewarding but not always easy. In one example, he went over in some detail what he wanted the author to say in a three minute talk at a particular point in the upcoming worship service. When the service got under way "Doc," in executing the earlier part of the service, covered every item he had outlined to be said by the author. There was about one minute lead time for the author to generate a new three minute talk which would fit in with the theme. Cheville was so immersed in the spirit of the service that, when those ideas needed to be expressed, he forgot he had delegated their expression. The service went smoothly, and neither of us ever mentioned the experience.

He clearly liked the position of center stage. He liked to be the one to get an audience singing with gusto and on the right tempo. He liked to control the sequence of events in a meeting and interpret the various themes. Again he would work very hard over a period of time to be in a position of control. He thought things were moving in the right direction only when he was setting the agenda. He appeared to see only one right way to do some things—his. He preferred center stage and he preferred being in control, but the effort thus aimed was never in the direction of building allegiance to himself. The charismatic character of his leadership could have resulted in a personal following, if that had been his desire. If he was tempted, he resisted successfully.

One aspect of control can be seen in his bibliography in the appendices to this volume. No co-authored publications exist. Those for which his name and Charlotte

Gould's name appear were written and published first entirely by Cheville, and a later version was produced by Mrs. Gould simplified for younger students.

Although he tried hard to suppress it, he did display a superior attitude occasionally. For example, a bit of self-righteous annoyance with the ordinary tourist shows through one report he wrote after returning from Europe in 1949. He said,

> Since my return from Europe, I've come to feel even more deeply that many—ever so many—travelers would do well to stay at home. They have no commendable reason for going. Only those who go to understand—to understand with clear perspective—have a right to travel. [1949D]

Though he was strong-minded, Cheville seems never to have had any trouble as a faculty member dealing with presidents of the college. His relationship with the general officers of the church was not as harmonious. At least after the era of Fred M., when Cheville referred in private conversations on administrative and policy matters, to the church officials, he called them "the big boys." He might have been a bit envious of their power and a little prideful in the thought that he could perhaps do a better job. When he became one of them he did not always maintain smooth administrative relations. As he was a loner in his theology, he was sometimes a loner in his working relations.

Roy Cheville had a merry sense of humor. It made him a very pleasant companion. He used it readily in campfire sessions and informal meetings. He used it frequently in classroom situations, both to hold interest and to illustrate points. He wrote a book on *Humor in Gospel Living* when he was 81. This book gives evidence of his sense of humor but does not do it justice. He believed that "a laughless religion will never attract the young for long." [1941E]

Many students came to Graceland from congregations that regarded laughter and religion as antithetical. Cheville's sometimes irreverent humor poked sly fun at stodgy religious customs. A former student remembers his use at lunch of a phrase that was customarily heard in solemn communion services, "Has anyone missed their worthy portion?" He startled students by introducing them to the Latvian folk song, "My God and I." He sang it with a line which went, "We'd walk and talk and *jest* as good friends do." That line had a purpose in Cheville's religion and in his theology. He wanted youth to think about God not only as a person, but also as a friendly and interesting person. He said that his God has a sense of humor. He wrote in the 1930's that we should think of God as the ideal personality. He clearly believed that the ideal personality has a well-developed sense of humor.

Cheville's ability to hold a close relation between religion and levity seems implicit in an early story about his Religio class in 1925. "Anyone who thinks religion and fun cannot be mixed should have been at south woods last Tuesday evening," began a *Saints' Herald* article. It went on to describe a surprise picnic by Cheville's Religio class to express their gratitude to their instructor for his leadership throughout the year. As he neared the camp everyone greeted him with a song, "For he's a jolly good fellow." Then with appropriate ceremonies he was presented with a baby owl in remembrance of all the wise cracks he had made. [SH 10 June 25]

Cheville's humor did not include telling sex-related jokes. He neither told them nor gave them recognition if they were heard. Instead he gave abundant illustration that off-color subjects are not needed for laughter and

81

merry interaction. However, his humor sometimes had an earthy quality. Enid DeBarthe remembers his asking two male students in class, "Did you practice laying on of hands last night?"

He took deadly aim at pomposity and excess. During a preaching service one night during a general conference, an apostle, who was a good friend of Cheville's, was preaching a very long and very dry address. Cheville leaned over to his companion and said, "I move the previous question." Commenting on long-winded prayers, he would remark, "The brother's prayer included those who dwell in uninhabited places."

Cheville was never stuffy or pompous himself. He, Roscoe Faunce, and Bill Gould delighted college audiences on many occasions. Appearing in outlandish costumes, they usually brought down the house singing, "Cigareets and whusky and wild, wild women will drive you crazy, will drive you insane." After the new water tower arose above the campus, Roy Cheville wrote a humorous additional stanza to the Alma Mater hymn:

Through years and decades long to come
  Thy shiny, silvery tower
Shall give us ample pressure
  For the fountain and the shower.
And as the waters rise high
  Thy cubic feel will hold
Sufficient fire protection
  For the halls of the Blue and Gold. [1972F]

He recognized humor in many situations. In an article, "The Setting for the Sermon" in the *Priesthood Journal* of January 1936, he gave practical advice regarding the choice of music,

If the solos or anthems do not fit into the theme of the service, it is better to have a congregational hymn just before the sermon. . . I recall an account of Elder U. W. Greene. He had preached on HELL. A soloist arose and sang at the close, "Tell Mother, I'll Be There." Once in Lamoni several years ago an elder was rather long-winded in his sermon. He was followed by a duet, "Some Day 'Twill All Be Over." [1936B]

In the Zion's League Handbook he wrote,

Church work can be and must be colored in a springlike atmosphere if laughing eyes and enthusiastic spirits are to be created. Appeal to chivalry and adventure, and youth will move a mountain. The playless and funless youth is unhealthy. The cheery, red-blooded and enthusiastic person can be enlisted to give his energy to the church. When the heart is open with pure laughter and fellowship, response will be voluntary. [1941E]

His ability to generate humor and enthusiasm is evident in the log of Nauvoo Camp in 1946. Cheville was program director:

"I'm always blowing bubbles" or "Ring dem bells, cause I got one o' mah own now" could be Doc's theme song after last night. Appreciative campers presented him with a soap-bubble pipe, bell bank ("so you can use this one to wake up the kids if you don't have anything else") and a flashy necktie for "making the camp a real bang-up affair, and for helping us have so much fun." Doc confided to the staff that "this bell touched me more than anything else." [*Nauvoo Camp Log* 6 July 46]

In writing about the characteristics of good families he said,

They do not come by chance. . . One of the little-thought-of forces that hold a family together is the jokes. . . Our family has a stock of these joke possessions. There was the time when the mother was away that I had supper with the son and daughter. As we sat down to the meal, the son suggested that we pretend we were cats and have a cat supper. We agreed. Without thinking further about the implications, I asked him to return thanks. He spoke three reverent meows and said amen! There was the time my eight-year-old daughter told me my tie would look better if I held my stomach in. . . The

God I know has a sense of humor. I want him to have it when he deals with me. [1958A]

Cheville was not a plaster saint. He had some saint-like characteristics but he was a real person with defects. If we follow his theory of God, Cheville's complexity makes his life all the more important to study. If we want to find spirituality at work, he believed, we must learn how to see it in the lives of ordinary people in ordinary places. He put that thought into a poem:

If I could go away from here,
    Away from things I've always known,
I could find God. This place is marked
    With common things, like tree and stone.
        Among these trees the sunlight weaves
        Artistic patterns 'mong the leaves.
        These growing plants are Aaron's rods
        That witness visibly of God.
But this town is so commonplace.
    These folk have no prophetic flame;
They could not mount to Pisgah height.
    These men are truly halt and lame.
        The chosen are not always great
        In social life of wealth and state.
        Men thought that Nazareth could bear
        No prophet, yet the Christ lived there.
I search for God's revealment now—
    Some flaming word across the sky,
Some pentecostal fiery tongue—
    I'd like to see an angel fly.
        You see not as you look around
        This very place is holy ground.
        Attune thy soul and thou canst see
        Some common bush afire may be.
But I have wanted, oh, so much,
    Some revelation great to find,
That would remove my every doubt,

84

And fathom the eternal mind.
   A lad in youthful searchings strove
   And found God in his father's grove.
   So each can find revealment, too,
   Who reads the signs as God breaks through. [1950O]

Roy and Nell on Hill Cumorah in 1930. Picture from the files of Ina Campbell Crossan.

Roy, Nell, Dick and Charlotte about 1941.

Family Life

It may be a fancy that "real love matches are made in heaven," but surely if we would have God's blessing at any point in our lives, it is at the time when we choose a life companion. And our choice should have the deepest sanctions of our religious natures. [1933E]

Roy Cheville once said that he asked married couples he counseled where they met. That gave him a clue to the things they had in common. He and Nell met on the Graceland campus. They shared the church ideals and a commitment to education. Roy's professional preparation was greater and his career took priority over Nell's, but both believed that family living should nourish each person. They had a happy and effective companionship which was increased by the qualities of their two children. Achieving their goals took effort. Not every day went well, and they did not do everything right. They did support each other, and they left a rich legacy.

Roy Cheville and Nell (her real name was Nelle) Marie Weldon were married in Lamoni December 23, 1929. They had two children: Richard Arthur, born December 26, 1931, and Charlotte Estelle, born January 13, 1937. Dick married Lila Davis, and they have two children, Alan and Andrea. Charlotte married Robert Farrand, and they have two children, Christopher and Gregory. Nell died of cancer in Lamoni December 3, 1957.

Roy and Nell met in September 1927, when Nell came to Graceland College to be campus nurse and to study in the field of religion. She was born on September 19, 1903, in Lafayette, Contra Costa County, California, the daughter of George and Estelle Sweet Weldon. She was baptized into the RLDS Church September 5, 1910, in Irvington, California and confirmed by E. L. Kelly. She

89

had two sisters: Rachel and Ruby (married Charlie York), and four brothers: Roy, Walter, L.D., and Chester. Nell had completed nurse's training at Merritt Hospital in Oakland, California, before going to Graceland.

Nell's family extended themselves to help her attend Graceland. This was done in the context of their devotion to the RLDS Church and the expectancy that the Graceland experience would be beneficial to Nell, to the family, and to the local California church branch. She wrote,

> But frequently our thoughts turn toward the little church at home, to the faithful ones who are waiting for our help, and to the sacrificing parents who have so confidently sent us forth to take advantage of the opportunities denied to them. If those home folks could only hear the fervently expressed desires to be true to home, to coming responsibilities, and to the church, they would know that their sacrifices are not in vain and that their confidences have not been misplaced. Nell Weldon [SH 28 Nov 28]

Roy Cheville was a bachelor faculty member at Graceland for more than six years. Julia (Judy) Travis Closson, who had known him since 1924, did not remember that Roy dated before Nell arrived on the scene. She said that he was always with a group and that things were lively when he was around. Agnes Adams Fisher, who also had known him since 1924, said that she was surprised when she heard that Roy was married because she did not think he was interested in dating.

Nell was a serious professional and a devout Christian. She wrote a short article entitled "An Interview on the Subject of My Vocation" which advocated two years of college study in the social sciences as preparation for nurse's training and displays a practical realism about her profession: "The average girl just out of high school has not enough stability of character to stand the shocks she will receive upon looking into the raw wounds and festered spots of human life." [SH 19 Oct 27]

She reveals a depth of religious commitment in the following report on the Easter Vesper Service at Graceland:

A short Easter drama, 'Those who saw him living,' carried our thoughts back to the time of the resurrection of Jesus. As we listened to the testimonies of those who had seen and talked with Him, who testified that 'He that was dead is risen,' we were touched by that same spirit of faith and trust that has been the hope of the followers of Christ in all ages. [SH 11 April 28]

Another article by Nell reported on Graceland prayer meetings and their effect on her:

Among the many excellent features of college life at Graceland, the Wednesday evening prayer service is most enjoyed by the majority of students. It is there, in our little chapel, that we can withdraw our minds from the confusion and stress of active school life, and under the influence of that peaceful spirit that meets with us, regain our spiritual values and get an insight into the deeper meanings of life. Under the sympathetic guidance of consecrated leaders, we can share our problems and aspirations as we worship and meditate together. [SH 28 Nov 28]

Still another article by Nell described the challenges and dedications expressed in the last prayer meeting of the college year:

Departing students spoke regretfully of the small heritage they felt they were leaving in comparison with the greatness of the things Graceland had given them in their stay on the College Hill; and new and old students voiced a fervent desire to strive to attain higher planes of life in the years to come. Through all the meeting, binding the whole group to a closer unity, ran the earnestly expressed desires to be true to the Graceland ideals, to the folks at home, and to the church. [SH 29 May 29]

With the student picture of Nell Weldon in the 1929 *Acacia* was the note "Always there when help is needed." Her activities were listed as Victorian, OOH, and Crescent Club. Female students selected women who had demonstrated personal integrity and a genuine spirit of service to be Crescents. It was a great honor.

Nell and Roy became engaged in May, 1929, at the North Door (outside) of the Administration building. Roy commented that it was the only place where they could find privacy. Somehow Roy's club brothers in the Royal 13 found out about the engagement. They cut two long poles, built a rather precarious throne draped with a club blanket, and lay in ambush. As Roy left class that afternoon he was quickly surrounded, placed on the throne and hoisted to the shoulders of the enthusiastic students. Others had abducted Nell, and she was hoisted to a shaky position beside him where, to keep from falling, she had to cling to his embarrassingly public embrace. Then the parade started, picking up more students by the second, until the campus had been covered and classes for the afternoon hopelessly interrupted.

Nell returned to California in the summer of 1929 to attend to economic concerns. During that summer Roy's thoughts were clearly concerned with family. On Father's Day he gave a family night address. He said,

> The family as a unit should follow the same general trend as all of the great Creator's works. No two flowers are alike, no two people, yet there is a similarity of symmetrical beauty in the flower, and there should be a condition of unity and interest in the family and in the church which creates a similarity of purpose, and a common goal toward which to center the efforts of each group. The interest must not be temporary or forced, but come from a desire to accomplish the things which are of greatest good for the whole. [SH 29 June 29]

With Roy's engagement to Nell and a wedding planned for December, he relinquished the role of head resident at Herald Hall. A news item noted that the little "angels" down at Herald Hall are starting their earthly sojourn with a new "head angel," Voas Meredith, in charge. An item in the *Graceland Record*, December 17, 1929, announced, "Marriage of Unk to be on December 23."

"It won't be long now! Uncle Roy and Nell are waiting patiently or otherwise for that day of all days when they shall be united in marriage. The people whom most Graceland students are envying are those few who will get to stay over and enjoy the thrill that comes from watching two of their close friends, experience so happy an occasion."

The Lamoni Chronicle for December 26, 1929, described the ceremony:

The marriage of Miss Nell Weldon, daughter of Mr. and Mrs. George Weldon, of Lafayette, Calif. to Mr. Roy A. Cheville of Lamoni, was solemnized Monday afternoon at 3:30 in the Brick church in the presence of a large number of friends and relatives. A navy and old gold altar in the center of the rostrum was banked with ferns and greenery and lighted with yellow and white candles. The service, employing the single ring ceremony, was read by Elder W. E. Prall.

The bride entered on the arm of her brother, L. D. Weldon, of Iowa City. She wore a gown of ivory satin fashioned with oval neck and tight bodice, and full skirt with uneven hem line hanging in graceful folds. Her three-quarters-length veil was held in place with two bands of tiny white flowers, and she carried a large shower bouquet of white roses and ferns.

The bride's sister, Miss Rae Weldon, acted as maid of honor, and wore a gown of apricot colored moire designed with oval neck cut low in the back, snug bodice and long full skirt. The bridesmaids were Miss Ruby Weldon and Miss Beatrice Gates of Philadelphia, who were attractively gowned in green and pink moire of similar style. . .

The groom was attended by his brother, Fred Cheville, of Rhodes, Iowa, Frank Parsons of Goodland, Kansas., and Leslie Flowers of

93

Independence, Mo. Hilliard Cox and Richard Anderson acted as ushers.

Preceding the ceremony Arthur Oakman, of London, England, sang "O Promise Me," by Reginald DeKoven and "Ah Sweet Mystery of Life," by Victor Herbert. A quartet composed of Mrs. Gertrude White Walden, Arthur Oakman, Miss Rae Lysinger and Evan Walden sang "Now the Day is Over," "Believe me if all Those Endearing Young Charms," and a prayer response. They were accompanied by Verna Schaar. The wedding march from Lohengrin was played by Miss Mabel Carlile at the piano and Evan Fry at the organ. Mendelssohn's wedding march was used at the close of the ceremony. . .

Mr. and Mrs. Cheville departed on the evening train for Chicago, where they will spend a brief honeymoon, and they expect to visit at the home of the groom's parents, near Rhodes before their return. They will be at home in Lamoni after January 6.

Out of town guests at the wedding included: Mr. and Mrs. George Cheville, and son Fred, parents and brother of the groom, Rhodes, Iowa; Rae Weldon, of Oakland, Calif.; and L. D. Weldon, of Iowa City, sister and brother of the bride; Evan Fry and Leslie Flowers, Independence, Mo.; Doris Mitchell, Aledo, Ill.; Richard Anderson, Des Moines; Irene Johnson, Plano Ill.; and Marie Nelson.

From the beginning of their marriage they shared many appointments for ministry. In June of 1930 the Chevilles chaperoned a group of young people camping out at Radnich's Bend near Davis City. In July 1930, they were on the staff of Nauvoo Camp. In July 1932, Roy was the program director at Nauvoo Camp and Nell conducted a class in health rules for girls. In the summer of 1933 Roy was again program director and Nell was camp nurse.

Ina Campbell Crossan remembers a trip taken by Roy and Nell during their first year of marriage:

In the summer of 1930 Roy and wife Nell took a 10 day trip with our (Robert Campbell family). We went to places of historic interest (to members of the RLDS Church.) Roy often mentioned to our family that that trip was Roy and Nell's honeymoon trip as they had no car

94

(it was during depression days) and they never had a honeymoon until they made that 10 day trip with our family.

The trip began on August 18, 1930, with 10 people in two cars. At night a haystack cover between the two cars housed the men and a side tent housed the women. Meals were cooked where they camped for the night. The tour included Nauvoo, Kirtland, and Palmyra.

On December 26, 1931, Roy and Nell's son, Richard Arthur Cheville, was born. As a baby, Dick was in poor health. He had asthma and some other ailments. Now a physician himself, Dick believes that he probably would not have survived his early years without his mother's nursing competence and constant devotion. Judy Closson said, "It took Nell and the doctors a while to determine what was wrong with Dick. He couldn't tolerate milk. He just cried continually. He was just hungry, I suppose. He would take milk then lose it. Nell said, 'Why on earth do I have all this milk?'"

The depression hit the Cheville family hardest in 1932. Between April and October, 1932, the Cheville family received a total of $14 from Graceland College. They and other faculty members bought groceries on credit from the store of Arthur Lane who reported that eventually every one of them paid him in full. It was characteristic of their loyalty and gratitude that they continued to shop there even after a larger store opened in Lamoni.

Some time in 1932 the Farmer's State Bank of Lamoni failed and the Cheville family lost its home. The three Cheville's moved into the upstairs of the house in which the Blair Jensen family occupied the first floor. Jensen was president of Lamoni Stake and Cheville was his counselor.

During the depression Roy Cheville charged a standard fee of $5 for performing weddings for non church members. When strangers who had been referred for this purpose would knock on the door, there was joy in the house because $5 would buy a lot of groceries.

On January 13, 1937, a daughter was born to Roy and Nell Cheville. She was named Charlotte Estelle. Among Roy Cheville's notes there was a story about Charlotte's blessing. Roy told five-year old Dick that his new baby sister was born, and she and his mother were well. Dick asked how much she weighed at birth. When told the weight he noted that he had weighed two ounces more when he was born. Roy recognized that Dick was happy about the new arrival but did not want to lose his place. Roy worked on a plan for arranging a service of blessing for Charlotte which included Dick in the planning. They decided to hold the blessing in the children's church for ages five, six, and seven. Dick agreed that Earl Higdon would be the minister. The hymns were all chosen to be appreciated by the children and have a message of love and dedication. At the end of the service Roy reported, "More than one child, boys and girls came to me and said, 'We want to help Charlotte and all of us to be good friends with Jesus.' Several drew near to Charlotte to pat her head, her hand or her shoulder."

Enid DeBarthe remembers that, shortly after the birth of Enid's first child, Nell asked her to come over to learn some techniques about bathing babies. Enid said, "Nell was a very sensitive woman. She seemed to understand when you had problems without having to be told." Katherine Condit, a frequent Cheville baby sitter, said, "I always enjoyed going early and staying after Nell came home because she was the nicest person to visit with. I always felt I could share problems with her. I thought she was a good mother. She was considerate and thoughtful as a nurse; very tender." Katie added,

> She was a very understanding person. She could relate to children and young people. I always felt grateful for the association I had with her. I have always felt of Nell as a "mother in Israel." She would take care of the kids on the block as well as her own. She was a very nice lady. A Christian lady.

After 1939 Nell Cheville's health seems to have been fragile. She suffered what was described as a "heart attack" by the then young physician Dr. E. E. Gamet. She was taken in an ambulance to the Sanitarium in Independence. After returning home she was in bed for several months.

Nell was nurse for the Lamoni schools when Priscilla Boeckman Siler was a teacher there about 1940. Priscilla describes an incident that was occasioned by a polio scare. Nell came into the classroom and visited with the children, tousling their hair and touching each one. Without their being aware of it, she had touched each of the children under the chin or in some place where she could detect a fever if they had one.

Bill Higdon was a boyhood friend of Dick Cheville and was in the Cheville home frequently. He remembers Mrs. Cheville as being very friendly and compassionate. But he said she was a straight shooter. She would not hesitate to speak frankly if something was not right.

Nell was mature and a professional in her own right when she and Roy met. That she was a committed idealist can be seen in the articles quoted above. Her love for Roy was accompanied by a strong respect for his mission. Roy was already well known and highly respected throughout the church. His teaching and his ministry were already considered outstanding. He put his whole self into the activities which fulfilled that mission. Although he drew upon the resources of those about him, he took a major role in all his activities. Much of what he did he could not share with anyone, and that would not change. Nell gladly dedicated her life to him as a person, and to him as a man with a mission in which she believed whole-heartedly. Her role would be that of companionship in those things they could share and support for him in the parts of his mission they could not share.

Enid DeBarthe said, "They had a happy and very understanding relationship. Nell was of the old school. She kept the house and took care of the children. On Sunday Roy would go to church early. Nell would take care of the kitchen, get the children ready, and then come later. Both intellectually and emotionally they had a close relationship, but it was not confining. They gave each other space."

When Judy Closson was asked how Nell handled Roy's long absences in the summer, she said, "How did the rest of us handle it? We kept house, took care of the children, mowed the lawn. You had to. We had parties with our women friends, and we all would bring our children."

Roy was very appreciative of the companionship which he and Nell shared. That companionship is reflected in his approach to writing about Joseph and Emma Smith in his book, *Joseph and Emma, Companions* [1977A]. However, he proceeded with the activities which took a great deal of his time in Lamoni, and increasingly took him out of town. That he would do so was apparently a part of their shared agreement.

In the summer of 1947 Charlotte Cheville was 10 and Dick was 15. Roy was apparently giving thought to the time he spent with them in relation to the other demands on his time. In an article which appeared in the Septem-

98

ber 20, 1947 issue of the Herald, he articulated the concept known as "quality time:"

> Perhaps I have exaggerated my own busyness, but I have classified myself as a dad who does not have much time to spend with his family. I made a discovery that has given me heart. I found that having lots of time does not insure good parenthood. . . I came to conclude that it is not *how much* but *how* that matters most. Fifteen minutes wisely utilized can be more fruitful than five hours of aimless or misaimed association. [1947H]

Roy clearly attempted to combine his ministerial and family responsibilities. For example, in the summer of 1947 Roy was at Camp Couchdale near Hot Springs, Ark., on the staff of the RLDS reunion of the Arkansas-Louisiana area. His daughter Charlotte accompanied him. (Nell was visiting her father and sister at Warrensburg, Mo.) However sound his ideas on the subject were, Roy never really solved his own problem.

Nell continued to find joy in the life of her family and in Roy's accomplishments and their reflection on her ideals. Though she did not complain, she was aware, as the years went by, of the cost to her of maintaining his mission. For a long time the stresses remained inside her, rather than between them. She developed a number of illnesses which frequently limited what she could do. It is likely that some of these were psychogenic. In a conversation with Barbara McFarlane in 1949, she said, "Whenever I start getting into too many activities I get sick, and I think it is the Lord telling me I should not get over involved because it interferes with Roy's ministry."

Some of these stresses between them came out into the open in 1949 when Roy was preparing for a ministerial trip to Europe. President Gleazer had succeeded in working out support for Roy to go to Europe for three months in 1949. He got approval from the Board of Trustees and received an allocation of $1,000 to finance the trip. In the Cheville home there was a discussion of a different kind. Roy had assumed that he was going alone; Nell had assumed she would accompany him. According to the children, Richard and Charlotte, their mother became aware that Roy felt that her presence on the trip would dilute Roy's ministry. This realization hurt her deeply. It was probably too late to make any changes in the Europe trip plan by the time "Doc" learned that he had an intense personal problem. We have described the complexity of the process by which President Gleazer had obtained funding and approval for "Doc" to make the trip. Though parts of him were now being pulled in two different ways, Roy Cheville went to Europe as a minister in the summer of 1949.

Roy's going alone was not a new pattern. It had become standard procedure that Nell and Roy hardly saw each other during general conferences, sometimes even staying in different places in Independence. But this time Nell objected. Discussion about this issue appear to have brought to the surface other unresolved issues between them. There was not a satisfactory healing experience. Some of these strains were still not resolved at Nell's death in 1957.

When Katherine Condit was teaching in the Lamoni schools [probably 1953–54] Nell was the school nurse. Katie said,

> I enjoyed visiting with her between classes, before or after school. One day when we were visiting she said that it was a hard job being the wife of Roy Cheville. I remember being surprised at her statement.

Dick and Charlotte felt as children and feel now that they were fortunate to grow up in the Cheville home.

They were well-cared for emotionally and stimulated intellectually. According to Priscilla Boeckman Siler, Nell tried to reserve Thursday evenings for family time. She discouraged drop-in visitors and phone calls. Both Dick and Charlotte felt the effect on their mother and the somewhat lesser effects on themselves of their father's high intensity mission. Both of them loved their father and have great respect for his accomplishments.

Dick and Charlotte were affected somewhat differently by the strains between their parents. Dick was then preparing to enter college and was in the process of separating himself from family affairs. And it was his nature to be able to separate himself from such an issue. This he proceeded to do. He concluded that his mother received both rewards and costs from being the spouse of Roy Cheville, and that her rewards amply outweighed the costs.

Charlotte was five years younger than Dick and was much more involved with the family emotional climate and balance. And it was not her nature to withdraw. She became involved in the discussions and defended her mother's position. She was and is of the opinion that her mother paid a rather large price in support of her father's ministry. Both Dick and Charlotte have advanced degrees and have been successful professionally and personally.

Cheville recognized that he had paid a high cost. In 1983 he wrote a book about his endowing experiences in Kirtland Temple. In that book he told of a number of different trips to Kirtland, each with a different group of people. Then, among these factual accounts of trips to the Temple, he wrote an account of an imaginary trip that he wished had occurred. He wrote,

Often, after our family became 'scattered,' I wished that we four Chevilles had taken a journey to Kirtland Temple. The most promising time for such an excursion would have been in the summer when we could have camped along the way and become acquainted with the countryside between Kirtland and Nauvoo and Independence. In so doing we could have 'relived' some happenings in church history. This would have led to meaningful explorations by all of us, but especially by the two junior members of the family.

I wish we had gone the summer after our son Dick was graduated from high school. Our daughter Charlotte was five years younger, but she, too, was inclined to inquire and explore. We would have spent two months in getting ready, enjoyed the days of traveling to Kirtland, visited the temple and surrounding area, and then returned to our home in Lamoni. Nell, my wife-companion and their mother, would have helped with the planning. As a family we would have increased our historical background, considering the function of a temple in the life of our church, and more. A day in Nauvoo would have helped us in our research. [1983]

That trip remained imaginary.

In June of 1951 Roy was at the Kansas reunion in Wichita. He gave 30 patriarchal blessings in seven days. Nell went along to do stenographic work. Roy reported that she was gradually picking up some skill and doing quite well. Often, however, their schedules took them in different directions. He wrote to President Gleazer, "The Cheville family has been quite modern the last couple of weeks. Nell went with Ruth Scott down into Arkansas and Texas, Charlotte was at Nauvoo Camp, Dick was in France, and I was in Lamoni. We received a letter from Dick yesterday, not very newsy but assuring us that he was all right."

When Dick Cheville completed a two-year assignment in the Army in 1954, he bought his mother a car and taught her how to drive it. She did not have very long to enjoy it before she discovered in 1955 the malignancy which took her life. Her friends remember that she did not give in to self-pity. Nell Cheville died of cancer December 3, 1957. Thus ended a marriage which had begun December 23, 1929. Her wedding and her funeral took place in the church building of the Lamoni Branch, though the buildings were different. Earl T. Hidgon officiated at the funeral.

Roy Cheville had referred to Nell as his "companion" and he would continue to use that word. He expressed a high regard for their companionship, and mourned its end deeply. Dick Cheville says that his father had a difficult time in emotional adjustment for about a year after Nell's death. He moved out of their home into smaller quarters near the campus. In the process he threw away a great many of his collected papers.

A few years after Nell had died, Roy commented to Enid DeBarthe about the efforts of some women to find him another wife. He said, "I wish they would leave me alone. I loved Nell. I don't have the time to give a woman the attention she would deserve. I don't want another relationship."

An overview of Nell's life should consider what her objectives were. She considered Roy to be the most outstanding man she had ever met. She had dedicated herself foremost to supporting him and enabling his ministry. She appears to have taken the long view of "support" and "enable." If his capability expanded and his effectiveness enlarged while she was functioning in her role, then she was successful in her lifetime commitment.

Nell and Roy were married when Roy was rapidly developing the powers and the capability for which he became justly famous. He helped a large number of people to interpret personal religion in functional terms, and he wrote two sets of remarkable quarterlies and his first book in the first decade of their marriage.

Nell lived through nearly all of the period in which Cheville did his most effective and creative work. He wrote nearly all of the hymns which have endeared him to Saints around the world. He became what has been described as, "The Guiding Genius of Graceland." He put together most of the concepts that guided the rest of his career and which guide hundreds or thousands of Saints today. In a real sense Roy's career may be seen as Nell's monument. What she dedicated herself to support is what came to pass.

Enid DeBarthe remembers Nell as "one of the most sensitive, loving, sweetest people I have known. She had an awareness of the divine presence; a true spirituality." Judy Closson remarked, "Nell was a caring person. She had much more depth than people usually realized. I really miss Nell now that she is gone."

Late in his life Roy said, "If I had it to do over again, I would spend more time with my family."

Career Path

The most potent religious fact in a college lies in the personality of its leadership. There is no program or machinery that will make up for men. So the Graceland faculty includes men and women of religious influence, in personal life and breadth of viewpoint. This must be the fundamental factor. [1928E]

Roy Cheville became a member of the RLDS Church in 1914 to test the relation between divinity and humanity and see if it was functional as the group claimed. By 1918 he had clearly decided it was functional, for he accepted appointment as a full-time minister. He accepted successive assignments in the church and its institutions for the rest of his life. He seems never to have looked back.

Roy Cheville was a Graceland student in the academic year 1920–21, studying for a missionary assignment. Upon graduation from Graceland, his assignment was changed. He went immediately to the University of Chicago to study religion and theology. The objective was to return to Graceland as a faculty member qualified to teach in those areas.

He earned the Bachelor of Philosophy Degree at Chicago in May of 1922, and the Master of Arts in Religion in May of 1923. He completed an additional summer of graduate work at Chicago before joining the Graceland faculty to begin his professional career in September of 1923. That professional career divides into three segments of approximately equal length: 1) the "Unk" period 1923–1940, 2) the "Doc" period 1941–1958, and 3) the Patriarch period 1959–1986. (Not long after joining the Graceland faculty he acquired the nickname "Unk." He was regarded as wise and friendly as an uncle might be. After he earned the Ph. D. he became known as "Doc.")

In 1980 Cheville spent two days with the author as an observer in a meeting of a Scientific Advisory Team for the Federal Aviation Technical Center in Atlantic City, New Jersey. As he was introduced to the seven members of the team, two of them, not church members, recognized his name immediately. One said, "I'm glad to shake hands with a man who is a legend in his own time." (One, a Purdue Ph.D. had been married to a church member and the other was a Ph. D. from the State University of Iowa.) After leaving the meeting Cheville mused, "I have often wondered what would have happened if I had taken a different path. I'm not dumb and with my work habits I might have been a success at some other endeavors."

"UNK"

In the years 1923 through 1940 on the Graceland faculty he developed the abilities for which he is remembered. This was the period in which he was known as "Unk" Cheville. On the faculty he taught courses in history, philosophy, religion, and sociology. "Unk" wrote the Graceland College Alma Mater Hymn in 1926. By the late 1920's he had developed the Wednesday evening fellowship meetings into the most important religious influence on the campus.

The first of a series of church school study materials "Unk" wrote for senior high students appeared in 1932. The year-long series had the titles, *The Relation of Our Church To Other Churches* [1932A], *Beliefs of Our Church* [1933D], *Membership Qualifications* [1933E], and *The Program of the Church* [1933H]. These definitive pamphlets were used throughout the church. They were reprinted, re-edited and reissued regularly until 1959.

The first of a series of church school materials "Unk" wrote for study of the Bible appeared in 1934. Their titles were, *How the Bible Came To Be* [1934A], *How To Read the Bible* [1935B], *How the Bible Reveals God* [1935C], and *How Shall We Use the Bible?* [1935D]. These pamphlets were used church-wide until he incorporated material from them into a book, *The Bible In Everyday Living* [1939A], which first appeared in 1939. This book was reissued in 1944, 1948, 1951, 1956, and 1961. It ranks among the Restoration's most influential books. As the title suggests, its focus was on the functional use of the Bible. He said he put his "heart and soul" into writing it. By the end of 1940 "Unk" had written 82 published articles, 10 published hymns, and 19 published pamphlets.

"DOC"

The second period of Roy Cheville's professional career began in the year 1941 even though the doctorate itself would not be awarded until 1942. From about 1941 until the end of his Graceland faculty service in 1958, Roy Cheville's abilities and performance were in full flower. These were the years when he was called "Doc" Cheville. He was everywhere on the campus, elevating the performance of all aspects of the institution. In demonstration and in writing he taught that effective religion and religious thought must be integrated with knowledge from all the sciences and be compatible with experiences from the arts.

In the "Doc" period were published nearly all of his well-known hymns. The first of these, "Open My Eyes" [1941G], appeared in 1941. In this 1941–1958 period also were written "Hast Thou Heard It?" [1950I], "All Things Are Thine" [1950K], "Master, Speak! Thy Servant Heareth" [1950L], "Sacred Books, the Church's Treasure [1950AA]," "Conviction" [1953D], "Afar in Old Judea" [1955G], "O Lord, Thy People Gathered Here" [1956K], "For Bread Before Us Broken" [1956O], and "Send Forth Thy Light, O Zion" [1956W]. The most important single source of "Doc's" hymns and worship materials is *The Hymnal For Youth* [1950G].

Seven major books were written by "Doc" during this 1941–1958 period; *Through the West Door* [1946A], *Growing Up in Religion* [1951B], *When They Seek Counsel* [1954A], *They Sang of the Restoration* [1955A], *The Latter Day Saints and Family Life* [1955P], *By What Authority?* [1956B], and *Ten Considerations For Family Living* [1958A].

In a 1947 *Saints Herald* article, "One World and One Church" [1947F], "Doc" introduced the whole church to the ideas of world outreach which he had been developing on the Graceland campus. In 1947 also appeared the first of a set of materials for church school study laying the foundation for that world outreach. These pamphlets were entitled, *How Shall We Look At Our World?* [1947A], *What Kind of World Shall We See?* [1947B], *What Is Our Church's Mission To the World?* [1948O], and *How Shall We Equip the Church For Her World Mission?* [1948P]. (The series was reissued in 1950 and 1951.) A careful reading of these materials reveals that he was developing a religionist's long-range plan for world peace with a social scientist's plan for its achievement. In 1949 his perspective was enriched by his first trip to Europe.

By the end of 1958 "Doc" had written 12 published books, 35 published pamphlets, 45 published hymns, and 174 published articles.

Roy Cheville signing Acacias in the 1920's.

Roy Cheville as cheer leader in 1925.

Cheville with Eugene Closson in front of the campus congregation in Zimmermann Hall about 1949.

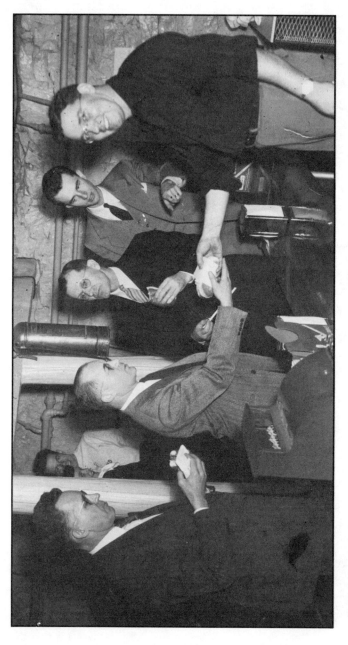

Cheville in snack bar and bookstore in the basement of the Ad building in 1951. In the foreground left to right are Alva Gilbert, Neal Deaver, Roy Cheville, Edwin Browne, and Jack Gernhart.

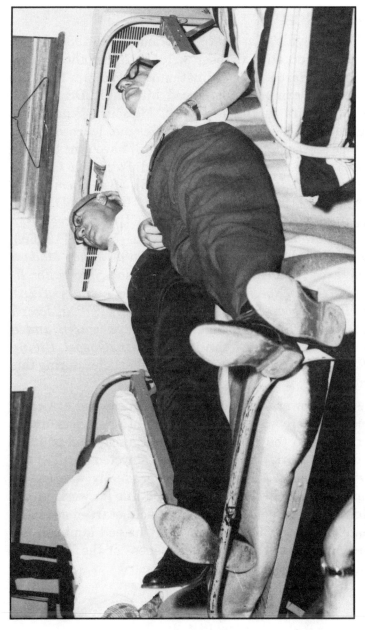

Roscoe Faunce and Roy Cheville take a break from nursing duties during 1957 flu epidemic.

PATRIARCH

Roy Cheville's last career period, 1959–1986, began with his ordination October 8, 1958, to the office of Presiding Patriarch. This ordination removed him from the Graceland campus and placed him in RLDS Church Headquarters in Independence, Missouri. When Tess Morgan, his long-time faculty colleague, learned of the change she said, "Now maybe Roy will have time to write more." And he did. In this period Patriarch Cheville wrote *The Field of Theology* [1959B], *Meet Them in the Scriptures* [1960A], *Did the Light Go Out?* [1962A], *Spirituality in the Space Age* [1962C], *Scriptures From Ancient America* [1964A], *Spiritual Health* [1966A], *When Teen-Agers Talk Theology* [1968A], *They Made a Difference* [1970A], *The Book of Mormon Speaks For Itself* [1971A], *Expectations For Endowed Living* [1972A], *Spiritual Resources Are Available Today* [1975A], *Joseph and Emma Smith; Companions For Seventeen and a Half Years* [1977A], and *Humor in Gospel Living* [1978A]. He also wrote 171 published articles during this period.

As his powers had developed and increased at Graceland, so there was a gradual loss of sharpness and a narrowing in the Patriarch phase. He had said in 1952, "I do good work when all of me is devoted to all of the divine endeavor." Perhaps there gradually was less of him to use. It became difficult for him to work in the midst of a resurgence of ideas he had discarded as inadequate by the 1930's. Perhaps that helped diminish the personhood and thus the effectiveness of the Patriarch. And he no longer had a congregation.

Graceland Service

Any young person who goes to college finds himself in a new world. His world is expanded in literature, peoples, physical surroundings, animal life, art, and philosophy... In this period it is highly essential that the youth shall live in a college environment that will stimulate wholesome religious thinking and living. [1928F]

Roy Cheville arrived on the Graceland College campus as a new faculty member in September, 1923. He was 25 years old. It had been one summer more than two years since he had been there as a student. Though absent he had been a part of the institution. He had been in regular contact with President George N. Briggs. Briggs was his supervisor in the ministerial service to which Roy was committed. Briggs had sent him to Chicago on assignment, and now Roy was back for the next assignment— as a teaching faculty member. His Graceland service developed as follows:

1923–59 Faculty member at Graceland College,
1023–29 Dean of Men, staff resident at Herald Hall
1925–59 Director of Religious Education/Activities
1949–53 Dean of Faculty
1951–52 Acting President
1959 Retired from Graceland College
1967 Received Distinguished Alumni Award at Graceland College
1968 Became Emeritus Professor of Graceland College
1968 Received Honorary D.D. at Graceland College

The *Saints' Herald* noted in September, 1923, that Graceland faculty appointments included R. A. Cheville in religious education. At the same time the college catalog listed his teaching field as history. The Catalog noted that administrative officials included G. N. Briggs, President, F. M. McDowell, Dean, R. A. Cheville, Dean of Men, and Vida Smith, Dean of Women. Cheville was also staff resident in Herald Hall, which position he would hold until 1929, the year of his marriage.

Those years in the dormitory were important to young professor Cheville. He maintained an easy and effective relationship with the students. His front room was the gathering place, especially on Sunday evenings. He said later that the student who has never lived in a dormitory missed something. Of his years at Herald Hall he wrote, ". . . those six years were invaluable. The personal contacts, the insight into human nature, and the free expression of boyish spirit could never have been obtained elsewhere." [1930D]

It was through his role as dormitory supervisor and counselor that he acquired the name "Unk," an acknowledgement of his relationship with students not much younger than himself. "Unk" was also a counterpart to the Dean of Women who had long been known as "Aunt Vida" Smith. Cheville was always ready to talk with any student, and he wanted them to be comfortable in addressing him. "Mr. Cheville" and "Professor Cheville" were too formal and too distant. So Roy Cheville became "Unk," the name used by his friends and students until he earned the Ph.D. in 1942, when he became "Doc."

On Sunday mornings in 1923, the college faculty and students were in the Brick Church as a part of the Lamoni congregation. On Wednesday evenings the college people met in the Graceland Chapel for prayer meetings. "Unk" had been an Elder for five years and was an innovative leader in worship services. He identified this Wednesday evening service as the center of worship for the college community. He attended and participated in these meetings. With his talents and his industry he began to make significant input and in due time assumed responsibility for them. Although he always in-

116

cluded other faculty and students in planning and conduct, he was primarily responsible for the structure and content of the meetings. At some point he changed the name from "prayer" to "fellowship" meetings to better reflect his view of the nature of the experiences.

The effectiveness of these services was soon recognized. In 1927 George Lewis expressed the view of many when he wrote that,

> No one has ever really been to Graceland unless he has entered into the weekly prayer meetings. . . The quiet influence of meditation which pervades the whole assembly, the meaningful expressions of ideals, hopes, and aims, told in the characteristic way of the students, make these meetings the dynamo from which energy is generated for the carrying out of purposes. It is here that one sees the other side of a fellow's nature. [AL Aug 27][1]

"Unk" became director of the academic religious education program and soon became leader, then director, of religious activities on campus. He went on to exercise both of these functions nearly all the time he was a regular member of the faculty.

The college utilized Roy's abilities in other ways as well. In 1925 he participated in a fund drive to provide an endowment for Graceland College. A *Herald* article noted that "Unk" "summed up in a very interesting way the inspiration offered which leads her students to give the best that is in them to humanity." "Unk" spent a weekend in the Des Moines Branch working with local campaign directors Stephen Robinson and Henry Castings. In his evening message Roy Cheville "in an inspiring and forceful manner, spoke of the message of Christ, Graceland College, and stewardship." "Unk" identified the real individuality of Graceland in the general tone of its men and women, whose association and standard of living tend to renew simple faith and the spirit of the church. He said that Graceland endeavors to meet its responsibility as no other school in the shaping, directing, and stimulating of religious living. [SH 4 Nov 25] W. D. Tordoff reported further on the campaign trip, "It has been a pleasure to be once again associated with Brother Cheville. He carries with him the Spirit of Graceland." [SH 18 Nov 25]

The late 1920's were busy for him. He taught religious education and history, and participated in many campus activities. He was called the most versatile man on the campus.

The 1928 *Acacia* said, "Mr. Cheville is at ease in any worthwhile group. He is Graceland's true friend—ever willing to lend his unreserved ability toward anything that consummates the best student life. In class he is open-minded and thorough, ever ready with his delightful conversation." He was president of the 150 member Lamoni-Graceland Oratorio Society and sang in the A Capella Chorus of 22 members, Mabel Carlile, Director.

The 1929 *ACACIA* recognized the importance of his contribution to campus life by choosing him for its dedication faculty member. There was a full-page picture of him in the front of the book opposite this dedicatory statement:

> In recognition of the services so fully rendered this college by "Uncle Roy"; in admiration of his geniality and versatility; in appreciation of his attitude in the class room and in chapel; in acknowledgment of his generosity and understanding and in commendation of his unfaltering and consistent efforts to the end that Graceland might be made a better institution, we respectfully dedicate this *Acacia* of 1929.

The Great Depression caused serious disruptions in the lives and careers of Graceland's faculty and staff. Tess Morgan, dean of women, and James Evans, faculty member, were released from the faculty in 1933. Other members of the faculty assumed their teaching duties. Tess Morgan would rejoin the faculty later but James Evans would not. The loss of good faculty members to these economic circumstances had a profound effect not only on those leaving but also on those who remained. "Unk" said that it made those still on the faculty increase their work level as a stewardship.

The *Lamoni Chronicle* provides a window on the economic effects of the depression in 1933 on the little community. In March of 1933 merchants were offering only 6 cents per dozen for eggs. In March also the banks reopened, ending the catastrophic bank holiday. The *Chronicle* noted that the "Local bank holiday is ended." The *Chronicle* reported that the Decatur County State Bank was one of only 32 banks in Iowa that reopened. [LC 16 Mar 33]

Roy engaged in a wide range of activities in the early thirties. In 1934, he was head chef for a men's supper at the Coliseum. He planned the meal and cooked meat loaf and escalloped potatoes. The meal was voted a success by the ladies. The *Lamoni Chronicle* observed, "We are glad to add this role to his already long list of accomplishments." [LC 4 Jan 34] Roy frequently assisted Nell with the meals at home.

He gave a lecture in the chapel on the cause of World War I. He led his audience through the acts leading to the war, pointing out the jealousies and the "wholly insignificant incidents which brought to a most disastrous head the trouble which had been brewing for over a century." In closing he repeated the pleas and ideals of Woodrow Wilson that some day the world might become entirely free from any more intentional catastrophes like those of 1914 to 1918. [LC 8 Feb 34]

For Graceland College night at the RLDS General Conference of 1938, "Unk" developed a program about the Latter Day Saints at Far West in 1838. He wrote the historical narrative and selected music presented by the A Capella Chorus, supported by organ and piano music. The *Herald* said the presentation was an experiment that will bear repetition. "Unk" also gave a daily class at the conference entitled, "Teaching Values in Church History." [1938E,F,G,H,I,J]

In the fall of 1938 "Unk" taught three new courses, The Church and Leisure Occupations, Principles and Administration of Religious Education, and Church Doctrine and Program. That fall Graceland enrolled 255.

A frequent summer assignment for Graceland faculty was to attend one or more reunions in the interest of student recruitment. In August of 1939 "Unk" and Mabel Carlile were at the Kirtland reunion, "where they advised and counseled prospective Graceland students."

As the school year began it was noted that "Unk," besides teaching, plans the interesting assembly programs and open forums, the inspiring Wednesday evening fellowship services, and many church activities, including the Religion Club. [LC 4 Aug 39]

In December of 1939 "Unk" flew to Chicago to speak at a Graceland Alumni rally. He spent the morning of December 9 in Independence with church officials planning for general conference, then represented Graceland in Chicago at the alumni banquet. The *Tower* for April 19, 1940 printed a picture of "Unk" alighting from the TWA airplane, a DC3.

In January of 1946 the enrollment at Graceland increased significantly over the fall semester as World War II soldiers returned to become students. The Wednesday evening fellowship services were still held in the chapel, but the room was now full. A much larger increase was expected for the fall of 1946. "Doc" was very much concerned about maintaining the quality of campus life. He knew that many a school had enlarged until it lost its soul. When the fall 1946 semester opened both the Sunday morning church services and the Wednesday evening Fellowship services were held in Zimmerman Hall on the basketball court.

One of the significant services in 1946 was the Graceland Gold Star Memorial service for former students killed in action during the war. "Doc" had said that early in the war when news of former students who had been killed in action began to come back, the question of whether to have a memorial service for each one arose and it was decided on the campus to wait until the war was over and have one service for all of them. The memorial service was held during homecoming.

In the Alumni magazine, "Doc" reported that the challenges of the enlarged student body had been met. "I wish alums might have shared these opening days of this college year. Staff meetings, academic, social and devotional, had 'soul' in them . . I am expecting this year to be one of the most creative and contributive years in the Graceland I have known. The heart of the college is growing to carry its life stream into further places." [1948F]

In 1949 "Doc" was appointed Dean of the Faculty in addition to his other duties. He was Dean of Faculty and Instruction, Director of Religious Life, and teacher of social science and religion. He was active as usual in community and church affairs.

In October of 1950 "Doc" was ordained to the office of patriarch. As a patriarch he was to be freed from the administration of church activities. He would thus have time to devote to the personal ministry of the patriarch.

On July 1, 1951, with President E. J. Gleazer, Jr., away at Harvard working toward his doctorate, "Doc" became Acting President of Graceland for one year. He had been reluctant to take the assignment, having rejected other administrative appointments. He knew he could do a good administrative job given his sensitivity and his prodigious work habits. He felt, however, that even though administrative appointments brought significant rewards they detracted from his major commitments. "Doc" asked in 1953 to be released from his assignment as Dean of Faculty and Instruction in order to devote more time to teaching.

In September of 1956 Graceland began offering the third-year courses of a four-year liberal arts curriculum in religion. This event brought into being a long-standing dream for "Doc." He wrote, "I see the introduction of this curriculum as something highly significant in the life of the church." [1956G] Dr. William S. Gould, Acting President, expanded on the announcement,

> Dr. Roy A. Cheville, who has taught religion at Graceland for nearly 30 years, will head the instructional staff for the department of religion. His creative thinking has stimulated the church around the world, for his influence has always been far wider than the circle of Graceland students. His academic training insures that Graceland's courses in religion will be accepted by other colleges and accrediting agencies. Other qualified teachers are being trained to assist him. [LC 7 Mar 57]

Three events followed which had far reaching consequences for Graceland. Dr. Edmund J. Gleazer Jr. was elected President of the American Association of Junior Colleges at the annual national convention held March 8, 1957. Harvey Grice became President of Graceland in

1958. On October 8, 1958 "Doc" was ordained to the office of Presiding Patriarch of the RLDS Church.

After the ordination he began to revise his activities and terminate his service at Graceland. He scheduled retirement from Graceland to be effective at the end of the 1958–59 school year. Lloyd Young was appointed to replace "Doc" as Director of Religious Life on the campus beginning with the 1959–60 school year. "Doc" asked Lloyd to accept some major responsibilities for that program during the remainder of the 1958–59 school year.

Graceland President Grice obtained approval from the Church to have "Doc" serve as guest professor during the first semester of the 1959–60 year and also during the first semester in 1960–1961. He was to teach two courses, Introduction to Religious Education for juniors and Christian Theology for seniors. A major part of his assignment was to advise new members of the staff appointed in the field of religion. At the end of the Fall semester of 1960, Roy A. Cheville finished his career as a Graceland College faculty member.

Notes

1. AL is the abbreviation for *Autumn Leaves*, a periodical of the RLDS Church.

Teaching Fields

In his 35 years on the Graceland faculty Roy Cheville's teaching fields were history, philosophy, religion, and sociology. He had taken graduate courses in all four of these fields in his studies at the University of Chicago before he began teaching at Graceland in 1923. He would take many more as he continued summer study at Chicago until 1942.

Most of the time he taught freshmen and sophomores. By the time Cheville arrived, Graceland had changed from a four year baccalaureate college to a two year junior college. As a four year institution it had not been able to achieve accreditation. By converting to a junior college it became accredited. Courses which students took then could be transferred to other colleges and universities across the country. Its leaders hoped that Graceland would again become a four year college when it had built enough strength to allow accreditation at that level. In his last year on the faculty, Cheville taught junior and senior courses in religion, aiding in the transition back to a four year college.

HISTORY

It is one thing to affirm God's hand in history, it is another thing to interpret the function of God in history. [1938J]

History was the first subject Roy Cheville taught as he began his Graceland faculty service. He taught American history, European history, and other general history courses. He would later teach the history of Christianity and Latter Day Saint History. In time he yielded the teaching of general history courses to other faculty members, but he would teach the histories of Christianity and of the Latter Day Saints until the end of his Graceland faculty years.

He approached the study of the Bible and of the Book of Mormon as histories. That is, he looked upon both as the accounts by real people describing their experiences and their understanding of events. He said at one point that we should use the Bible as we use any other library (1933D). The distinctiveness of the Bible and the Book of Mormon is that they deal with religious experiences and the interpretations of those experiences. This principle of seeing the persons in the scriptural accounts is at the heart of his book, *Meet Them in the Scriptures*. [1960A] The purpose of the book is to bring the individuals to life so the reader can see and understand them as persons.

He refined his understanding of history in teaching the subject. Soon he began to write some aspects of history himself. He was a member of a committee which produced a 40 page history of the town of Lamoni in 1929. [1929E] Given the way Cheville usually worked on committees, it is likely that he did the writing himself, with editorial review and approval by the rest of the committee. A year later he wrote a 58 page pamphlet on the history and place of education among the Latter Day Saints. [1930J] In 1931 he gave a lecture on the greatness of Washington and Lincoln, which was reported in detail in the college newspaper. [1931H] In 1933 he wrote an article on the history of High Priests. [1933B] In 1934 he wrote a 64 page pamphlet about the origins of the Bible as a book. [1934A] In 1936 he wrote a pamphlet on the setting and times of the Book of Mormon story. [1936I] This was followed a year later by another pamphlet about the people of Book of Mormon times. [1937A]

For the 1938 General Conference he gave a class for young people entitled, *Teaching Values in Church His-*

tory. [1938E, F, G, H, I, J] In 1946 he wrote a history of Graceland College, with the title, *Through the West Door*. [1946A] In 1955 he wrote a history of hymns and hymn-singing in the RLDS church, with the title, *They Sang of the Restoration*. [1955A]

In 1962 he wrote about the status of Christianity in the Middle Ages in Europe. In RLDS literature this period had frequently been described as the period in which the quality of spiritual living was reduced and the light of the gospel went out. Cheville's book about this period was entitled, *Did the Light Go Out?* [1962A] A part of his research for the writing was done in a monastery in Dubuque, Iowa. In a series of articles for young people in 1963 he wrote one on seeing God's purpose and plan in history. [1963Q] In 1977 Cheville wrote his last book on a historical subject, this one about the marital companionship of Joseph and Emma Smith. [1977A]

RELIGION

Before I can answer the question whether or why I believe in God, I should first answer what kind of God I believe God to be... certainly every young person should have some workable idea of God, that will function in his life. For God is at the heart of religion. How, then, shall we believe in him? [1933D]

Religion is that phase of human experience in which men are endeavoring to make personal contact with their universe. [1951B]

The program of religious education for which Cheville had prepared to teach had begun in 1919. In that year the First Presidency appointed a committee to map out and install a course in religion at Graceland. This committee appointed C. E. Wight, who was already on the faculty, to take charge as head of the department. The idea was to secure the leaders of the church to give a series of lectures on various subjects. A class was given in the history of religion, and the students took other general subjects.

A number of appointee ministers were picked as students. They were a diversified group, and the task of the teacher was challenging, since some of the students had previously attended college, some had not finished high school, while others had not even finished grade school.

When Cheville arrived as a faculty member in 1923, Cyril Wight was still responsible for the program. Five years later "Unk" was in charge. He wrote the report on the program that appeared in the Conference Daily Edition of the *Saints' Herald*. In that report he gave this outline of the course work which should comprise the program:

    History and Theology
       Modern Religious Thought
       History of Religious
       American Christianity
       History of Latter Day Saintism
       History of Christianity
       Church Theology
    Church Administration and Laboratory
    Bible
       Old Testament History and Literature
       New Testament History and Literature
       Other courses
    Religious Education
       Principles of Religious Education
       Psychology of Religious Development
       Organization and Administration of Religious Education
       Materials of Religious Education [1928E]

In that article he said that his own interests were developing in the fields of religious history, religious philosophy, and theology. He proposed that another faculty member should prepare to teach religious education and

Bible. Despite that proposal he was to teach courses in Bible throughout his teaching career.

In 1934 Cheville noted that some courses had been introduced with rather specific Latter Day Saint content. These included the History of Latter Day Saintism and the Principles and Administration of Religious Education. At various times he conducted a course which involved the students in developing materials for religious education. One such course in resulted in the production of the *Official Zion's League Handbook* in 1941, [1941E] another in 1944 addressed the curriculum needs of junior high youth, age 12–14. This class spent one semester in establishing the needs of the students, then a following semester helping to write the materials needed, particularly quarterly study guides. This group included Bernice Fleeharty, Frank Shank, Eldon Winters, Myron LaPointe, Faith Millman, Jane Ross, Georgia Metcalf, Thelma Sintz, Alice Zion, Charles Kornman, Wayne Jackel and Lillian Maxwell.

In his last years on the faculty, Cheville developed Junior and Senior level courses in religion in the transition to a four-year curriculum in religion.

PHILOSOPHY

Philosophy sees things comprehensively. It emphasizes inconclusiveness. The man who sees things philosophically sees beyond a five-minute glance or a one-mile measure. He stretches out to see the totality of himself or anything else in the light of the totality of the universe. [1961C]

Through the "Unk" period, Cheville regularly taught courses in philosophy. We can see some of the effects on him of this experience in some of his later writings. In the 1950 quotation above we see him looking at philosophy as an attempt to see life's experiences as a whole.

His later writings are strongly influenced by his immersion in philosophic subject matter. In a series of articles beginning in 1961, Cheville laid out some useful ways of looking at philosophy and described some important philosophers. The title of the lead article was, "The common man is a philosopher." The subtitle was "Men and life's meaning: A study of philosophy." He wrote early in the article,

> Historically the word "philosophy" combines two Greek words that together make it mean "love of wisdom." It implies that a man will place high the quest for understanding and meaning. . . It ought to be concerned with problems of meaning, and value, and foundations of existence. . [1961C]

Other titles in this series were, "Socrates: He turned to man himself," [1961E] "Plato: He sought the enduring," [1961F] "Augustine: He sought for the unchanging amid change," [1961J] "Aquinas: He sought to bring reason and faith together," [1961K] "Descartes: He dared to think and thought a dualism," [1961L] "Kant: He stayed at home and saw a world view," [1961P] "Nietzsche: He took apart and did not put together," [1961Q] "William James: He affirmed the right to believe," [1961U] "Henry Bergson: He perceived something vital in the Universe," [1961W] "Alfred North Whitehead: He perceived a Universe of process," [1962E] and "Karl Jaspers: He asks whether man will continue." [1962F] At the end of the series he wrote a summary article entitled, "A Time for Philosophy." [1962G]

In the article on Whitehead, Cheville wrote,

> This British-American philosopher spoke to his age in terms science was using. His key words were *process, organism, possibility*, and *universe*. He gave to these a spiritual significance. He saw the cosmos as dynamic and pulsating. His is a foremost voice in using the major concepts of his times (1861–1948). . .

Our times are richer because Alfred North Whitehead thought and conversed and wrote. He spoke the language of our times. These things he furthered:

1. A spiritual conception of the universe that is truly *one*.

2. The inherence in the universe of creative power, available for furthering beauty and harmony.

3. The richness of *possibility* in the resources of the universe.

4. The reliability of God, describable in terms of natural law.

5. The universal and comprehensive aspect of beauty and truth and goodness.

6. The incorporation of so-called spiritual phenomena into the natural order making it the not-yet-explored, the not-yet-understood.

7. The interpretation of happenings as pulsations in the universal process, related to the totality of experience.

8. The essential quality of adventure in the universe in religious living. Many of us will keep hearing Whitehead reminding us, "The death of religion comes with the repression of the high hope of adventure." Many of us will be stirred by his zest and faith in great spiritual questings.

Cheville's own views were in essential agreement with these ideas of Whitehead. But he went on to list several things Whitehead did not do. These had to do with personalism in the universe—a characteristic of the universe with which humans may be in personal contact. These issues about personal contact are things which are at the heart of Cheville's own views and his practices. They are discussed in the section on Cheville's theory of God.

SOCIOLOGY

Lamenting over the passing of yesterday's family is useless. It is gone. We cannot return to it, for conditions have changed. We should not want to return. Let us rather analyze the situation, see things as they are, and in the methods of science, in the idealism and spirit of religions at their best, lay the foundation for the family that is to be. [1939B.]

By the early 1930's the Graceland College Catalog listed Roy Cheville's teaching fields as social science and religion. He taught both Introduction to Sociology and Marriage and the Family. He also maintained association with professional sociologists.

In sociology he did not spend much time on such concepts as "social disorganization," which presumed an earlier and better state of affairs. He taught objective approaches to analysis and description. These can provide scientific principles on which one can hope to develop more effective group living. This forward-looking positive aspect of sociology fit Cheville's general outlook.

In scientific sociology he saw the grass roots principles which could be used as the basis for implementing the ideals of Zion. In this field, as in other fields, he took the long view. He did not engage in, nor did he advocate that others engage in, short term battles about social problems. Over and over in his classes he turned back student suggestions that the way to solve a particular problem was to "pass a law." He saw that approach as short range and more likely to make the problem worse than to solve it.

In 1939 Cheville wrote a pamphlet for RLDS church school use entitled, "History and Significance of the Family in the Work of the Church." In the foreword he wrote,

> More thoughtful students will realize that some background is necessary. They also know that we cannot separate the present family from all that has produced it, and from the social world of which it is a part. [1939B]

In 1950 Cheville invited Evelyn Mills Duvall to Graceland as a visiting speaker. For years Duvall had been executive secretary for the National Council on Family Relations. Cheville was one of the members of the council. Mrs. Duvall was invited again to campus in 1953 as guest lecturer for a two day Dating and Marrying Conference. In 1953 also Cheville attended the annual meeting of the Mid-West Sociological Society in Omaha. The program included papers and discussions in the general fields of urban sociology, sociology, general education, the family, race and ethnic relations, research methods, social theory, population, crime and delinquency, and social psychology.

In 1955 Cheville wrote a book entitled, *The Latter Day Saints and Family Life*. [1955P] In it he wrote,

> The major objective of the church and of the family is the same. Both set out to develop personalism of eternal quality. . The family is the primary group for developing the child's personalism. The family and the Zionic community combine in a complementary way in the education of the child. . .
>
> Family life is conceived as the natural way of developing persons in this good life. Salvation—that is, the pulling up of the person from forces that would drag him down—would not be furthered by mere union in marriage with priesthood sanction; it would come to the degree that marriage furthers spiritual development in persons. .
>
> Building family life is important enough to merit divine enlightenment. . . [1955P]

In 1958 he published another book on the family. This one was entitled, *Ten Considerations for Family Living*. The book was an extension of a series of evening presentations made at the Far West Reunion in August 1957. He wrote in part,

> Good families do not come by chance; they are planned. Foundations of today's family living go deep into yesterday's life; we are laying the groundwork for tomorrow's homes. . . as a child I heard two phrases associated, "getting married" and "settling down." I gathered that they were supposed to go together in some way. . . I did not get married to settle down. . [1958A]

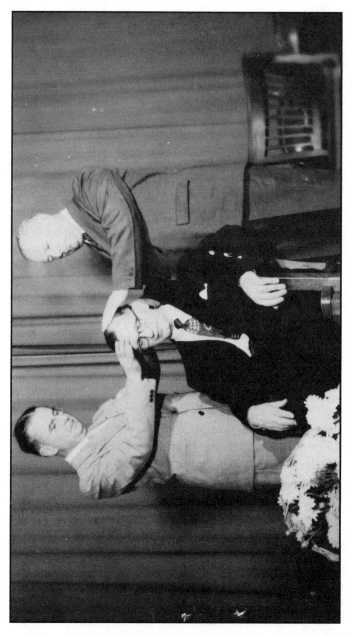

Roy Cheville being ordained to the office of patriarch in 1950 by Apostles Charles Hield, left and Arthur Oakman, right.

*Roy Cheville leading the singing in the new Lamoni Church,
1952. He had insisted on having the words from Joseph
Smith's grove experience represented on the front of the
church building.*

135

World Church Service

We need the Church—
> for association and friendship in religious living. . .
>
> to stabilize our beliefs and behavior. . .
>
> in order to work together in large world projects. . .
>
> that we may have a home in which we can grow with others whose characters are wholesome and helpful. [1933D]

From the time he joined the church in 1914, Roy Cheville was committed to the RLDS Church as an organization. He never wavered from that allegiance and he never tried to bend any allegiance to himself. As he began service on the Graceland faculty in 1923, he saw his teaching and his ministerial duties as one commitment. They were two aspects of the same stewardship.

As he had done while at the University of Chicago, Roy matched his faculty activities with a full schedule of ministerial activities. On campus he became active in the Wednesday evening fellowship services, and soon became responsible for their planning and conduct. In town he exercised an elder's priesthood functions in preaching, organizing, and administering the church program. He had focused his graduate studies on youth and junior church. He quickly became responsible for many of the youth and junior functions for the Lamoni branch and Lamoni stake. These youth activities included classes and programs for the college students.

RLDS Church President Fred M. Smith made a point of making personal contact with young appointee ministers. He seemed particularly interested in visiting with those who showed promise of intellectual contributions. Fred M. was especially interested in the use the scientific tools of psychology and sociology to study inspiration and social organization. Fred M. challenged Cheville with a specific task:

> You are called and directed to keep in vital touch with trends and happenings in our Church. You will not be a hasty, forward speaker and teacher. You are to be reliable. As you move forward exploringly you will not always receive agreement and statements of support. This will range from ordinary members to ordained men in significant administrative positions. You are advised to move ahead with charity and courage.

When Lamoni Stake President C. E. Wight resigned in May of 1925, the First Presidency of the Church, E. A. Smith as spokesman, nominated Brother W. E. Prall to fill the position. Elders D. A. Dowker and Roy Cheville became his counselors. An announcement of the stake reorganization in the *Saints' Herald* of June 10, 1925, written by Elbert A. Smith stated,

> Brother Cheville is a young man, and his contribution probably will be to the young people in Graceland College, to whom he will be in a sense a student pastor. He has really occupied that position in an informal way for some time and is loved and respected by them, and will thus in an official way join the stake presidency with the important work to be done at Graceland College.

Cheville was also ordained to the office of high priest. At this time he was 27 years old. It was quite unusual for one so young to be a member of the stake presidency and quite unusual to be ordained a high priest. Neither would have happened without explicit approval by Fred M. This seal of approval by Fred M. was reinforced by other functional assignments. The young Cheville was expanding on the visions of Fred M. in employing scientific methods to study the experiences of inspiration and routes to the goal of social righteousness. Once when Cheville was asked if he was criticized for use of his unusual ideas in his religious work, he began by stating that he was in the stake presidency and thus was a part of the establishment.

Cheville served in the Lamoni Stake presidency from 1925 until 1940. He was counselor to a succession of stake presidents. During one gap in 1942–43, he was acting stake president. The Lamoni Branch had its own presidency. Usually the stake president was also the branch president, but the counselors were frequently different. Cheville was a member of the branch presidency until he was ordained to the office of patriarch in 1950.

The summer of 1926 was a typical one for Cheville. In June, in the church's Summer Institute of Religious Education at Graceland College, two of the six courses were taught by Cheville: "Bible Appreciation," and "The Junior Church in Theory and Practice." (The other courses were taught by F. Henry Edwards, A. M. Carmichael, C. B. Woodstock, Blanche Edwards, and F. M. McDowell.) After summer school at Berkeley, Cheville was back in Lamoni directing youth activities for the stake reunion. Each morning at 7:45 an average of 110 youth met in prayer service directed by Cheville. The theme of these services was "What young people of Zion live by."

By 1927 Cheville had become established as the leader of singing for the church general conferences. The *Herald* reported on the afternoon song service and business session of April 8:

> Shortly before two o'clock Elder Roy Cheville, one of the presidency of Lamoni Stake, took the baton, and aided by the chorus of missionaries sang such songs as, "Father, when in love to thee," "Let us walk in the light," a missionary song, "Master, use me," which was truly phenomenal. As we sat at the press table the spirit of devotion and harmony took possession and warmed us through and through. It seemed the congregation was at the fusing point. . .
>
> Then as a crown to the song service there was announced by Brother Cheville, "Admonition," the song dearly loved by the people

of the church. Oh, what a world of feeling was manifested by the huge assembly as in perfect time and chord they sang, filling the audience room with wonderful harmony of sweet sound and beautiful sentiment. [SH 8 April 27]

In 1929 Cheville was appointed Director of the Lamoni Branch Church School, which covered all ages and all activities. The name was changed to "Department of Religious Education." In that year also he was listed as Associate Editor of *Autumn Leaves*.

In January of 1931 the old Brick Church in Lamoni burned to the ground. Roy Cheville was named to the building committee to plan and arrange for rebuilding. The work of the committee was delayed first by the depression then by World War II. When the new church was built in 1952, Cheville had been a member of the committee for 21 years. The committee was beset not only by the depression and by the war, but by strong differences of opinion among the members of the committee and the congregation. Service on that committee was the source of much personal stress for Cheville. He left his mark on the sanctuary with the choice of scripture to be displayed on the platform: "This is my beloved son, hear him."

"What it means to be a Latter Day Saint," was the theme of a set of four pamphlets by Cheville which the church published in 1932 and 1933. These quarterlies established a new level of relationship between Roy Cheville and the membership of the church. The four quarterlies were, "The Relation of Our Church to Other Churches" [1932A], "Beliefs of Our Church" [1933D], "Membership Qualifications" [1933E], and "The Program of the Church" [1933H]. They were revised and reprinted by the church, and issued a total of 11 times, the latest in the 1959.

In 1933 the church held a youth conference at Graceland. Cheville taught a class, "Worship in the Young People's Program." In that summer Cheville was program director for Nauvoo Camp. He became a regular at the youth conferences and at Nauvoo Camp.

"We have waited many years for this type of approach to be made to the study of the scriptures," said Charles B. Woodstock of the church's Department of Religious Education, in his introduction to a set of four pamphlets by Cheville which constituted a year-long study of the Bible. The title of the series was, "The Bible in Everyday Living." The four quarterlies were, "How the Bible Came to Be" [1934A], "How to Read the Bible" [1935B], "How the Bible Reveals God" [1935C], and "How Shall We Use the Bible?" [1935D]. These quarterlies were used church-wide until Cheville used their contents in writing his 1939 book, *The Bible in Everyday Living.* [1939A] This book was reprinted in 1944, 1948, 1951, 1956, and 1961.

A study of the Book of Mormon was the next church school textbook series from Cheville in 1936 and 1937. This year-long series was written for intermediate grade youth. The four quarterlies were, "A Journey into Ancient Times and Places" [1936I], "People Who Lived in Book of Mormon Times" [1937A], "How the Book of Mormon Helps Us Today" [1937B], and "How the Book of Mormon Helps Us in Everyday Living" [1937C]. In 1945 this series was rewritten for younger students by Charlotte Gould.

Cheville was a busy contributor to each RLDS general conference. In the 1938 conference, for example, in addition to leading the daily congregational singing, he conducted a class each morning on "Teaching Values in Church History." He wrote and produced for Graceland night a special program on the story of Far West, to mark

141

its centennial. In that conference he was named a member of the First Presidency's Advisory Council on Religious Education.

Roy Cheville directed the program for the 1939 church-wide youth conference at Graceland College. He prepared an extensive program, which included writing several hymns and other material to be used in the evening pageants. He edited the pamphlet which described the results of the conference. [1939G] About 700 people attended the classes each day. Clifford Cole remembers that Cheville said during one session that he did not know what his mission would be. McDowell responded wryly, "When you find it I hope it amounts to something."

The Tenth Biennial Youth Conference was held at Graceland in June of 1941. A member of the general committee, Cheville wrote a small book (160 pages) as the official report of the conference, *The Branch of Today and Tomorrow*. [1941A]

In 1941 the church released a book by Cheville with the title, *Official Zion's League Handbook*. [1941E] It was written by a class in religious education, directed by Cheville, and edited for publication by Floyd M. McDowell. The Foreword was written by Fred M. Smith and the Introduction by F. M. McDowell. This volume contained several original hymns by Cheville, including one of his most popular hymns, "Open My Eyes."

In the school year 1943–44 Cheville conducted a religious education curriculum class for the general church. A study was made of the needs of junior high youth, age 12–14. The first semester was devoted to the discovery of the needs and wants of normal junior high youths and to the formulation of aims and objectives which in their realization would contribute to their wholesome development. In the second semester the class began writing on the quarterlies and expressional materials.

An article about him in 1947 summarized some of his contributions to the general church:

Roy Cheville's influence has been felt far beyond the bounds of Graceland's campus. As the only professionally trained specialist in religious education in the church, he has generously contributed to the educational materials used by the general church. He has helped shape courses, has written innumerable quarterlies for all ages form junior high to adult, has written the church's only scholarly book on the Bible, has contributed frequently to the *Saints' Herald*, has planned youth programs for the entire church for a complete year, time after time, and has served unofficially and without recognition as an adviser to the general church Department of Religious Education. He has traveled all over the United States and parts of Canada to reunions, institutes, and youth conventions. [SH 16 Aug 47]

In a 1947 *Herald* article, "One World and One Church" [1947F], Cheville introduced the whole church to the ideas for world outreach he had been developing on the Graceland campus. That was followed by the release by the church of four pamphlets by Cheville with the theme, "The Latter Day Saint Youth Looks at His World." The four quarterlies were, "How Shall We Look at Our World?" [1947A], "What Kind of World Shall We See?" [1947B], "What is Our Church's Mission to the World?" [1948O], and "How Shall We Equip the Church For Her World Mission?" [1948P].

In 1950 the church issued a *Hymnal for Youth* [1950G] which contained six of Cheville's hymns, and several poems and responsive readings. He had been a member of the committee to produce the hymnal.

In October 1950 Cheville was ordained to the office of patriarch. He gave 1,979 blessings, the first in 1950 and the last in 1985.

In 1951 the church issued a book by Cheville with the title, *Growing Up in Religion*. [1951B] Its subtitle was, "A Text for Explorers Who Are in the Quest for Spiritual Development." It encourages readers to re-examine basic ideas about religion. He defines religion as "that phase of human experience in which men are endeavoring to make personal contact with their universe." The material invites readers to avoid using such terms as "grace" and "salvation," which may turn out to be thought stoppers. It urges instead that readers focus attention on religious experience, personal and historical, and consider rigorous thought processes in dealing with them.

The opening of the new Lamoni Church was celebrated March 2, 1952. The bulletin for the service listed the 27 persons who had served on the building committee. By Roy Cheville's name was a symbol with a note that he had served continuously since February 1931. Of the 27 persons who had served, six were deceased at the building's opening.

In 1953 Cheville presided over a discussion for the first professional and businessmen's institute, sponsored by the Presiding Bishopric of the RLDS Church. The theme was, "Building for a Zionic Community." At that time he was also a member of the general church Curriculum Planning Committee, for which he was working on a five-year plan.

A new hymnal for the church was published in 1956. It included 11 hymns by Cheville.

On October 8, 1958 Roy Cheville was ordained Presiding Patriarch of the RLDS church by President W. Wallace Smith, D. O. Chesworth, and D. V. Lents. The ordination took place in the Auditorium during General Conference.

The setting for Patriarch Cheville's ministry was significantly different from that of "Unk" and of "Doc." At

Graceland his congregation was nearly the same group for a year at a time. It was possible to build group experiences over that period. But, in his new field he could not stay long with any one congregation. At the college most in his congregation was about the same age, and, of course, all had some college education. With them his major focus was on the integration of religious theory and practice in the planning and preparation for a wholesome and effective life. In his new field the congregations ranged widely in age, in education, and in many other factors. Since there was no built-in single focus, it was harder to meet on common ground.

The Patriarch also had to do his work in the context of the church's administrative structure. Nearly everything he did touched on an area that was someone else's responsibility. None of these cohorts was his equal in scholarship, particularly in religion, theology, and social science (the areas in which he had been commended by Fred M. Smith). But many of them had administrative control over matters which affected his ministry, including editorial power over things he wrote. As "Unk" and as "Doc" he had worked effectively with many colleagues, as well as congregation members who knew much less than he did. But never before were they in control of the environment in which he worked. For example, he was informed by the Hymnal Committee in 1980 that they had made several changes in his hymns to make them "reflect the best present understandings of the church theologically and linguistically."

Only one of his well-known and published hymns, "Let Us Sing a World-Wide Chorus" [1979A], was written after 1958. He wrote and used many hymns during this period, but with that one exception, they were not promoted for general use. As time went on he saw himself as being surrounded by people with untestable theories of God which were not based on the religious experiences of the Saints. Those feelings were private and they did not rule him. All his conversations, sermons, and writings were positive and upbeat.

As the Presiding Patriarch he was able to emphasize the brotherhood of all the saints world-wide. He wrote a series of articles in the *Saints' Herald*, under the title, "These Are My People." (He said, "I single out the company of the Saints, and I say as I walk with them, 'These are my People!'") [1959E] He ministered extensively abroad; to Europe, to Africa, to Asia, and to Latin America. He maintained two-way correspondence with friends on all these continents. When he wrote to some he would usually enclose a dollar in the letter so the respondents could buy postage to write back. When ministering in U.S. congregations, he would frequently draft a letter to be sent to a person in some foreign land and have it signed by all the members of the U.S. congregation. The objective was to provide friendly contacts and a demonstration that they, in their far-flung locations, were connected in a world-wide fellowship. Underlying these efforts was the conviction that world peace is possible through the leavening effect of his church's message and program in changing the lives of persons. That affirmation is expressed in the Patriarch's 1979 hymn, "Let Us Sing A Worldwide Anthem" [1979A], "We are one, for we are thine."

On April 4, 1974 Roy Cheville was released from assignment as Presiding Patriarch and given the "title" "Presiding Patriarch Emeritus." The *World Conference Bulletin* of that date said,

> In recognition of past and continuing ministry through the years we honor Roy A. Cheville for service which is distinctive by the nature of his gifts and personality. In response to the word of the

Lord, as acted on by this World Conference, and by action of the Joint Council of the First Presidency, Council of Twelve, and Presiding Bishopric, we pay tribute to Brother Cheville in his retirement. . .

Many lives have been influenced for good by the personal ministry of Brother Roy Cheville. His concern and interest in the individual goes beyond race or creed and know no bounds. As pastor-at-large of the church he has indeed served as one of God's chosen ministers in these last days.

We honor Brother Cheville for his many gifts to the church and know he will continue in faithful service as Presiding Patriarch Emeritus.

Cheville counseling Gerry Westwood in the hall, 1958.

Cheville counseling June Lendrie and Gary Beil in his office, 1958.

The Chevilles and the Gleazers share a Madrigal dinner.

Counseling

. . answering a letter from a lonely, bewildered young person. . During the day, there is a constant stream of students trickling into his office. . Students with romantic problems, students confused about life in general, student committees wanting help, students just wanting to talk, students of former years returning for a visit . . [SH 16 Aug 47]

Roy Cheville was much in demand as a personal counselor. During his "Doc" period, particularly, there were always people seeking him. Even though he was an easy person to visit with, it seems clear that he would not have been sought out so often by so many if they had not felt rewarded by the contact. Something must have happened inside them as a consequence of their contact with him.

By its very nature personal counseling is private and ephemeral, thus not easily documented. Two examples of Cheville's concern for and nurture of individual students are typical. Dick Dunlap was a sophomore student from New Westminster, British Columbia, when he met with an accident which caused the loss of his left foot in 1943. The accident occurred at 2:30 a.m. in Davenport, Iowa, as he jumped from the freight train he had been riding. Roy Cheville and Alva Gilbert were soon on their way to Davenport to see Dick's condition and give him support. In the spring of 1951 "Doc" met Kisuke Sekine at the train station in Osceola, when "Seki" came from Japan to be a Graceland student. "Seki" and Cheville became good friends. Seki was Japanese with a Buddhist background. The fatherhood of God and the personhood of Christ were concepts that did not have immediate meaning for him. Seki's own father had died when Seki was two years old. Seki said in 1986 that he felt that he had found a new

151

father when he came to Graceland and Cheville took him under his wing. "This father-son relationship in due course of time turned into a brotherly care in a circle of Christian fellowship." He went on,

> Brother Cheville worked with me very patiently and brought into my life "awareness" of the eternal nature of life and made my life profoundly meaningful. He enabled me to see God and Buddha not some "beings" dwelling aloof in some remote heavens, but representing the fundamental entity, fundamental life, that created the universe and keeps it alive and operating, linking the East and the West...
>
> Under his tutorship, Brother Cheville serving as my mentor, I made slow but steady growth in understanding the universal nature of the gospel of Jesus Christ, blending beautifully with the good elements which I brought in from my Buddhist background, enhancing and enriching...
>
> Thank you, Brother Cheville! If it were not for your fatherly/brotherly care, I would not have become what I am today. I would not even be here today. I shall always remember you and try to follow your step.

Cheville was also concerned with prevailing societal problems which could be addressed in writing. For example, out of his personal experiences, his sociological studies, and his ministerial activity, Cheville wrote a book in 1954 that he called a marriage-counseling manual for ministers. Its title was *When They Seek Counsel*. [1954A] He said it had risen out of a realization of what had been happening in our own church during the past 30 years— a time of marked transition in family life. He said that "things are not as they used to be when young people went a-courting and a-marrying."

The theme of the benedictory Graceland Christmas service in 1958 reveals the importance with which Cheville regarded the ministry of letters. The theme was, "We send around the world, through our letters, the light and love of the Everliving Christ." Roy Cheville planned and presided over the service. He regarded his own letter writing as a serious activity. Estimates of the number of people who received such ministry from him runs into the hundreds, and perhaps more. He spent long hours preparing responses, often hand-written.

Not infrequently Cheville would get a letter out of the blue from a former student he had not heard from in years. Many times individual were experiencing personal problems—so personal that they felt they had no one else to turn to. The letters would start out asking if "Doc" remembered the person, then go on to describe the nature of the problem—a potential divorce, behavior gone wrong, confusion which was becoming evident in dysfunctional behavior, etc. The writer would shortly receive a letter establishing recognition through some remembered event or relationship. Cheville's response would then go on to do some structuring of the problem and lay the basis for continued correspondence or contact of some kind. Not all divorces were prevented nor were all personal behavior patterns turned around. But, in a significant number of cases, something constructive took place in the life of the person who had initiated the contact. There was a renewed sense in the person of greater strength than before to meet the current challenges.

Nor was it only former students who wrote. Sometimes it would be a person who felt free to write by having heard a Cheville sermon. Sometimes the person who wrote felt free to write on the basis of the way he or she felt after reading something Cheville had written. For example a person wrote to Cheville saying in essence, "Over the past few years I have often been tempted to write to or meet with you about my problems. . . My question is how do I find God in a way which convinces me of his existence?" In his reply Cheville wrote,

I start out with this salutation, "dear friend" for it brings this kind of sense of relationship when some one inquires and indicates personal condition and outlook as you have done. No pretense. Straightforward concern and honesty.

You get right to the problem of believing in God. This is basic and foremost today. With thinking, exploring persons, the much-heard injunction, "Have faith in God!" often does not elicit an affirmative response. Nor would this get such a response from me. If some one asks me if I believe in God, I would need to ascertain what they mean by God. I could not and would not say "Yes" to some persons until I should find out what this term "God" meant to them. I could not respond affirmatively to some notions of God. These notions would be opposite to the genuine nature of God. This is not being finicky: this is being honest. Today persons of inquiring mind are wondering about the kind of God they can and do believe in, in the light of the universe and of the history of things as they see things. These persons ask, What kind of God can I believe in?

In the letter Cheville went on set the stage for understanding God working through discoverable processes. And he posed the problem of childish conceptions of God. He noted the need to use personal experience to interpret God. He talked about the concept of the person. He talked about the nature of spirituality and the concept of "spirit" and "element" as aspects of one reality. He continued,

And getting with God and knowing God requires more than looking on from the bleachers or observation platform. We have to get in the game with God and adventure in the laboratory of living. This seeking is more than asking questions. This calls for searching and applying in the quest. God has never given me ready-made, finalized answers. I was directed to the counsel to Oliver Cowdery (D. & C. 9) and I have always had to explore. And the exploring continues. What a thrill!

Here is a start. If this quest of yours needs more, we shall try again.

Sincerely and Expectantly Yours, Roy A. Cheville

Cheville sometimes initiated the correspondence. One of the persons who received Cheville's ministry by letter was E. J. Gleazer, Jr. Ed has said that on some occasions when he was confronting troubling choices, he would receive out of the blue a letter from Cheville providing penetrating insights to the problems at hand. The first of these letters was written August 20, 1957. Ed had gone to Washington on a year's leave of absence to head a project for the American Association of Junior Colleges. During that year he was offered the position of executive officer of that organization. He wrestled with the decision and finally decided to leave Graceland and to take the new job. That was the setting into which this letter arrived from Cheville:

August 20, 1957
E.J. Gleazer, Jr.

Dear Ed.

I understand you will be coming back to Lamoni in a week or so, but I have wanted to write you before that time. Last Saturday Nell and Charlotte drove down to the Far West Stake reunion to bring me home—they brought the letter announcing your resignation and your appointment to the secretaryship of the junior college association.

Last fall when you left for the special assignment with the junior college association I said to myself that you would not be returning. I mentioned this view to Bill Gould and to Tess [Morgan]. I think there was something of insight in it.

At that time I was concerned about your going. I sensed so many administrative problems that needed to be clarified. After your absence during last summer I felt there were so many questions calling for solution that I thought you could ill afford to go.

At announcement of your resignation and of your future work, my reaction was quite otherwise. It will be the type of work you will enjoy. After being in this recent assignment I am sure that you will be more at home in this type of work with its general aspects, contact with persons who appeal to you, travel, and concern with the large

155

questions rather than details of administration. And you will do well in it.

As to the future of Graceland, I have nothing to say just now. I have not had time to think. My own role in the college is confused just now. It is not one of complaint but of uncertainty as to the way and place for making my contribution to the church in the next ten and more years. I have a sense of theological mission which I question may have fulfillment here at Graceland. I say this so you will understand my attitude. I do not speak of this here—I would not be understood.

I presume you will continue to live in Washington. You will represent the Church well in the capital city. You have a breadth and an analytical viewpoint that we are needing so very much right now.

We need men and women who will move out in key places and bring the fruits of their experience into the larger body. You can have such a mission through these coming years.

I saw Allen [Gleazer] at Stewartsville. He came up to me and spoke very cordially. He seemed happy in the reunion life.

Good wishes to you Ed. I wanted to say this without the pressure of mass meetings during the convention.

Sincerely, Roy

In that letter are insights which allowed Ed to sense more clearly the mission before him. He had been struggling with the opportunities he could see before him to represent the church in a larger context—through professional educational activities rather than as a minister from the outside. His friends in the church hierarchy had been almost unanimous in counseling him to stay within the framework of the full-time ministry. But the insights in Cheville's letter recognized the mission Gleazer could perform in the context of a broad and growing service. The accuracy of Cheville's understanding of the potential in Gleazer's decision has been validated by the frequency with which the church and the college have called on him for specialized service in the areas of education and peace, contributions which he would not have been qualified to make had he chosen the more parochial road. That letter is representative of the many hundreds of counseling letters Cheville wrote to his friends.

As Cheville began the transition from faculty member to Presiding Patriarch in 1960, the steady stream of visitors continued. One evening in his room on the third floor of Gunsolley Hall, a men's dormitory, as he was about to turn in for the night at 9:30, two fellows came in. As they left, another came. At that visitor's departure Cheville got into bed when he heard a rap on the door—another visitor. It was just before 12 when he got to bed to stay. He wrote,

> These visits brought me into the lives of some more of my people— young men. I met occupational questions, educational plans, romantic strains, concerns about friends, pranks of high school days, views on church life. When one of the fellows was leaving he extended his hand and said, "I'd like to give a good night handshake to you as my friend!" Experiences like these cannot be purchased with money. Occasionally friends express sympathy to me because I am rooming in Gunsolley Hall. They are pitying me for having to put up with noise and confusion. Not at all! In three months not once has noise disturbed me. [1960E]

Patriarchal Ministry

> It is a good experience to place hands on the head of a youth and sense the illuminating presence of God, indicating that the life is clean and worthy of God's approval. Many a time I have experienced this sanction as a Saint has come before me clean and consecrated. [1978D]

The ordained patriarch in the RLDS Church is a special minister to individuals within the church. The role is that of a spiritual parent. The patriarch is a counselor who works toward lifting the aspirations and the accomplishments of the recipients of the ministry. Roy Cheville had already been ministering in the direction of the special functions of the Patriarch. The *Graceland Alumni Magazine* said that "Doc's" ordination to this office "is a symbol of the ministry which already has been given and a ministry which shall yet extend itself beyond present expectations."[1] The unique function of the Patriarch is that of delivering the Patriarchal Blessing. This blessing is normally a once-in-a-lifetime event. In preparation both the member and the Patriarch make preparation to qualify for the presence of the Holy Spirit in the experience of the blessing.

On October 1, 1950 Roy Cheville was ordained to the office of Patriarch at a special meeting of Lamoni Stake in the Lamoni Coliseum. Church President Israel A. Smith presided; the ordaining ministers were Arthur Oakman and Charles Hield; Apostles. E. J. Gleazer, Jr. gave the invocation and the benediction. Apostle Hield spoke on "The Significance of Patriarchal Ministry."

The ordination prayer by Arthur Oakman was a very special experience for both Oakman and Cheville. In preparation Oakman sought guidance for what to say to "this holy man"(his phrase). He saw in vision an iceberg of considerable size on the extending ocean. He sensed the iceberg was representing the spiritual brother to whom, about whom, he was to speak in prophetic message. Then he sensed with clear awareness that the large part of the iceberg was below the surface of the water and was not visible to casual onlookers. Oakman said to Cheville that as a patriarch "you will minister as an evangelist, as a revivalist, as a father living with the saints."

Israel A. Smith, President of the RLDS Church, also spoke to Cheville in counsel, "You will live among the Saints in spiritual fellowship. You will receive confidences and confessions that only you and God will know." A note found in Cheville's desk said that Elbert A. Smith had testified to him that through many preceding years God had been prompting him and guiding him for this ministry with specific expressions in counseling and encouraging adults, youth, and children with the guiding light of the Holy Spirit.

On October 15, 1950, Roy Cheville gave his first Patriarchal Blessing to Jack Fears in Lamoni. He had given 12 blessings by the end of 1950. In all he gave 1,979 blessings, the last one on July 10, 1985.

Cheville described some aspects of his patriarchal work in a newsy letter to E. J. Gleazer, Jr. Cheville concluded on a personal note:

In your letter you hoped I would find recuperation at the Kansas reunion. I took this Kansas reunion because I thought I needed one where I would function as the patriarchal minister. It was the best organized for patriarchal work of any I have ever seen. The days were busy and exacting but fruitful in inspiration and service to the membership. [In Wichita in June he gave 30 blessings in 7 days]

Nelle went along with me to do stenographic work. She is gradually picking up some of her skills and doing quite well.

In 1952 Cheville made a presentation in the Graceland chapel to some students about preparation for a patriarchal blessing, which reveals his understanding of the sacrament. He complimented the students on inquiring about preparation that could equip them for a rich experience in receiving the patriarchal blessing. He said that many think of something they ought to do in the last two or three hours to give them a specific fitness. Instead, he said, "It is the total pattern of an outlook on life that we shall be looking to . . You ought to look toward a patriarchal blessing with high anticipation. Effective religion must have sound expectancies. Life without these aims and hopes is anemic and colorless. It is not enough, however, that you must expect. These expectancies must be sound and realizable."

He believed that the recipient of the blessing should expect to assume responsibility for problem-solving. The patriarchal blessing is no escape from decision-making, it is no fortune-telling device to unveil the future. Those who expect to shift the responsibility to God for decision-making will probably be disappointed. God wants disciples of understanding and ability who choose to go along with him. The blessing will set forth guidelines for life planning. The actual choosing must be ours.

Cheville noted that he had found the college student days particularly well suited for patriarchal ministry in blessings. He said further that the spirit of dedication is indispensable. One cannot expect God to give counsel unless one is disposed to respond. He noted from his own experience that he was able to do good work when all of him was devoted to the divine endeavor.

He pointed out that the word "blessed" means "happy." Essentially a blessing is a counsel for a commitment to a way of life what will achieve enduring happiness. Persons would do well, then, to think through what values they prize most and ask themselves whether these will bring Zionic well-being. A blessing's purpose is not to bestow gifts and hold out spiritual allurements. Our prayer should be that God will help us to see the good way.

He counseled candidates to be clean and effective in personal living, for God cannot place a benediction on sordid, smutty living. However, one does not have to be perfect before being blessed. The blessing is designed to help achieve quality of character. He said there is no hurry about receiving a patriarchal blessing. One does not rush up to a patriarch and ask if there are a few minutes to spare for a blessing. We do not rush hastily into the presence of God. We come step by step until we feel ready to commune with our heavenly parent.

He did not ignore the responsibility for preparation on the part of the patriarch:

> The patriarch must follow a well-ordered pattern of living. Here, again, it is the total pattern of life that matters. I shall be frank to acknowledge that the ministry is exacting. One cannot come to the hour of blessing with animosities and ranklings in his soul. He must come clean "before the Lord." He must come with faculties alert. And finally, he must expect confidently that God will meet him at the appointed place. [1978D]

He saw the work of the patriarch essentially serving the membership in contrast to the seventy who reaches to those outside the church.

Notes

1. *Graceland Alumni Magazine* for October 1950.

BOOK V.

Personal Principles

BOOK V.
PERSONAL PRINCIPLES
Philosophy and Practice
of Education

Great teachers set out to develop the personalism of their disciples. They free the spirit. They do not bend the loyalties of their pupils to them. They stimulate the maturing learners to attach their allegiances to something eternally worthful. [1956E]

During his academic career Roy Cheville taught courses and developed and managed curricula and degree programs. But that is not where he put his emphasis in education. With regard to courses (as with worship services) he believed that teachers need to have clearly in mind what they want to have happen in the lives of students. For Cheville the heart of education was development in the person. Each course, each degree program, and each worship service could play a part in helping the person grow in a positive direction. Furthermore, education was not just what went on in the classroom and in the library. Students also spent time in dormitories and in a variety of other activities. All these experiences affected the person and were a part of education.

Cheville was a master teacher. He was able to make himself understood by the youngest and the oldest persons in his audience. The classroom presented a range, not so much in age, but in variety of outlook and degree of attention. His ability to hold his students' attention was in part due to his lighthearted approach which was always ready to see humorous elements in the topic being discussed. Sometimes startling and sometimes irreverent, these techniques resulted in students learning to look at serious issues from more than one angle. He discouraged narrow and simple views. Many student papers were returned with the note, "Other factors, also."

Some of his ability to hold the student's attention was in his practice of diving more deeply into the subject matter than the student expected. Cheville made this an adventure. Students seldom had the feeling that they were just being fed from the vast stores of information of this superior scholar. Instead, the student had the feeling of being a member of a discovery party. Something new and unexpected just kept showing up. A thoughtful student who lived through that kind of experience understood thoroughly the words of his hymn, "Hast thou heard it? . . something for you; go and find it."

Cheville believed that great teaching came from great character:

> Teachers of this order must have insights and convictions and loyalties that make them stand upright and certain concerning things worth living for. Such persons will have something in them worth radiating. [1956E]

One thing that radiated from Roy Cheville as a teacher was his enthusiasm. Nothing he did or taught seemed like an afterthought or a secondary task. His students could feel his love for his subject, his love for teaching, and his love for them. He showed that in part by the degree of preparation he had made—over long years. In part he showed his enthusiasm by his attention to each student. He understood and respected student questions, and he understood the implications of different ways of responding to them. He seemed never to shut out an honest searching question and seemed to be willing to take whatever time was needed to answer it. He did not ridicule or belittle curiosity that was immature or ill-informed.

He believed that the good teacher functioned as a mentor (older brother) for the student, not as an autocrat. Cheville's belief in the worth and development of persons is the same thing as his educational philosophy which focused on the worth and development of persons. It is the same philosophy he saw in Jesus of Nazareth, one of the greatest teachers of all time.

Cheville fit comfortably into a church which believed that God is continually revealing his word, his ways, and his truth. No matter how much has been revealed and established, there is always more light and truth to be apprehended. Thus he could say,

> The principles of the educational theory of the church are inseparably connected with the belief in inspiration, personal development, and its social gospel. [1930J]

Approach and Methods

The understanding teacher has a love of humanity and a comprehension of human relations. The wholesome teacher has habits of life which give him the maximum physical, mental, and spiritual effectiveness. The effective teacher possesses more than good intentions. [1931B]

Roy Cheville had a legendary ability to remember student's names, to remember where they came from, their family tree, and which branch of the tree they were connected with. That trait reveals his commitment to know students in depth and to track their personal growth. He was genuinely interested in each student as a person. In class he made it easy for students to speak up in participation. In doing that he was no pushover. If a student repeatedly introduced a comment with "don't you think —," Cheville often responded, "No I don't." Even so, he was gentle and encouraged students to speak up. He wanted their involvement because he was sure it helped the learning process. Once in after-hours reflections in 1946, Joe Sage said, "at test time I remember best the things I said in class."

In sociology classes where there were a number of concepts Cheville wanted his students to understand, he would assign relatively short reading assignments from a variety of sources. He had chosen each one as a succinct but comprehensive presentation of the concept he wanted understood. In that manner, also, the student was exposed to a number of different authors and writing styles. The result was a broader and more thorough understanding of the concepts.

He took course and class planning seriously. He was always thoroughly prepared. Without diluting the content, he looked for ways to engage the interests of the students. One student describing a class on Bible appreciation called it "pleasantly different but no less interesting and helpful." The student, Sara Gardner, continued,

> With his rich background of religious history and his unique method of presentation, the Bible ceases to be a book to marvel at or to be superstitiously handled, and becomes a book to read, understood, and loved for the beauty of its literature and its portrayal of the principles of the more abundant life in everyday living. . . his whole-hearted enthusiasm, which is undeniably contagious. [SH 23 May 28]

A student wrote of a 1934 lecture that "it was presented in such a new and interesting way that each listener gave his undivided attention through the entire discussion." The subject was the World War. The account continued,

> He then led his audience dramatically through the various acts of the "play" stressing at every point the jealousy and the wholly insignificant incidents which brought to a most disastrous head the trouble which had been brewing for over a century. [LC 8 Feb 34]

Cheville used his knowledge of the students as persons in figuring out how to inspire them. Three qualities he said a good teacher must have: know the subject, have ability and love for teaching, and have the ability to inspire students. By inspiring he meant that he wanted the student to make a personal response to the material. That response could be a sudden insight into what the student might be able to do as a personal mission—including the qualifying steps. The goal of the mission could motivate the student for years of preparation.

Good students were impressed with the rigor of his thought processes. His use of language was precise. His examples were well thought out, and he took no logical short-cuts in their use or description. That was a revelation for many who had come from small branches where there were few church members of intellectual accomplishments. In that situation they had become accustomed to viewing their church people as somewhat deficient compared to others in the community. Now they were learning to know one of their own church leaders who could hold his own in any intellectual group. Not only could he hold his own in affairs relating to religion, but in science as well. But with all that, he was like the members of their own branches in that he, too, was a friend.

He did not restrict his interest to good students. He knew and understood students with a variety of abilities. One not particularly good student was Jack Fears. By his own description Jack had lived through several years of enthusiastic pursuit of rather unworthy objectives. He had come to Graceland in the process of getting lined up with better ones, still with enthusiasm. Cheville became his friend as a matter of course. When Cheville was ordained a patriarch in 1950, Jack's was the first patriarchal blessing he gave. Fears spent many years in enthusiastic ministry before succumbing to ill health.

The student characteristic which appealed to Cheville most was intellectual honesty. The trait he had the most difficulty tolerating was laziness. He spent much of his time with male students; however, he felt strong bonds of friendship with many women students. He could be unrestrained in expressing friendship with the men, but he had to be much more careful in the way he related with the women. However, he held many women students in high regard and offered them unrestrained encouragement.

When Cheville made his first trip to the Kirtland Temple [he wrote that it was in 1929, but it was probably in

1930] he climbed to the second-story room, originally designed to be a teaching area. He described a confirming experience in which,

> The Master Teacher reminded me of my teaching stewardship. It was to be directed toward those who would go forth as "living teachers" in "the great and marvelous work." [1983]

Whole Life Approach

A hundred years ago the play life of people was not looked upon as having much educational significance. . . We have come to see the soundness of the statement that "there can be no Christian civilization without the Christian use of leisure time." We have come to see that our true selves find expression in the spontaneous activity of play. [1933E]

Cheville "viewed life steadily and viewed it whole." He honored the totality of human experience as God-given resources for personal development. For example, at one Lamoni Stake Conference he gave a lecture on religion and play. He said that play is essential to rounding out personality. He said that church leaders and members need to understand the function of play and its place in the church's program. He would say the same thing about play in the college program and in the educational process in general. What he called the "quiet factor" in the college experience was the general association of students and faculty in the common life, study, play, and conversation. The college experience should educate the whole person.

Dormitory life had a special place not only in his theory of education but in the warmth of his own personal experience. He said that,

. . dormitory life teaches one a certain "give-and-take" and a communal aspect that is a good formative influence for character. The recognition of established routine for the welfare of all adds something valuable to social experience. The intimacy of contacts gives an expanding circle of friendships such as can not be found under other conditions. [1930D]

He felt that the six years he spent in Herald Hall were invaluable to him. The personal contacts, the insight into human nature, and the free expression of boyish spirit could never have been obtained elsewhere. Residents in his hall claimed they had more dormitory spirit and more real fun than any other group in the college. They described a good dorm organization which allowed them to have well organized parties. They boasted that they were the only dormitory with a full-fledged musical organization furnishing music for church services and radio programs.

Cheville addressed wholeness in discussing the place of religion at Graceland. He said that religion is not a veneer to be plastered on the surface, nor is it a compartment of one's life. Jesus compared it indirectly to leaven that should permeate the wholeness of things. He said it should permeate economics, science, art, social intercourse, philosophy, recreation and every other field. Graceland may be considered an experiment toward this end—becoming both a laboratory and a fellowship. [1936H] He wrote at more length about this wholeness in his 1966 book, *Spiritual Health*.

Cheville paid attention to the issues which were in the minds of the students. "We may stand or fall in life on the vocational choice we make," was one bit of his counsel. He would note than many youth get into a line of work for which they are not fitted and blunder along through life. Some young people never choose but go blindly along responding to circumstances. The wise youth studies native capabilities and seeks to develop strengths to provide the basis for a vocation that fits.

He did not duck the issue of human sexuality He recognized sex as a strong influence in the lives of young people especially. As such it deserved attention in education for life. Such teaching was a part of his sociology courses, particularly Marriage and The Family. But sex also was a religious matter. He wrote,

174

Sex is no accident in our nature. God must have had some great purpose when he created men and women with a claimant sex instinct at the center of them. We do not call these urges good or bad: they become so, according to the way they are directed. Rightly controlled, they make possible a rich spiritual and aesthetic nature, a strong, healthy mind and body. Misused, they can undermine our characters and dull our sensitivities to that which is noble and beautiful. [1933E]

He addressed the balanced life in many different ways. In 1938 he took a stand for temperance as part of an anti-liquor campaign in Decatur County. He defined temperance as a philosophy of the wholeness of things. Anything that is pushed to excess defeats some other areas of life. He took the position that liquor can and does crush out other sides of life. But, he said, it is not the business of the church to tell people specifically what to do. "We can't build a community that way." [1938A]

In 1941 Cheville explored the relation between general education and religious education. He defined religious education as the development of persons through co-operative relations with the spiritual powers and purposes of the universe. He looked at educational institutions across the country and found little substantive agreement on a good definition of general education. He believed that as we develop toward higher community life, general education and religious education would become the same. [1941C]

Building a student body into a community was his objective every college year in his "Doc" period. The junior college had two classes, so somewhat more than half the students were new to the college each September. Cheville arranged for the sophomores to arrive a few days before the freshmen came. In those few days the sophomores went through some experiences designed to help them be the carriers of Graceland values and counselors to the new arrivals. In 1948, with the second of the suddenly large student bodies, Cheville noted that 600 students would arrive. They would be built into a community that would last nine months. "That is so much to expect in so short a time," he wrote. "Without the common heritage of the church, this could hardly be possible. There is no other group like this in the church." [1948Q]

Cheville believed that sound education trains us in decision-making. In his view decision-making is the hallmark of personhood. Making choices means self-management, and that distinguishes persons from animals. There are decisions to be made in all aspects of a person's life. Some church people have had the view that religion should relieve them of responsibility for making decisions. When they turn their lives over to God, they can let God direct them. Former students will remember that the Dubuzzys waited for God to make all their decisions. Mrs. DuBuzzy, for example, would pray for divine guidance as to which dress fabric to purchase. Cheville abhorred this kind of abdication. For him being religious meant making quality choices. Growth in religion meant refinement in ability to make choices. However, he cautioned that well-meaning choices based on faulty data can have bad consequences. A good life requires both pure motives and educated views of the consequences of the alternatives in the choice.

Youth-Centered Emphasis

Now you are putting life together. Now you are working on life objectives. Here you are pushing out the boundaries of your world. Today you are reinterpreting your theology. Now you are working on plans for vocations, family mates, church participation, advanced education. [1978D]

Should the most talented and most scholarly personnel of a church be assigned to the service of its youth? That is a question which the career of Roy Cheville should bring to full attention. In his 35 Graceland years, he had an enormous impact not only on the college but also on the church. He stimulated youth to take a large view of what they might become and how they might serve. His influence was directed toward making the established RLDS Church and its objectives the vehicle of their service. Toward the end of his faculty years Roy Cheville was the strongest voice in interpreting the RLDS religion at Graceland and to the youth of the church.

Most church groups use their best talent in ministry to adults. There is more prestige and more visibility in working with adults. Youth are served by ministers who are left over after the best have been assigned elsewhere. The result is that adult groups get better quality ministry and the youth receive ministry of lesser quality. But it is the youth who are more ready and willing to receive ministry. It is they who are much more likely to change. It is they who will have longer years in which to express in their lives the effects of the ministry given.

One way to measure the influence of Graceland on the church is suggested by an event that took place in the Church's World Conference in 1994. The Conference assembled represented the primary force of personnel performing the work of the church. The delegates who had been students at Graceland were asked to stand. When these former Gracelanders stood they were the overwhelming majority of those in the Conference chamber. Not only was that a tribute to Graceland's influence but also to Cheville's. Many of those standing would have been his students.

Cheville became an active priesthood member while he was still quite young. It is understandable that he would direct a reasonable portion of his ministry to youth while he was himself at or near that stage. The unusual thing is that he stayed focused on youth long after he became one of the foremost theologians and thinkers in the church and was no longer young himself.

Cheville addressed the needs of youth in the planning of his academic work. He wrote the paper required for the Bachelor of Divinity, his second graduate degree, on the junior church. He continued that work by writing articles about youth work and the junior church in church periodicals. He not only carried on his direct work with Graceland students, he also assumed increasing responsibility for youth work in the Lamoni congregation.

At a church-wide young people's convention on the Graceland campus in 1924, he gave a course on the junior church. He said,

> The junior church is not a place for merely holding the children while their parents enjoy an adult service; it is not a place of entertainment; it is not a place for talking down to children. . . merely translating an adult problem into simple terms or child language does not make of it a child problem. Children have problems of their own, and the junior church should discuss these in such a way as to make a continuity of experience between their week-day and Sunday activities. [SH 11 June 1924]

He matched his academic studies of religious education for youth with practice in the religious services
which targeted young people. At the Lamoni reunions he
was in charge of social and recreational activities for the
juniors. He designed and led Graceland students in activities on the campus. One Saturday night in October he
gathered the Athenians for a campus frolic:

'Uncle Roy,' being the group leader, divided the crowd into two
circles, and a few short moments were spent in playing 'Flying
Dutchman.' This was followed by several other lively games. Finally
we gathered into one large circle; all-day suckers were passed, and
'Uncle Roy' led us in our 'Agriculture Song' and several Graceland
songs before we bade each other a happy good night. [SH 17 Oct 28]

He used the religion club at Graceland as a planning
and service unit for ventures such as a series of missionary services for young people. Student members of the
club planned worship, prepared special numbers, arranged advertising, and did the ushering. Cheville delivered the sermons. He defined worship in 1933, noting
that "fundamentally the worship experience is a harmonious communion with God." [1933A] He expanded and
enlarged the concept in 1936 as a re-interpretation of
religion for youth. He wrote,

The up-and-coming college student always demands—and he has a
right to ask it—that his religion square with the facts of his growing
educational experience and that it be functional in the current
world. . . If there is an outstanding calling that I believe belongs to
our college, it is the stewardship of interpreting our religion in terms
that can command the respect of alert minds and can supply the
foundations for living in the modern world. [1936A]

By this time his outlook on ministry for youth combined the experiences that made religious activities enjoyable with a serious and analytic approach to study of
life and the functions of religion. His mature theology

supported whole-life ministry for youth. His effectiveness is shown in the report of crowds of young people in his classes at general conferences:

> The Stone Church Annex was filled to capacity with the youth of the church at the eleven o'clock hour when Roy Cheville led them in discussing "Youth at Work in Evangelism." This was the first in a series of classes to be held at this hour every morning during the Conference. [SH 10 April 40]

He could have ministered in person to groups of any age as he did in his books, his pamphlets, and his articles, and as he would later do with his hymns. But he chose to stay with his teaching and ministering to youth. However, by 1946 he was indicating in private discussions that he did not know what his continuing mission would be. And he said, about 1955, that he felt that he had a calling to teach theology to a broader audience. And, in 1959, he did move on to a position to do just that.

In his Graceland years he was devoted to serving youth. Their response to him provided a wonderful energizing force for him. In turn, he achieved his objectives of enlarging the aspirations and the quality of life for many, many Graceland students and other church young people.

BOOK VI.

The Practice of
Religion

BOOK VI. THE PRACTICE OF RELIGION
Growing Up in Religion

A difficulty with many of us is that we have not learned how to grow up in religion. It is possible for us to be in the last year of high school, and yet be about five years old in some of our ideas and practices. [1933D]

In his Graceland College years (1923–1959) Cheville was *growing up in religion*, a phrase he had used to title two publications, an article in 1930 [1930H], and a book in 1951. [1951B] His thesis is that childish ideas about God are acceptable for children, but will not serve mature persons. Many people who mature in their knowledge about the sciences, business, and people do not mature in their understanding of God. Instead they wind up as generally mature individuals with childish ideas about God. Religious maturity is required to understand a theory of God involving the interaction of spiritual forces with humans. Religious maturity is required to leave childish theories about God behind and develop a higher level theory of the nature of God and how divinity works.

In the 21 years between the 1930 article and the 1951 book, Roy Cheville's theology developed dramatically. In the foreword to the book he explained that it "emerges out of my life with those who live on the growing edge." Two experiences of spiritual counsel in the summer of 1925, which Roy remembered for the rest of his life, influenced his spiritual growth. The first of these took place in a reunion west of Chicago. Roy was probably at the reunion on the weekend, while attending summer session at the University. In a prayer meeting one brother had spoken in counsel with what Roy described as a simple message, in simple tongue. Roy seems to have felt that such a simple message could not be ascribed to the Holy Spirit, as there was no profound guidance involved. But Roy's friend H.P.W. Keir, a senior priesthood member, pointed out to Roy that the event may have had a very profound effect on the life of the brother who spoke. Roy remembered the lesson:

> After the meeting H. P. W. Keir of Chicago walked aside with me. He placed his hand on my shoulder and gave prophetic counsel, "Brother Roy, you are advised to perceive how God speaks to his Saints. He speaks on their level so they will understand. This applies to the content of what he says and to the words used to express what he wants his people to hear. Sometimes, as today, God's message will be simple and self-evident to you. Sometimes it will not meet your needs."

That experience was illuminating with regard to the nature of inspiration. Inspiration could come to one who is an earnest seeker and whose life is clean and worthy. That person may not be very learned. A genuine spiritual experience may illuminate his or her life, but contain no elements that are new or instructive to other hearers of the same words.

The other experience took place a few weeks later. Roy made a trip from Chicago to Lamoni to be ordained a high priest at the Lamoni Stake Reunion August 9, 1925. The officiating ministers for the ordination were E. J. Gleazer, Sr. and A. B. Phillips. It was an unusual occurrence: ordaining a man so young to be a high priest. He had already been ordained a counselor to the president of Lamoni Stake, Wilbur Prall. This ordination contained very significant counsel for 27-year-old Roy Cheville. He was not well acquainted with Apostle Edmund J.

Gleazer, Sr., who was to be the spokesman in the ordination. But the experience which they shared on this occasion helped engender a long-lasting spiritual comradeship between them. Cheville described the experience later:

> One bit of instruction has been very beneficial to me. I have sought to remember and utilize it. . . I remember little of the ordination prayer, but one sentence of admonition burned into my spirit—"Go on in the work of preparation and in the work of thy ministry." With such spiritual power was it spoken that it stood out in relief. In my reflection I pondered why such advice was necessary. At that very time I was engaged in "preparation" and no admonition in that direction seemed needed. I had just entered into the stake presidency—the work of "ministry." Then with one of those illuminating touches well known to the people of God, the realization of the meaning of it all came to me. It was not only a continuation of academic studies of religion, nor a further participation in ministerial work that was intended. It was a combination of the two, into one service, that was advised. Study and experience were to go hand in hand. No scriptural statement ever came to me with more force than did that prayer with its insight. [1931F]

That combination of study and experience were to characterize his activities for the rest of his life. He was to see relevance in his studies as he reviewed the lessons of his personal experience. He was to evaluate those experiences by the use of the best intellectual tools he gained from his studies.

Commitment

There are those who are capable of giving little to a cause and so require little assurance about it, but those who are willing to give of all their energies demand that the foundations are sound and solid. .. He who loves his church in a genuine way will always be searching to make sure of his foundations and to expand his views. [1933E]

Roy had been told in high school that he had the potential of becoming a zealot. He must have shown signs that early of a remarkable drive and ability to hold to an objective. He was baptized with the conviction that the RLDS Church could teach him to make contact with divinity and have that contact guide his life. That, he concluded, was the most important principle to which he could devote his energies. He learned to balance religious service with study and other person-developing pursuits. He learned to keep his religion broadly defined and his study broad-based.

Not all of Roy's compatriots in the church and on the Graceland faculty shared this breadth of focus. But Roy chose to follow the path of those who did, particularly Fred M. Smith and Floyd McDowell. McDowell probably wrote for the 1930 *RLDS Centennial Year Book* the affirmation that "the Church has nothing to fear from the developments of modern science on the grounds that all truth ultimately converges."

Two sets of influences follow from such teachings by a church. One is that a young person growing up in such an environment is motivated to develop capabilities on a broad front that lead to success in many kinds of endeavors. Such development generally produces many attractive opportunities in a wide variety of enterprises. The other influence is that such open teachings by the church make it easy for the young person to move away from the church. Few teachings bind the person to the church with bands of guilt. These two sets of influences can combine to make it easy for a capable and diligent person to leave the church by preparing him or her for many attractive alternatives. The church commitment which leads the person to be successful leads also to opportunities to follow other avenues.

Roy Cheville's church commitment caused him to go to graduate school and become a professor. It helped him to be successful as a scholar and to gain stature in his profession. He had ample opportunity to follow other avenues of rewarding pursuits for which he was well qualified. Although he was clearly aware of some of these, he seems never to have wavered a moment from the path of his original commitment.

As a new and young faculty member, he had to establish himself. As the only theology scholar with a graduate degree, he was at some disadvantage among some faculty and church personnel. He soon sensed in some quarters either unspoken hostility or open antagonism to Graceland's religious life and her religious studies. This antagonism complicated the work he felt necessary to the development of the academic programs. He saw a need to replace Graceland's special religious education courses with a standard collegiate-quality department, and he knew this would need to be done carefully.

Though he had a Master's degree in religion, the official college catalogs for several years showed his teaching field to be history. For a number of years the *Acacia* listed his teaching fields as religious education and history. He established himself by teaching well the courses to which he was assigned, by going more than half-way in the many incidental things faculty must do, by being very active in the religious activities on campus and in the Lamoni Branch. He did so well that he was named in 1925 counselor to the Lamoni Stake president. At that time he was also ordained a high priest. These two actions made it clear that he had the support of the First Presidency of the RLDS Church.

When he was in summer school in Berkeley in 1926, he got to know a second major university campus. Having now been a graduate student at Chicago and Berkeley, he could see the way to develop a career in such prestigious institutions. There is no evidence that he was tempted in that direction, but there is evidence that he did think about it. In a description of his writing the Alma Mater Hymn he sat overlooking the majestic Berkeley campus. In his mind's eye, however, he could see the Graceland campus as the scene for the realization of his ideals.

"The loyalties of life" was the theme of the baccalaureate sermon "Unk" gave for the Lamoni High School 1927 graduating class. He talked about loyalty to home, to friends, and loyalty to ideals. Ideals are a necessary factor in keeping one going. He referred to the life of Paul, the great biblical adventurer, who remained true to his ideals throughout his entire life. In an article he was writing about the same time, he gave an understanding view of the difficult situation of the new college student who finds himself or herself in the midst of new materials, strange theories, enlarged social life, and a seemingly changed universe. He noted that it was the role of Graceland not to shield the student from any of this, but to provide resources which will allow the student to master the wealth of this new learning and these new experiences in the context of long-range values. "Graceland endeavors to meet its responsibility as no other school in shaping, directing, and stimulating of religious living," he said. [1927F]

Among Cheville's notes was a reference to spiritual counsel through John Martin at Graceland College. The content was, "You are called to minister to my Church in increasing radius. Now your stewardship is here on college hill. Put into your work here the quality that expresses the Church in and for all the world."

By 1928 he was established on the campus. Though the catalog still listed his teaching field as history, he wrote the section on religious education for the report of Graceland College to the RLDS General Conference. That made it clear that he had the support of Graceland's president George N. Briggs. Here was recognition of success in the work he was performing to nourish his commitment.

In 1928 he reflected on carrying on pastoral work in the stake presidency while doing all the things he was committed to do on campus. That was an idea that kept coming to his attention. He dealt with it in terms of his overall commitment:

> Yet, such arrangement proves sound from the collegiate viewpoint. Men of any college field must carry on laboratory work, if they are to retain reality. Theological professors do so in order to counteract professional aloofness. Such connection hooks up with active ministry in such a way as to be satisfying to the onlooking membership. It gives a point of contact. And lastly, it furnishes the needed connection when we are ready for it. The final study of those in religious training should be in actual doing under supervision, for which there is college credit. My visionary eye tells me I shall see it some day. [1928E]

In the 1929 baccalaureate sermon for Lamoni High School, his title was "Nothing in Excess," after an inscription over the door of an ancient Greek temple. It was the underlying principle on which the Greeks sought a balanced life. It was they who first asked the question, "What is the ideal life?" He said that there must be a unified purpose which makes a life something worthwhile.

By 1930 he was writing regularly in church publications and was an editor of *Autumn Leaves.* One conference edition of the *Saints' Herald* in 1930 contained a profile article about him with the title, "Roy A. Cheville—A Friend of the Young." It noted that Cheville was by this time a familiar figure to everyone who attended the business sessions, and it noted that those who know him wonder at his versatility.

In the 1930's he began serving in the church's youth conferences and youth camps in increasingly important roles. Some of these stimulated his writing of hymns. In the 1930's also he developed a more extensive role in each of the general conferences of the church. These included daily classes and prayer services for youth. He continued in his role as hymn leader for the business meetings. All of these activities extended beyond the time of his Graceland service.

During the depression years the college found it necessary to let go of some very good faculty members. The remaining faculty had to cover all the work. Cheville and others felt an increased sense of stewardship in being retained to carry on the work. Here was more evidence that work coming from his commitment was appreciated and rewarded.

In 1938 Cheville was appointed to an advisory council on religious education by President Fred M. Smith. Later he would be appointed to the committee for the 1950 *Hymnal for Youth* and to the committee for the 1956

191

Hymnal. General church responsibilities continued to increase during his faculty years.

In 1942 Cheville became acting president of Lamoni Stake for a year, and in 1951 he became acting president of Graceland College for a year. He did very well in these functions, even though he maintained a very heavy schedule of his regular responsibilities. He said once that the opportunities to become an administrator kept coming up, and he had to give them serious attention. However he continued to make the decision that direct ministry and indirect ministry through theory development were the ideals to which he must remain loyal.

In 1950 his major commitment was expressed in terms of young lives unfolding:

> Dr. Cheville loves to "watch young people unfold their potentialities." He states that perhaps his main purpose in life is "the interpretation of religion in terms of contemporary patterns of thought" in an attempt to make religion practical and meaningful to youth. [LC 16 Jan 50]

Personal Discipline

"Live honestly!" . . Lying and self-deceit are self-killing. If people in a group do not practice honesty among themselves, they cannot carry on their daily existence. There must be mutual confidence if members are going to live together. Treachery may go on between hostile groups, but it cannot flourish within a group. This holds for the person, too. He will disintegrate if he is dishonest with himself. [1957H]

"Live honestly" was the advice Cheville gave in 1957 to readers of *Stride* magazine. He described a requirement for personal living which in his view is essential if a person is to maintain personal integration and be able to function from day to day in society. This same characteristic in greater degree is necessary for a person to qualify for interaction with the Holy Spirit. He presented several guidelines which he had found functional that came from his own experience. They explained different aspects of living honestly: One must not kid oneself, one must be intellectually honest—refrain for example, from choosing those points with which we agree and disregarding others; One should practice occupational honesty, always earn your wages; One should behave honestly in dating—there is disaster in misleading a boy or girl in order to take advantage of him or her; One should be honest with God. We say to God, "This is the way I am. This is all of me." [1957H]

These points about living honestly can describe the kind of personal discipline involved in developing and maintaining the person of Roy Cheville. He had made a commitment at age 16, which commitment was still in place and only enlarged at the time of his death. It is clear that he exercised personal discipline over that productive lifetime to keep his energies and his activities applied to the nourishment of his ideals.

His diary of his first year at Chicago gives a day-to-day picture of his activities, which are busy and consistent. He took his courses in an orderly manner and finished them all on schedule. On the side he took some additional courses by correspondence to make his compressed schedule work out. He finished all of those on schedule also. He maintained a regular pattern of church attendance which included leadership of several activities.

He did all these things at Chicago while confronting all kinds of perplexities and doubts as his courses raised new questions and new ways of looking at things. Some of these issues required that he release old religious beliefs and reconstruct belief in a larger framework. At the same time he was in a most uncertain status about finances. The church and college had promised to underwrite his university expenses, but money came to him irregularly and in smaller amounts than needed. He was continually unsure how that would work out. He took odd jobs; he developed sources of scholarship funds; he borrowed money from his father; and he did without many things. In spite of these problems he seems to have finished up his degree requirements in the shortest time he could have and to have accomplished the work with a credible academic record.

His Chicago experience was appropriate training for membership on the Graceland faculty. Money was always short, and sometimes non-existent. The work required to accomplish his lofty ideals was always very great. The ministerial activities to which he was committed seemed unlimited in their scope. And their scope increased until he was traveling all over the country and finally all over the world.

At Graceland he wrote his books, his articles, his hymns, and his quarterlies with a fountain pen. He made commitments for such things as reunions and camps months and years ahead of time. In the early years he could travel by train on a minister's pass. Later he had to go by auto. He never owned or drove a car. In order to meet his schedules he arranged for somebody to drive him. Many times that would be a student. Frequently such trips enabled him to develop friendship to a greater degree over the long hours of travel. But always it took time to make sure that he would have somebody lined up to take him where he was committed to go.

He could have been more efficient in the use of his time on campus if he had closed his office door even occasionally. But that would have reduced his availability to talk with students and others who would drop by. So that door stayed open, and his time and attention were available to those who had their own interests in mind. He was a great listener, and that listening provided him with information about what was going on in individuals and through them in the life of the church. He was a good listener also when he was on a train or airplane trip. He said once that he always heard one or two life stories while on such a trip.

Typically he was an integral part of evening campus activities, always present and always up to date on what the campus group had been doing. But as the activity continued he would often disappear. He judged when his useful contribution ended and was off to home and family. The next morning his office light was the first one on. He would be doing his writing and other work requiring concentration before others arrived on campus.

Worship

At Graceland anything that passes by the term religious must have vital relation to student life or it will not endure... Observers have noted the vitality and the spirit of hope and enthusiasm in the college prayer meetings. Religion on the campus centers about current problems and visions, and tasks. [1930D]

Hundreds of students thought of Cheville as the one who guided them to an understanding of their church, and the one who represented "religion" and "the church" at Graceland. Important components of that reputation were the group religious services he developed and conducted on the campus. In these services Graceland students frequently found themselves moved to a deeper understanding of divinity. There they made internal commitments leading to lives of better quality. They came face to face with divinity and went forward in newness of life.

When Cheville began faculty service he was one of several ministers on the faculty. He found a developed set of religious services with ongoing patterns. He began by participating in all of them, but soon recognized that the Wednesday evening prayer services held the greatest potential. He worked very hard to contribute to these services. He put his considerable talents and his knowledge to work in making these services go. Within two years he was effectively in charge of these meetings, and that would be true until he retired from the faculty.

The sentiment was expressed in 1926 that, "the prayer meetings under the leadership of Mr. Cheville have been a source of inspiration throughout the year, and have given to the students that unbreakable bond which has made Graceland's prayer service justly renowned."

197

Throughout the time that Cheville was on the faculty these gatherings were perhaps his most important and most effective laboratory.

Priscilla Boeckman Siler remembers that in the late 1930's there would be a three by five card on the bulletin board each Wednesday morning. This card, in "Unk's" handwriting, would contain a scripture or theme reference and an invitation to participate in the fellowship meeting.

Early on he communicated his intention for these gatherings by changing the name from *prayer* meetings to *fellowship* meetings. Each meetings had a carefully and thoughtfully chosen theme. That choice was made in the light of the conditions and outlooks of his student congregation which he knew and understood to a remarkable degree. He developed the theme in accordance with his growing understanding of the dynamics of spiritual reality. Then he chose supporting references, poems, and hymns. If he could not find a poem or hymn which carried exactly the thought he needed, he wrote one to the exact specifications he had in mind. In later years he said that he never wrote a hymn just because it was something he wanted to write.

He always conducted the singing himself. He knew what effect he wanted from the hymns, and he knew how to achieve that effect as the conductor. "Sometimes we seem to view the hymns as a trimming rather than an essential part of the meeting itself," he wrote in a 1936. He emphasized that the minister should have a clear conception of the goal and purpose of the meeting and a familiarity with the congregation. Then the leader fits the hymns into the theme, word, and spirit of the service. Cheville wrote about special moments in connection with hymns:

Some rather exalted moments have come to me in the selection and singing of hymns in prayer meetings. . . The spiritually attuned preacher inquires about the needs and interests of his flock and opening his soul to God seeks illumination in his choice and treatment of this theme. The same applies to the ministry of music. I have sensed that touch of inspiration leading and assuring in hymn selection. I also know what it is to be without it. [1936D]

In conducting the meetings themselves he conveyed the theme's thoughts to his congregation. At the same time he developed the tempo and the tone of the group experience. Some have described these aspects as showing his flair for the dramatic. He had a clear feeling for the way such a meeting should go. His normal tolerance for stupidity and ignorance did not extend to failures of his fellow participants to fit in with the tempo and tone of the meeting.

In planning these meetings he put forth the best talents and abilities he had. He tried to look at the plan as he thought God might look at it. He tried to see what divine purposes could be accomplished in the lives of the students. He was frequently pushing himself to the limit of his creative abilities. That is a recipe for what he later called "seeing with God." And the effect was that he grew rapidly in spiritual insight. In the language of his later years he would say that he was drawing on spiritual resources. He sensed the inspirational effect on the hundreds of participants: "The walls of this chapel speak to me the words and scenes of lives remade and life decisions pledged. Often God met us here." [1928H]

The fellowship services were held in the chapel until the fall of 1946 when they were moved to the basketball floor of Zimmerman Hall to accommodate the greatly enlarged student body. They were moved again after the Memorial Student Center was completed in 1950.

With the enlarged enrollment in 1946, the college students quit going to town on Sunday mornings to meet with the Lamoni Branch. Now Sunday morning church services as well as Wednesday night services were held on the campus for the campus congregation. These meetings were also under Cheville's direction. They were conducted according to the same techniques he had developed for the fellowship meetings, except that testimonies were seldom a part of these meetings.

A special kind of service was planned for each Graceland night at general conference. These services frequently took the form of a pageant with many spokespersons and many musical numbers. They were usually written in their entirety by Cheville. For example, the 1938 Graceland night presented historical narrative of the Latter Day Saints at Far West. For Graceland night at the conference of 1950, Cheville wrote and directed the pageant "Finding God Through the Beautiful." William Graves, Joy Harder Browne, R. Edwin Browne, Henry Anderson, Myron Curry, D. B. Sorden, Roscoe Faunce, Delmar Goode, and E. J. Gleazer, Jr., participated. A number of the elements of this pageant are preserved in the 1950 *Hymnal for Youth*, including the poem, "Conversation of a Youth with his Inner Self," the hymn, "Truth has no Single Voice," and the poem, "The Voices of Science, Philosophy, Art, and Religion."

Music

It has been said that music makes everything go. It makes a peace meeting more peaceful; it intensifies the spirit of courage in soldiers; it makes drunkards drink more; it seduces; it uplifts, it stimulates workers; it soothes and it heals. It can touch every phase of our life. [1933H]

It is a fascinating experience to stand before a group of people and see them welded together into social unity. It is a rare technique, and I have marveled at the ability of certain song leaders to accomplish remarkable results. A genuine song leader has precious possibilities in his baton. [1927E]

Roy Cheville understood the power of music early in his life. He had permanent memories of the hymns his mother sang as she went about her work. He and his sister Cora sang for the missionary services that resulted in his baptism in 1914. At that time Orman Salisbury called him "a young musician." His first official function in the branch was that of music director. The title of his 1923 Master's thesis was, "The Function of Music in Religious Education." Much of the material of his thesis is to be found in an article entitled, "The Place of Music in the Church." [1927E]

Cheville's use of music expressed itself in three ways: leading group singing, using music in group worship, and writing hymns.

LEADING GROUP SINGING

The largest regular gatherings of the Saints during Cheville's career were the whole-church conferences. Through most of his career Roy Cheville led the singing at these conferences—first called general, then world conferences. He was highly visible in this role, and many of the Saints have retained the visual image of him as he

201

used his whole body to synchronize and energize the large group's vocal contributions. Perhaps some have remembered him only in this role.

Though he was very much at home in leading the songs of the conference body, he was equally at home leading campfire songs and hymns at college prayer meetings. Around a campfire he could get a group active in singing well-known "fun" songs—those with simple words, singable tunes, and negligible cognitive content. He would progress through songs with more and more serious content and end up transitioning (he used the word "transish") to a time of thoughtful worship and testimony.

In this role as singing leader Cheville was very much in charge. When the tempo of singing got too slow he would stop the music suddenly and say something like, "Folks, this is not funeral music. Let's sing it as if we enjoy it." His manner and tone of voice made clear this was a good-natured rebuke. Then he would start the song again and make sure that all were singing at the faster pace. He would use both his body language and his strong voice to set the pace. If necessary he would stop the music again and say something to get the attention of the stragglers. Eventually he would get his way, and the group would be singing together enthusiastically at the pace he wanted. In the end the group would have discovered that full and enthusiastic participation at his pace was what they wanted too. Many people remember his habit of coming in a fraction of a beat ahead of the group in an attempt to quicken the tempo.

USING MUSIC IN GROUP WORSHIP

Every time Cheville planned a worship service he had a set of objectives in mind for that service. He would build a service with units of theme introduction, group hymns, theme talks, special group music, prayers, and testimonies. In the development of the worship, he would want to have individuals grasp some new level of understanding and reach some new level of personal commitment. In order to achieve these lofty results, both the tunes and the words of the music were important. He chose both very carefully.

Cheville's understanding of the nature of God was critical to his choice of hymns. He would not choose hymns which abdicated personal decision making and turned everything over to God. He knew God as a friendly parent and refused to use "King" and "Lord" in referring to God. He also avoided the supernatural implications of "salvation" and "grace." What he sought were personal challenges in response to the spirit of God. He sought to encourage the spirit of adventure in uplifting and expanding service. He was convinced that religion can not be a spectator activity. One had to act on the implications of spirituality if one is to learn about divinity. He sought hymns which would embody these principles in their message.

He avoided hymns of praise. As a parent himself he did not want his children to sit around telling him repeatedly how great he was. Instead he wanted them to show their regard and respect by putting into their own lives the things he had taught them, thus showing tangible thanks for his guidance. He believed those principles should apply to our relations with our cosmic parent.

WRITING HYMNS

In the "Unk" phase, Roy Cheville matured rapidly in his understanding of God and in his planning of group worship services. He became more precise in the concepts he wanted embodied in the hymns he used. He turned to writing his own hymns, thus achieving the meaning and feeling he sought.

His first published hymn appeared in 1921, and is found in the section, "The Commission." His second published hymn was the "Alma Mater Hymn" which he wrote in 1926 and published in 1928. [1928D] It seems to be the only hymn for which he also composed the tune. Franklyn Weddle made the first arrangement of the music and Verna Schaar made the arrangement which appeared in the 1933 *Saints' Hymnal* [1933C] and subsequent publications. Several hymns in poem form were published in the quarterlies he wrote in the 1930's. These include "A Youth's Prayer of Thanksgiving" [1932B], "I Know that My Redeemer Lives" [1933F], "Speak of the Best" [1933G], and "God Send Us Men" [1933I].

Not very many of the hymns he wrote for use in services before 1939 have survived. He typically wrote to fit the needs for a particular theme. Usually this did not take long. He gave little thought to preserving what he wrote because it was so simple for him to write a new one for a new theme or purpose.

One song he wrote for Nauvoo Camp was published under the title, "Dear Old Nauvoo." [1930K] Three of his hymns were published in the pamphlet he wrote describing the youth conference of 1939. These were, "Are You Able" [1939G], "O Lord of Life, of Light and Inspiration" [1939H], and "Our Homes We Dedicate to You." [1939I] Six of his hymns were published in 1941 in the *Zion's League Handbook*. These were, "The Church of Christ is Calling" [1941F], "Rise, O Youth" [1941G], "Forward" [1941H], "Come Up Higher" [1941I], "Open My Eyes" [1941J], and "Prayer of Dedication." "Open My Eyes" became a very popular hymn. It was included in the 1950 *Hymnal For Youth*, and in the 1956 and 1981 hymnals. It was translated into German for the 1953 German hymnal, *Lieder Der Heiligen*, and into Spanish for the 1975 Spanish hymnal, *Hinario*.

In the *Zion's League Handbook* he wrote that no materials for worship are in themselves religious. They become so by using them in divine communion. He wrote also that music is to be employed as a part of a balanced program of self-expression and enjoyment. Music may become demoralizing when it becomes an end in itself. The religious value in music lies in expressing the group's social values and articulating the higher concepts for which other means of expression fail.

Though Cheville gave a great deal of thoughtful attention to every service he planned, there were many occasions to which he made a special degree of preparation. Some of these became "mountain-top" experiences, which included many hymns with special meaning. Cheville maintained a folder entitled, "Songs of the Soul." The cover page of this folder noted that these Songs of the Soul "have come out of Searchings for insight, Concerns for ministry, Reflections over stewardships, and Times of high communion with God and his people."

Included in this folder were descriptions of the writing of the following 11 hymns:

1) "Alma Mater hymn," from 1926 [1928D]

2) "The Church of Christ is Calling," from 1939, [1941E]

3) "Prayer at Nauvoo Camp," 1938

4) "This is Our Hope," from the 1943 Lamoni Stake reunion

5) "Conviction," from the 1945 Graceland Religious Emphasis Week, [1953D], see following.

6) "The Day Has Come," undated

7) "The Spirit of Graceland," [1945H], see below.

8) "Master Speak!," undated, [1950L]

9) "Home of the Open Heart," from 1947, on p. 197.

10) "Open My Eyes," undated, [1941J]

11) "Prophetic Song," undated.

Five of these 11 hymns have been published: numbers 1, 2, 5, 8, and 10.

Number 5 was written for Religious Emphasis Week in 1945 when "Doc" addressed the uncertainties and disturbances brought about by the continuing intensity of the war. The theme for the week emerged as "We build for Spiritual Convictions." The first stanza voices the queries of college students as they meet the data and theory of natural science. The second stanza catches up the concerns about themselves. The hymn was introduced at the opening service, being sung to the tune, "I Know Whom I have Believed:"

CONVICTION

It may be I shall never trace
  The orbits in the sky,
Nor learn the myriad mysteries
  That in the planets lie.
Yet, whatever investigation,
  One revelation of cosmic order
Discloses through all creation
  A design that is divine.

I cannot tell to those I meet
  The eternal mind of God,
Yet I can speak of One I know
  The way of service trod.
And whenever in indecision
  About my mission, or worth, or fitness
I can hear with the youth of vision,
  "'Tis my Son, O hear ye Him!" [1953D]

On the closing Sunday morning, R. V. Hopkins sang this hymn in a language unknown to him or the group at the fellowship service. He prefaced it with the comment that he had sensed the spirit of inspiration indicating that the word of God had been caught up in the hymn, and that he was singing in confirmation of its prophetic message.

Number 7 in that folder has the following words:

THE SPIRIT OF GRACELAND
(Tune: Morecambe, Saints' Hymnal No. 198)

Here at this altar
Gather we once more,
Shrine where have come
The Graceland sons of yore,
Bringing an off'ring
Incense of the soul,
Bearing hence, treasure—
Some live altar coal.

Here, Alma Mater,
See we once again,
Vision and purpose,
May·they never wane,
Spirit of Graceland,
Those, thy paths have trod,
Found thee the spirit
Of the living God.

When Cheville was ordained a patriarch in October of 1950, Elbert A. Smith, Presiding Patriarch, spoke to him in counsel, "You will minister to the Saints in the singing life of our people. You will provide hymns that express the Restoration gospel. You will vitalize the singing of the Saints."

The best single source for Roy Cheville's original hymns is in the *Hymnal For Youth* [1950G], which was first published by Herald House in 1950. This hymnal was an adaptation of a hymnal for youth which was copyrighted in 1941 by the Westminster Press. The committee that made the adaptation was composed of Franklyn Weddle, Roy A. Cheville, Chris B. Hartshorn, Anne Morgan, and Aleta Runkle, with Norma Smith, secretary. Hymns by Roy A. Cheville in this section are No. 354, "Hast Thou Heard It?" No. 365, "Open My Eyes, O Lord," and No. 370, "Master Speak! Thy Servant Heareth!."

From page 359 through page 387 there is a section entitled ORDERS OF WORSHIP. This section was probably written in its entirety by Roy Cheville based on materials he had written and used elsewhere. The sections are entitled, "The Voices of Music," "On Frontiers with God," "Seeking God in the Near At Hand," "Heroes Who Kept the Faith," "The Church's Flag: Ensign of Peace," "Each in His Grove," "Walking With God in Common Places," "By These Witnesses," and "The Counsels of Our Scriptures."

Some of Cheville's best-known hymns appeared first in the *Hymnal For Youth*. These include "Hast Thou Heard It" [1950I], "All Things Are Thine" [1950K], and "Master, Speak! Thy Servant Heareth" [1950L], which were later published in the 1956 and 1981 hymnals. They were translated into German for the 1953 German hymnal. The first two were also translated into Spanish for the Spanish hymnal.

Cheville wrote the hymn, "Afar in Old Judea" [1955G] in the fall of 1953. It tells of the Christ in old Judea, in Zarahemla, in Palmyra, and in contemporary time. It was written for a special series of meetings entitled "Quest for Christ." Cheville could not find a hymn which expressed that the everliving Christ was available to all.

so he wrote the hymn which would express "The Christ of Every Age."

A new hymnal for the church was published in 1956. It included these hymns by Cheville: "Sacred Books, the Church's Treasure," "O Lord, Thy People Gathered Here," "O Master to All Children Dear," "For Bread Before Us Broken," "Afar in Old Judea," "Open My Eyes," "Master Speak! Thy Servant Heareth," "Hast Thou Heard It?," "All Things Are Thine," "Send Forth Thy Light, O Zion," and "O Come Ye Sons of Graceland All."

He had no use for hymns which suggested that Zion was something God would create and deliver to the earth. He was convinced that Zion was the goal for our development of better ways of living together, such as Jesus taught. So he wrote "Send Forth Thy Light, O Zion" [1956W] to indicate the radiance of a righteous society built on eternal principles.

In 1968 Dennis Steele sought Cheville's advice about selection of hymns representing the church to be sung by a Graceland music group. "Doc's" response reveals his personal preferences as well as his philosophy:

> I am trying to see and hear a hymn in terms of your singing group. Some of our hymns would not do at all. Here are some I recommend:
>
> 1. "The Spirit of God Like a Fire Is Burning," No. 287
>   This is distinctive of the movement and can be sung with a good rhythm. When Dr. Marcus Bach came to the Graceland Campus a few years ago to record typical music for the Library of Congress, this song was the first one chosen. I would select stanzas 1 and 3.
>
> 2. "Redeemer of Israel," No. 201
>   This is often called our most treasured hymn. It is worked over from an existing hymn. It sings well. If you wanted to make it speak an "around-the-world" tone you might sing a stanza in English, one in Spanish, one in German, and then sing the fourth stanza in English. This fourth is the strongest stanza.

3. "Master, Speak!" No. 367

This is really a two-stanza hymn. I suggest that you sing it to the tune, "Admonition," No. 297. This tune will give you better choral expression. Neither of the tunes in the Hymnal will do.

4. "You May Sing," No. 280

This has a home-spirited message. The music sings well in parts. It is a favorite of our people. I believe it would sing well.

5. "Thou Hast Been Our Guide," No. 520

This was written for the campus and sung on the campus. Its tune, "Spanish Chant" is essentially folk music origin.

6. "This Is My Home," Tune, Finlandia

I consider this the most moving of our Graceland Songs. I believe your group could do this very well. I consider "Finlandia" comes out of a long Finnish background.

7. "Afar in Old Judea"

This could be sung to the tune Ewing, No. 287 or to the tune, Webb, No. 312. Since I am involved in this, you are free to sing it any time as far as I am concerned. I think "Webb" gets more ring to it.

He had a limited appreciation for the hymn "What a Friend We Have in Jesus." It was to him an inadequate expression of the friendship of Jesus that his role was "all our sins and griefs to bear." He saw an even more important role as Jesus the friend "all our joys and hopes to share." In 1979 he put his ideas into this form:

What a friend we have in Jesus!
  He is steadfast, kind, and sure,
Reaching out with understanding,
  With a love that will endure.
With his confidence he calls us
  To cooperate with him;
And he promises his guidance
  With the light that will not dim.

Jesus wants us as companions
  As we walk along life's way.
Working with him on his mission,
  Building for a better day.

For the things of worthful purpose,
    God's resources he'll supply,
Standing by us in our sorrow,
    Smiling with us in our joy.

What a friend we have in Jesus!
    Will direct us when we'll hear.
He will guide us through the darkness,
    Lift us from uncert'ning fear.
With him we make lasting cov'nant;
    Always on him we depend.
Now this testament we offer:
    "Jesus is our loyal friend!"

Cheville's last published hymn, "Let Us Sing a World-Wide Anthem," came out of his concern and exertions for a world-wide color-blind society which honors the worth of all human beings. All persons who acknowledge that they have the same heavenly parent are siblings. This gives global scope for our sharing the gospel's good news. As we do so in the spirit of comradeship, he believed, we are laying the foundation for a solid and lasting world peace. [1979A]

Writing

Once a recluse chose to live apart in his own cottage, avoiding communication with other living persons. But on his table was his well-worn Bible through which he associated with ever so many acquaintances. He was dwelling with their reflections, their experiences, their revelations. And in his library were copies from Plato to William James. [1975A]

Roy Cheville integrated to a remarkable degree the many broad facets of his life and career. They were all aspects of the core commitment which tied the various elements of his life into a unitary whole. Many teachers spend their summers earning money to supplement their meager income, but Cheville spent his learning and teaching different members of his church in different settings. Many scholars do their writing to earn money and to enhance their reputations, but Cheville did his writing to broaden the audience of his teaching ministry. That way he could reach more of his church's members with the same kind of messages he taught in person.

Some professionals write novels as a diversion and as an escape from the rigors of their professional discipline. Cheville's areas of concern were broad enough to provide ample opportunities for a change of pace. His rewards came from the satisfaction of living with rigorous intellectual discipline. He did not want to escape that.

Writing for publication takes a great deal of self-confidence. Once in print a work may be read by people anywhere in the world. It may be read by people who have spent long years mastering the subject matter. A potential author can be reluctant to write lest the work be roundly criticized by such acknowledged experts. Roy Cheville acquired the required self-confidence the patient and hard way. He studied in one of the best universities in the world in his field, and he earned the highest degree awarded by that university. He taught college courses in the subjects he was to write about. He knew that teaching a subject is a good way to learn a subject thoroughly, that the teacher always learns more than the pupil. He spent many years in laboratory observations in his field.

Though Cheville compiled a monumental list of publications, he did not exactly rush into print. He published his first book, *The Bible in Everyday Living*, 24 years after he took his first college course in Bible, 16 years after he completed a Master's degree in Religion, and had taught religion and the Bible during the same period.

His first substantive published writings appeared in 1926. They were four articles dealing with the junior church. [1926A,B,C,D] These articles were adaptations for use in the church of the study he had done under supervision in 1925 in partial fulfillment of the requirements for the Bachelor of Divinity degree in the University of Chicago. That study had the same title, "The Junior Church." In 1927 the *Saints' Herald* published his article entitled "The Place of Music in the Church." [1927E] That article was an adaptation of the thesis he had written in 1923 for his Master's degree at Chicago.

In 1929 he was one of a committee of who wrote a 40 page booklet on the history of Lamoni. [1929E] Cheville probably wrote most of the booklet. In 1930 he wrote an article with the title "Growing Up in Religion." [1930H] This title was a phrase he used a number of times. In 1951 he wrote a book with the same title. In 1930 he also edited a pamphlet (quarterly) on the history and place of education among Latter Day Saints. [1930J]

In 1931 he wrote an article about the theory and practice of revelation. [1931E] He wrote another on the function of theology. [1931F] In 1932 and 1933 the church released a set of four quarterly study guides by Cheville with the theme "What it Means to be a Latter Day Saint." [1932A, 1933D, 1933E, 1933D] These were revised and republished and used by the church until 1959. These pamphlets became very influential in the thought of the church, and they spread the name and reputation of Roy Cheville. In 1934 and 1935 the church released another set of four quarterly study guides with the theme "The Bible in Everyday Living." [1934A, 1935B, 1935C, 1935D] These quarterlies were used regularly by the church until they were incorporated into Cheville's 1939 book, *The Bible in Everyday Living*. The book is one of the most influential books in the history of the Reorganization.

In this manner Cheville's writing began and developed. At the end of his career he had written 26 published books [listed in Appendix A], 49 published hymns [listed in Appendix B], 36 published pamphlets [listed in Appendix C], and 346 published articles [listed in Appendix D]. Many of his writings are discussed in various chapters of this book.

In addition to his prose, which was clear and stylistically memorable in his prime, Cheville composed a large amount of poetry. His best efforts found their way into hymns. Most of the rest is of relatively poor quality, serving to commemorate some group experience or to preserve a funny moment.

The program to send colorful ties to the Saints in Germany, c. 1949.

Toward World Peace

I am a religionist who believes that "God made of one blood all nations." As such, I speak out for good will and brotherhood. I also am a sociologist. In this role, I insist that good intentions are not enough. Programs of action must be constructed on the data of research; they must gear to the natural laws of social relationships. [1947F]

Cheville tied several strands of thought and action together to form a design for world peace. On the one hand was the church's work in personal and societal development. On the other hand were Christian ideals for world-wide fellowship under God. Through numerous essays, many special programs, and a number of special purpose institutes, he conveyed these ideas. He involved a great many people, and this effort lasted several decades under his personal direction.

He noted that many attempts to achieve world peace were long on good intentions and short on effective constructive grass roots activities. Without both, idealistic programs have frequently failed to achieve their objectives. Some end in results that are nothing like those intended. As an example Cheville noted that one idealistic effort, the Children's Crusade of the year 1212, resulted in death or slavery for nearly all the innocent participants. Ideals are necessary, but a solid program of action is also essential.

Cheville did not start with the objective and then construct a program. Rather he seems to have realized that the activities he and the church had been promoting constituted the means for achieving world peace. Through much of the "Unk" period, Cheville was primarily concerned with the grass roots mission of the church. That consisted, he taught, in carrying forward the mission of Jesus, helping people to make those choices which elevated their level of living, resulting in lives of eternal quality. In that teaching, all persons are children of the same God and thus all are brothers and sisters. The more persons incorporate spirituality into their living the more refined is the quality of brotherhood and sisterhood.

Cheville continued to think about the broad implications of the church message. In 1929, in writing about the central theme of the book of Jonah, he stated,

> In no place is Jehovah seen in more world-wide interests. Even the Ninevites, most hated by Jews, could come under His love. Jonah, zealous for his religion as he saw it, was not unlike many of us who are more interested in self-vindication than in world-evangelization. He pouted under a gourd; we peeve in the back pew. [1929E]

During General Conference of 1930 he talked on the theme world brotherhood and the realization that we are an international church. In the General Conference of 1934 he called the youth to "the bigness, the oneness, the fellowship of the world-wide church." One section of his pamphlet for the 1939 Youth Conference [1939F] was "Youth Shares in World Fellowship." In that section he wrote that the church of Christ was set up as an agency for world service.

In 1940 Cheville responded to the question, "To whom shall the gospel go?" The answer was, "To all the world." But, to this ideal, he appended a study of the means. He wrote,

> Basically, the gospel must know no limitations of caste or color or culture. Translated into a program of action, however, it must reckon with realities of society, and these will condition the operation of this idealistic evangel.

Even Jesus seems to have exercised a certain qualifying of his world-wide plan. He demonstrated how the Divine must operate through human channels. Two factors hemmed him in: (1) the social mindedness of his times, and (2) the demand for concentration and selectiveness for effectiveness. It is well known that Jesus did not try to convert the Samaritans. We do not see him narrowed in spirit against them, but alert to situations as they were. Any student of society knows that if Jesus had gone to the Samaritans, he would likely have closed the way to his own people. The question is not what ought to have happened, but what would have happened. The fanatic idealist tends to disregard the latter. [1940C]

The theme for the 1940 religious emphasis week at Graceland was, "My Church and My World." Cheville noted the status of world affairs: Europe was at war; Japan was moving over territory step by step in the Pacific; the United States was providing moral support and some material for the democracies already involved. Religious Emphasis Week would be designed to help students relate themselves to the church in this changing world. He said, "In a word, this week is trying to help us think together on the Church's mission in today's world, to see the place of youth in today's spiritual confusion, and to develop common inspiration for taking some responsible place in a new emerging social order." [TWR 17 Jan 41][1]

Cheville's program for world peace crystallized in 1945. In the fall of that year the war was over and the church was sending four young couples to the European mission. Cheville arranged a special service around them:

The four couples assigned to the European mission came to the campus as they were en route to their new fields. Each spoke in testimony: Frank and Zeta Fry, Glen and Alice Johnson, Albert and Twyla Scherer, and Gene and Alma Theys. That night more than 500 young Latter Day Saints pledged to "keep the home fires burning." With organ and trumpeters, they filled the building with the stirring call to missions, "Heralds of Christ, Who Bear the King's Commands." It was a dramatic moment when these four couples, given the hand of fellowship by the president of our college, went down the center aisle as the congregations sang "God be with you." [1948B]

When Cheville launched his emphasis on world fellowship, as usual he had thought it through. He had looked over the sociological and religious characteristics of the world population. He noted fundamentally that under God all persons are brothers and sisters. He felt that a worldwide program to engender widespread relations with God would bring peace and harmony. The program of his own church provided the fundamental message and the structure of such a program. The church should and could move into a role that had the opportunity for expressing peace in a form that could do justice to the teachings of the Prince of Peace. Such was the logic behind his push toward world fellowship.

Typically Cheville linked theory to action. In 1946 Graceland students were preparing boxes of useful items to be sent to the families of saints in Holland. Nearly every student was involved, with personal possessions going into the boxes. A special service was held when all the boxes were ready to be mailed. Another project which Cheville organized came out of an experience from his 1949 trip to Europe. At a church gathering in Germany, to which he wore a flamboyant post-World War II tie, he overheard a small boy say to his mother, "Look at the man's beautiful tie." From that story, which Cheville loved to tell, came the idea to collect ties to send to the German saints to bring a little color to a drab post-war Germany. Representing the surplus of Graceland students (hundreds of ties), the project sent a message of brotherhood and hope.

Cheville described the program he was putting into motion. He spoke to the timing and the logic of world outreach:

> For the first time the world's entire population may be regarded as a unity. The best of today's religions are preaching that there is one common Father for all these peoples. It is saying, too, that the world family needs to learn how to live together happily and helpfully. [1947B]

He spoke to the issue of getting persons involved on a sound motivational and procedural basis:

> The Big Question . . is: What am I doing to build a world order in which war will be outmoded? How can we iron out tensions that bring on fighting? How can we get men to want a society in which every person will be respected as a son of God? [1948C]
>
> The young Latter Day Saint is out to discover how he can service this world with the gospel of Christ. Can anything be more important? [1947B]

He spoke to the essence of functioning religion as the basic dynamic which will make world fellowship work:

> When a person and God get together in working companionship, something constructive takes place in the life of the person. As this happens, the person comes to live with all others in brotherly relations. [1947C]

He spoke to the issue of "why us?":

> The Restoration gospel spoke to farmers and doctors and printers and men and women of every-day vocations. It dealt with the living now. This was something new: religions of that day were generally concerned with getting to heaven. The young prophet sensed that the world was behind in human relationships. [1947B]
>
> What are the fundamentals of our gospel that can unify different groups while they still maintain their own patterns? How does the gospel make possible "unity with diversity?" [1947B]

For the Graceland Homecoming of 1947 Cheville prepared a special program highlighting "World-wide Graceland." In preparation for that program he wrote the hymn, "Home of the Open-heart." In his folder, "Prophetic Songs," were these notes:

> On the Saturday night of the Homecoming of 1947, a pageant of the world-wide Graceland was presented. In the finale there came to the platform representatives from Australia, New Zealand, Hawaii, England, Canada, and the United States. There came, too, an American Indian and a Negro. Such an ensemble needed some message which all might join. Such a work must speak both welcome to youth from all parts of the world and commission to college youth to go out into the world. So this hymn with fervent feeling.

HOME OF THE OPEN HEART
(Tune: Russian Hymn)

Home of the open-heart,
Shrine of the world-soul,
Temple of wisdom and
Altar of truth;
Thus we salute thee [now],
Our own Alma Mater,
With loving pride and
The zest of our youth.

Rise, O beloved tower,
Symbol of Graceland,
Keep wide her portals
To youth of all lands.
Then send them forth
As apostles of learning,
Where'er the world
Needs their heart, mind and hand.

Cheville also wrote a year-long series of study materials for senior high school students dealing with world outreach. These were released by the church in October of 1947. The first of these was "How Shall We Look at Our World?" [1947A] It urged students to study the world situation with a long view to understanding the church's mission, using the tools of both science and religion. The second quarterly, "What Kind of World Shall We See?" [1947B] noted that we will see many religions, many social philosophies that clash, haves and have-nots, minorities wanted and unwanted, and yearnings for a new world now. The third quarterly was "What is Our Church's Mission to the World?" [1947C] We have to declare to our world today what will make a difference in human life. The development of lives is the first objective; then we have to consider the means. The fourth quarterly, "How Shall We Equip the Church for Her World Mission?" [1947D] proposed that we keep in touch with all the church, that we build branches that reach out, that we develop homes with world outlook, etc.

In a 1948 article about pacifism [1948C] Cheville said the big question is, "What am I doing to build a world order in which war will be outmoded?" Sub questions were, "How can we iron out tensions that bring on fighting?" and "How can we get men to want a society in which every person will be respected as a son of God?"

"I WENT TO EUROPE"

Roy Cheville's 1949 trip to Europe was not an ordinary experience. Connected to his deeply held convictions of long standing—from inception through personal complications to the experiences of trip itself and to writing about many aspects of the experiences—this was a watershed experience. "Doc" wrote of the depth of his long-standing desire to visit Europe dating back to his childhood. For almost five years "Doc" had been initiating programs of world outreach, writing about the church's mission to the world, and preaching about the Christian mission of peace to all the world. All this was being done with a personal objective of integrating many of his religious and theoretical ideas. Now he himself was

223

about to embark on a personal odyssey which would put him at the center of action in this dream.

He went to Europe in the summer of 1949. He was in Germany, [1949F] the Netherlands, [1949E] and the England. [1949G] He was on a ministerial mission and he ministered with his usual enthusiasm. He was an ambassador of the good news of the gospel. It was a very significant experience for him as a person.

The experiences of the trip stimulated him to even greater efforts toward world consciousness. The theme for Religious Emphasis Week in February of 1950 was, "Above color lines with Christ." Apostles Charles Hield and Reed Holmes were the visiting ministers. Problems concerning Tahiti, Hawaii, the Orient, the American Indian, and the Negro were reviewed and discussed.

In 1958 the outreach study unit was Latin America. Guest minister was Apostle Charles Hield. Hield was currently translating the *Book of Mormon* into Spanish with the help of Jose Aranda, a Spanish convert to the church.

Cheville described letters which had been coming to the Graceland campus as a result of the world outreach program:

These past four months letters have been coming to Graceland Campus that are significant enough to be shared with the church at large. They have crossed the Atlantic or the Pacific Oceans. . . Bill Ruoff . . had . . letters from the Berlin Branch . . Cecil Robbins . . as student pastor sent letters to the Nurnberg Branch . . Lynn Weldon . . led the group [which got replies] from Oslo . . A roll call of the "Branches abroad" reads like a roster of missions and list of youth about the church . . The student group that heard from Fred Becker of Kassel of the little group he is building there through his personal testimonials can hardly slink back into complacency. The group that followed the work in Tahiti can never think of "Whites Only" gospel. Those in the group that sent an autobiographical book to Enfield,

224

England, find some of their heart in Britain. Benny Simmons who corresponded for his group with Ken Hughes of Marazion will not forget the handful of Saints down on the Cornwall Coast. . . As in great spiritual ventures the blessings are two-direction. The salutation "Dear Brother" can be used and shared around the world. [1950A]

Cheville wrote about the value of Graceland's being the church college to which students came from all over the world. He recounted the campus experiences in world outreach and in providing reciprocal services for students from over the world to come to Graceland. [1951D]

THE ORIENT

Cheville planned a weekend youth institute for the Graceland campus which would emphasize China and Japan. The purpose of the institute was to develop insight into the life and culture of China and Japan and to help build an understanding for interpreting our message to people of Chinese and Japanese cultures. The staff included leaders of the general church. Held in March of 1953, this Sino-Japanese conference was open to selected delegations and to all Graceland students. One of the participants was Howard S. Sheehy, Jr.

In 1975 Sheehy, then an apostle, wrote to Cheville about the institute held 22 years earlier:

> I am sending this letter along from Hong Kong where I am participating with a number of ministers from the Asia/Pacific area in our Hong Kong Conference. Last night I could not help but reflect upon how many of the men that are gathered here have been touched very significantly by your own life and ministry. As for myself, it was almost 23 years ago at this time of year that we participated at Graceland in the Sino-Japanese Institute. I would mark that as the very beginning of my interest in communicating something about the "universals" of the gospel, and particularly with reference to non-Christian cultures and oriental people. I certainly would not have imagined at that time that I would be participating as a church

leader in an international conference, discussing in many ways exactly the same issues, but now, with a background of some years of experience of the church in the Orient and other Asian countries, and with the participation of deeply committed ministers from a variety of other cultures and races.

I simply wanted to take the time to express appreciation to you for the contribution you have made in my life which has helped me become in some part qualified for participation in this experience here, and recognize that that's true in the lives of the majority of the men who are here.

I trust this letter finds you in good health and continuing to enjoy a richness of the blessing of His spirit in your ministry. Very respectfully, Howard. S. Sheehy, Jr.

In recent correspondence with the author, President Sheehy continued:

I think that Roy Cheville was in a unique position as the Professor of Religion at Graceland College prior to and during the time that the World Church had an opportunity to expand the work in various countries. During that time the number of national churches increased at least four-fold and almost all of the persons involved in that would have had courses from Roy Cheville while they were students at Graceland which helped them to develop their theology which supported the expansion of the church among other cultures. Roy's own enthusiasm and interest in students "from abroad" gave all of us a sense that this was a very important dimension of the life of the church. There would be no question that his influence upon a number of persons who now serve as general officers of the church would still be bearing fruit in this regard... Very respectfully, THE FIRST PRESIDENCY, Bud, Howard S. Sheehy, Jr.

In 1957 Cheville wrote that each year for the past ten years as a planned unit in the program of religious activities, Graceland College had studied some mission field outside the United States and Canada. He stated the following objectives for this series of activities:

1. To develop the viewpoint of a church with a world mission and world message.

2. To achieve the ability to see a mission field in the light of the total program of the church.

3. To develop the long-time method of working in a mission of the church.

4. To establish friendly contacts with a mission abroad in a two-way relationship.

5. To give encouragement to those now working in a field abroad.

6. To contribute something to the church's study of this field.

7. To grow in worship and study through concern that is present tense and personal. [1957E]

For Cheville, the quintessential international experience involved Kisuke Sekine, who came to Graceland from Japan in March of 1950. "Seki" had a Buddhist background, and many things about Christianity were new to him. Some of the distinctive aspects of Latter Day Saintism were also new and complicated for him. He went through considerable development in order to understand the Christ of Latter Day Saint views in the framework of the Oriental. Later, Apostle Sekine would set out to translate Christian fundamentals into universal application meaningful for Japanese culture.

Cheville's effort to help the church see its world-wide mission was one of the stewardships of his life. For 40 years he worked on a grass-roots program aimed at world peace. What he accomplished should endure and enlarge because of its fundamental validity. He patterned his non-confrontational approach after the methods of Jesus. For Cheville the long view meant nourishing the spiritual roots of quality decision-making, and the short view meant urging specific action for specific social problems. He always took the long view.

Notes

1. TWR is an abbreviation for the *Graceland Tower*, the college newspaper.

BOOK VII.

The Theory of
Divinity

BOOK VII. THE THEORY OF DIVINITY
Theology—Theory of God

Latter Day Saints have never been much concerned with drawing
up creeds and then forcing them upon others. . . They said that men
who were led by the Holy Spirit would come into a unity of understanding. Consequently they taught men to seek this inspiration.
Men were not to be argued or compelled into a single belief about
God: they were to follow certain principles and *find* God for themselves. . . The church has given us a wonderful heritage in this field
of her teachings. [1933D]

Roy Cheville had a life-long commitment to the study
of theology. His transcript shows that he took 26 graduate courses in the Chicago Divinity School with the word
"theology" in the title. He wrote an article in 1961 about
the thrill of theology. [1961R] He said he felt the same
thrill Columbus must have felt when he first saw the
islands of the West Indies:

The field of theology brings this kind of excitement to me. . . I believe
God intends us to be spiritual adventurers in the realm of insights
and to enjoy the excitement of discovery. [1961R]

Some people observed the vast influence Cheville exerted on the lives of a great many people and concluded
that his effectiveness must be due to his understanding
of theology. The degree of understanding of theology was
a visible difference between him and his contemporaries.
It was fairly easy to draw the conclusion that theology
was the power behind his influence. It was not that simple. Knowledge of theology would have put him nowhere
if he had not developed his own theories to fit what he

learned and what he experienced. His own theories and the religion he based on them generated the power in Roy Cheville.

Many of his contemporaries had difficulty understanding the role that the scientific method played in the intellectual activities which undergirded his thought and his ministry. He used theology to formulate hypotheses about the nature of divinity. He used experience to evaluate those hypotheses—his own experience and the experiences of others, including biblical persons in interaction with divinity. The end product of his study of theology was to help in developing his own systematic and testable theories of the way God works.

As a social scientist he was aware of the pitfall of unanalyzed assumptions. One such assumption—frequently made and seldom analyzed—is supernaturalism. That concept assumes that there is a sharp dividing line between divinity and humanity. In the supernatural view divinity is part of the supernatural order and humanity is part of the natural order. It was Cheville's view that supernaturalism belongs with animism and other primitive explanations of experience. He believed we do not know enough to draw a line between what is natural and what is divine. Drawing such a line constitutes placing limits on God. In other words, making the assumption of supernaturalism limits the possibilities in understanding divinity.

Although Cheville addressed the creating aspect of divinity and the role of divinity in history, his primary focus was on interactions between God and humans. Perhaps his most succinct treatment of this issue is found in an article he wrote about the philosophy of Alfred North Whitehead. He was in general agreement with Whitehead's contributions, but noted that Whitehead did not address the interactions between God and humans.

He wrote, for example, in agreement with Whitehead's position on supernaturalism,

> Whitehead sees enormous damage done by separating reality into the natural and supernatural. . . We have assumed that the natural can be examined and explored, but that the supernatural is outside our diagnostic experience. . . Our notion of natural law must be enlarged to include phenomena other than those observable in terms of mechanistic operations. What men call spiritual is not a different reality but a different aspect of a single reality. [1962E]

After describing the major points of Whitehead's thought, Cheville notes that Whitehead did not visualize a personalism in the nature of God which might interact with human persons. Cheville put it this way:

> Some things Alfred North Whitehead never achieved. Perhaps he did not want to; perhaps he did not intend to. Maybe his framework of thinking prevented this.
> 1. He never posited personalism in the universe. There was no center of consciousness. So in a sense he made man with self-consciousness and personal vision superior to his God.
> 2. He never presented means or methods by which man is to tap the creative and sustaining and integrating forces inherent in the universe.
> 3. He never worked out any co-operative endeavor or fellowship for achieving the life that is to press toward beauty and truth and goodness.
> 4. He never set forth any universal and inclusive revelation of this universal creative power so man might have identifiable insight. It is this that Christians say Jesus Christ did and does.
> 5. He never pointed up clearly how man might be transformed in the process of becoming a worthy co-operating participant in achieving the good life suggested in the vision of the universe. [1962E]

These views are the heart and soul of Cheville's thought. To understand the interactions between divinity and humanity, Cheville focused upon the concept of the person—the sense in which we are created in the image of God. For this same reason also he focused on the working aspect of divinity called the Holy Spirit, and on the distinction between the physical Jesus and the spiritual Christ. Cheville rejected as inadequate concepts such as grace, as used in the thought of the Apostle Paul, grace being supernatural, and that puts it beyond the realm of examination and exploration.

The usefulness of theology lies in what it does for one's religion. One of the clearest expressions of Cheville's religion is in his small book, *Growing Up in Religion*. In this 1951 volume he wrote,

> Religion is natural to man. It is not something imposed artificially... It is in our human nature to want response and assurance, to seek meanings for life, and to find satisfaction in social activities. Religion is simply this lifted to a cosmic scale...
>
> To Christians the life and the personality of Jesus is the greatest miracle of the ages. He lived in intimate relations with his Father. He tapped the sources of spiritual power. He maintained contact always. He lived on a plane above our ken. Yet it was not outside the laws of God...
>
> How, then, is God infinitely personal? The answer lies in his plans, his purposes, his relation to other persons in his universe... He sees in the light of a total universe. He loves without warping toward any clique. He plans with an eternity in mind. He can be interested in any one person without losing concern for any others. .. In this light Jesus was divine. He was the fullness of personalism.
> ..
> This title, Jesus Christ, affirms how divinity was expressed in human terms that we can understand. This is the great revelation of Christianity. [1951B]

It seems accurate to refer to Cheville's systematic thought as a "theory of God." That can distinguish it from an untestable philosophical position. His theory of God was based on the experiences of his church, past and contemporary, as he had known and shared them.

Cheville's effectiveness came not only from his extensive theological knowledge but also from his use of that knowledge to develop his own theory. That theory grew out of the experiences of his religious group. It was testable and he tested it. The end result was his religion. That is what was effective.

Experience-Based Theory
of God

My religion is basically an experiential thing, rather than an interpretation of that experience. [1956F]

We build our concepts and conclusions out of our experience. We apprehend reality in terms of what has happened in our lives. . . I came to see the Scriptures as selected writings of those who had lived before me . . They phrased what they saw of the eternal and the universal in the most advanced forms they knew. . . One cannot interpret God by standing on the sidelines . . Theology, as interpretation of religious experience, should guide us in achieving ever-deepening experience with which to build expanding concepts. [1961R]

Roy Cheville's religion was not a set of beliefs, it was not a theology. Its basis was spiritual experience. That was what he looked at in his own life. That was what he looked for in the lives of people to whom he ministered. That was what he looked for when he sought to understand how God had worked with people in the scriptures.

His identification of his own and other people's religious or spiritual experiences became a part of the data which his theories were developed to understand. He sought the principles by which divinity interacts with humanity, deriving them from an analysis of the experiences. These principles were his theories. The statement of the principles was always tentative, as theories must be. Knowledge about the principles is always changing. As knowledge increases, the theories about the principles must be revised from time to time. There is no final statement, as there is no final experience.

Similar words could describe the development of theories in behavioral psychology. And that is exactly what Cheville intended. The methods of science are the best tools available for studying spiritual experience and establishing knowledge about the interaction between divinity and humanity.

Roy Cheville first learned to look to spiritual experience as the basic substance of religion from the small group of saints in Rhodes. He joined this group to develop his own experiences. He began to verify for himself that these interactions with divinity occurred as the Rhodes saints said their church believed and practiced.

When he went to Graceland College as a student in 1921, he encountered two persons with strong intellectual influence. The first of these was Frederick M. Smith, President of the RLDS Church. He was frequently on campus lecturing and ministering. He had studied scientific sociology to gain understanding of the social aspects of the church's mission, and in the process earned a Master's degree in sociology. He had studied the psychological aspects of religious experience, and in the process earned a Ph.D. in psychology. He understood spirituality and he understood the new science of psychology. He knew that it was possible for the first time to identify and even measure events which were not material in substance and were fleeting in duration. He used his time and influence at Graceland to encourage students to use the best tools available to study such spiritual events as revelation and prophecy.

Roy found the ideas of Fred M. Smith stimulating. These ideas inspired him to go further in the use of scientific methods for the study of the interaction between God and human. Though Fred M. seems never to have departed completely from supernatural ideas, he interacted approvingly as Cheville followed the implications of Fred M.'s visionary insights. In 1935 Cheville wrote,

Our modern world very frequently asks two questions: "Will it work?" and "How does it work?".. Let these inquirers take a survey of biblical history with such problems as these in mind: How has God worked through the centuries? How has he touched men's souls in past times? Such an investigation will tell the story of the work of the Holy Spirit. It will be a revelation of the way God operates in his world. [1935C]

Sixteen years later he likened the life of the church to a laboratory:

In review, let's look at the job designed for the church. It is not a museum of plaster saints nor an exhibit of angels. It is a laboratory in which men and women are busy at the experiment of living together—with God. Laboratories do not have the finished product. [1951C]

Cheville noted that the Latter Day Saint movement began with a specific religious experience. In a day when theology and rituals about Jesus were almost destroying the very heart of Christianity, the young Joseph Smith went into the grove at Palmyra to seek divine guidance. The initial experience of Joseph Smith gave the clarion watchword of the new movement, "This is my beloved Son, hear him."

In an important sense this experience was and is a call to basics. The advice was not, "Read what my servant the Apostle Paul said about Jesus." In the language of a historian the advice would be to reduce reliance on secondary sources. In 1944 Cheville said,

We who serve in the stewardship of teaching will do well to remember a slogan, peculiarly meaningful to Latter Day Saints: "This is My beloved Son, hear him." Then shall we turn toward the person and work of Christ, functioning in current life. Then shall we be truly Christian. [1944D]

He referred to this first experience of the young Joseph Smith frequently in his hymns and prose writings. He insisted that the words appear at the front of the Lamoni church. He considered this element of the grove experience to be the church's defining moment.

Cheville described a rich spiritual experience in the 1950 Kirtland conference of high priests. Presiding Patriarch Elbert A. Smith testified that God had prompted him to prepare to bring a message:

> He began by affirming that he was speaking for Christ Jesus. "I am no stranger in the building . . I have looked upon you and perceived the sincerity of your hearts, your humility, and your endeavor to approach close to God." Then came the salutation that Jesus Christ had given to eleven apostles in the Upper Room in Jerusalem: "I am pleased again to call you my friends."
>
> This prophetic message ended with: "I am he, who, before I ascended up, gave the missionary commission, Go ye into all the world and preach the gospel. That commission has been renewed to you in these days. This assembly came not by accident. It came by divinely inspired direction. It is a blessed privilege you have had to meet together in this holy temple." Then he gave a commissioning assignment for all of us who served in the high priesthood. We were told to minister with spiritual endowment to a needy world.
>
> Later Brother Elbert said of this occasion, "I think that I have never experienced before in my life a feeling of such spiritual light and conviction and power as I had in delivering that message." [1983A]

Cheville advised young ministers at Graceland to get a good foundational education, believing that the warm emotion of spiritual experience needs to be accompanied by the cool reason of careful analysis. "The basic courses of college curricula are considered basic training for the ministry. Communication, psychology, sociology, economics, science, literature, music, and so on are fundamental. To these may be added courses in religion and related subjects that apply more specifically to church endeavor." [1954C]

The focus on experience was expressed in his view of college life as a laboratory. He asked each youthful saint to exercise faith in the laboratory of living. He saw that some would prefer not to meet the perplexities of college explorations in science and philosophy (He remembered the struggles and turmoil of his own university years). He saw that some would avoid honest inquiry that led to an examination of their faith, preferring to find comfort in the teachings of childhood. Some simply separated their faith from their learning.

Joseph Smith's grove experience first expressed to Roy contemporary contact with divinity. The functional principle is stated in the book of James, "If any of you lack wisdom, let him ask of God . . and it shall be given him." (James 1:5) Joseph Smith knelt in the grove at Palmyra to ask guidance in choosing a religious path. The resulting experience provided the requested guidance. It also provided verification of the statement of James. Throughout his life Roy Cheville would use the experience of the young Joseph Smith in the grove at Palmyra to represent the ever-present opportunity of contact between God and humans.

Cheville did not believe that direct experience with God is or should be restricted to the leader of the church. Instead he thought such contact is inherent in the nature of God and humans. "Our church can never grow into its ideal until inspiration is diffused throughout the membership as well as expressed through the prophet," he wrote. [1933D] As each of us experiences contact with divinity we can understand better the experiences of persons in the past. That is one key to the use of the Bible. "Each of us should make a study of the Bible as we would any library, and then use it in our lives," he wrote. [1933D] But, useful as the Bible is, it is only one means by which we can apprehend the workings of divinity. As he frequently did, Cheville used poetry to express the range of avenues by which the truth of God can be learned:

> Truth has no single voice: Countless her spokesmen,
> Tho' she seems mute in the soul's searching hour.
> Light breaks at length through the dark and confusion,
> Bringing the seeker her glory and power.
>
> By all her witnesses would she speak to us,
> Through heart and mind as we cling to her rod.
> Bathed in the glow of her insight and vision,
> Youth stands as seers who have seen with their God. [1950Y]

To learn about God requires initiative. Spiritual experience comes only through participation. A person knows love only by loving, and faith only by "faithing." Some workings of divinity are always among us. Divinity does not sit on a throne or wear a crown. We can be in the midst of the action and not know it. We can be taken aback as was Philip when he asked Jesus to show them the Father and Jesus said, "Have I been so long time with you, and yet hast thou not known me, Philip?"(John 14:9) It frequently takes refinement of perception to recognize the spiritual Christ in action. One kind of perception recognizes that which is before our eyes. Cheville believed that we need also a perception which recognizes that which happens inside us.

Epistemology

> We have come to understand a miracle not as something that happens contrary to natural law, but as phenomena in accordance with laws that we do not yet understand. . .

> As we grow in experience we understand more and more how God operates the Universe with well established laws and how we are expected to discover and apply these. [1933D]

> . . investigations in the biological-chemical-psychological nature of man. God has to be in on this or he will be left out in matters of God-man relationship. [1968B]

No assumptions of supernaturalism are required to understand the concepts in Roy Cheville's theology and the practice of his religion. In fact such assumptions get in the way. To assume that certain events were the result of supernatural forces is to block the possibility of understanding those events. To acknowledge spiritual power does not require that we acknowledge supernaturalism. Cheville's position was that divine processes are just as orderly and lawful as the rest of the operations of the universe. There are many divine processes that we do not yet understand. But that is true also of physiological, psychological and social processes.

Cheville said clearly that we do not know enough to draw a line between what is natural and what is divine. He said that drawing any such line puts a limit on God. What he probably meant was that it puts a restriction on the possibilities of our understanding the way divine processes work. It restricts the growth of our understanding.

He said that every bit of help that science is able to contribute ought to be enlisted in the study of the Bible. He noted that some young people read the story of Saul's conversion in Acts 9 and have trouble in explaining it.

Then he said, "Why not utilize the laws of psychology and sociology that they have learned? Let there be added to this the understanding that comes through their own highest religious experiences." [1935D]

Cheville dealt most intensively with one aspect of divinity—that part which is in interaction with humans. He advised study of the scriptures by examining what happened to persons who reported experiences with divinity. That is the historical arm of investigation. Contemporary personal spiritual experience is the essential laboratory component of investigation. These two components were to him the essential meaning of the scriptural guidance to learn "by study and by faith."

For each person there are functional aspects of spirituality in interaction with the rest of the person. This wholeness of the person is best described in his book *Growing Up In Religion* [1951B] and in his book *Spiritual Health* [1966A]. A person can be described in terms of physics, chemistry, biology, physiology, psychology, and spirituality. These are all in interaction and are interdependent. A diagram of his conception of the dimensions of personhood may look something like that shown on the following page. The dividers are not solid. Each level of operation may interact with the others, and each may interact with external reality.

Lack of development in any one of these aspects affects the whole person. There is a hierarchy of operations, each level depending on the functioning of the ones below. Consciousness is achieved at the level of psychology, and spiritual awareness and sensitivity are achieved at the highest level. He defined the term "spirituality" and some conditions of its use in this context: "It is safe to say that thousands of people in our social order are spiritually stunted. . . Let us think of religion as the experience of making contact with the God of the universe—the Cosmic personality. The highly spiritual person develops his capacities to sense and live with God in as many fields as his capacity will permit." [1951A]

```
* * * * * * * * * * * * * *
*      SPIRITUALITY      *
* * * * * * * * * * * * * *
*       PSYCHOLOGY       *      Cheville's
* * * * * * * * * * * * * *      concept
*       PHYSIOLOGY       *      of the
* * * * * * * * * * * * * *      whole
*         BIOLOGY        *      person
* * * * * * * * * * * * * *
*        CHEMISTRY       *
* * * * * * * * * * * * * *
*         PHYSICS        *
* * * * * * * * * * * * * *
```

Floyd McDowell, who was dean of the college at Graceland (and later a member of the First Presidency), shared the rigorous ideas of Fred M. Smith. McDowell recommended the study of the emerging science of psychology. In a *Herald* article in 1920, he wrote,

Psychology is one of the youngest of the children of that great mother of sciences, philosophy. This is due, no doubt, to the very nature of the subject itself. Psychology deals, in the first place, with facts which are so closely bound to other facts that they seem to resist any attempt to separate them for scientific purposes. . . it has proven to us that the mind of man operates according to, rather than in violation of, law.[SH 15 Dec 20]

Psychology had thus pointed the way to scientific study of spirituality by showing that even fleeting and immaterial events could be subject to observation and even measurement. Such an approach appears at first glance to be inconsistent with the Biblical accounts of God's dealings with humans. But this seeming inconsistency should be seen in the context of the changes over these two millennia in the ways of establishing knowledge. About this seeming inconsistency Cheville wrote,

> It is hard for us to vision the barriers of ignorance and superstition that hedged in the ancient as he sought for light. When we remember such factors, the prophets became torch-bearers in the progress of God's revelation. One pauses to wonder what Isaiah or John would be preaching in this twentieth century of scientific achievement. We may well conjecture that they would be using every bit of information available to proclaim God to this generation. [1935D]

Taking into account the differences in background knowledge and in the ability to describe complex processes and relationships, Cheville pointed out the soundness in some of the early experiences committed to writing. In the Genesis story of beginnings, for example, "there is a kind of progress in the sequence of creative events. The emergence of continents from oceans, the appearance of plants before animals, the coming of water animals before terrestrial ones, all fit into the later description of science concerning the development of geological and biological forms." [1935B]

Cheville emphasized that the study of spiritual phenomena should utilize appropriate methods. Even though the social and behavioral sciences have developed a number of tools for study since the days when Cheville was active in the use of such tools, he did understand the basic logic of research in this area. He cautioned,

> We should not be concerned with trying to duplicate the operations of the Holy Spirit as described in some particular incident in the Bible. It is rather for us to discover the principles that governed their spiritual expression and by them cultivate the Holy Spirit for our own age. [1935C]

Personhood
The Person Is the Purpose
of Religion

Religion is concerned with the development of persons—utilizing the personhood-developing forces available.

The church is the integrating institution for achieving this development of persons. [1942G]

Just as I can interact with persons in my social world, so I can develop personal relations with the Cosmic Personality. If I develop my personalism through interaction with other persons, just so do I expand this personal relationship with the Great Person whom we usually call God. [1951B]

One cannot understand Roy Cheville's theology without knowing his concept of the person. "Person" is a sociological term. We become human through biology, but we become persons through interactions with other persons. In Cheville's thought it is in personhood that we are created in the image of God, and God is the most important person with whom we may interact. Cheville gave credit to Shailer Mathews at Chicago for introducing him to the concept of the person in its relation to theology. He enriched his conception of personhood under the teaching of the social psychologist George Herbert Mead. Personhood assumed a central position in Cheville's developing theology. Although the concept was in place during his Graceland College years, his most complete treatment of the concept is in *Spiritual Resources Are Available Today*. [1975A]

Personhood is something to be experienced. It is not tangible, but it is real. Cheville wrote,

What expandable possibilities throughout life are reflected in these expressions of personhood—self-awareness, self-identification, and self-management! The person may be thwarted by inadequate patterns of living, of looking at himself, or he may grow with ever enlarging notions of personhood and how to realize these. The person can include God in his development or leave God out. And he can include God with sound or unsound patterns. What he does about Deity can narrow or expand his personhood. [1975A]

The word *personality* refers to the qualities of a person that distinguish him or her from other persons. It is a matter of identity. Every person is measured by the kind of qualities that are identified in the personality of others. Personhood requires freedom. Without ability to choose, disposition to choose, and setting to choose, one cannot live as a person. If biological drives dominate, one is animal; if domineering direction controls, one is slave; if fear of God impels, one is a dumb devotee. Personalism calls for "the power of self-determination."

Among the first questions we need to ask about a religion are: "What is the nature of mankind? Is a human considered worthful? What kind of person is one to be? How are humans and God going to get together in this person-with-person relationship? What is the function of the Holy Spirit in all this?"

On a number of occasions Cheville referred to the instructions given by God to the young Ezekiel. In one he wrote,

> I thrill at this directive to young Ezekiel: "Son of man, stand upon thy feet!" Here God was asking for a youth to appear before him with erect bearing, with self-respect. This is a long way from the usual observances of slavish obeisance. It expresses a dignity that God expects of his people. This is the God I know, the God who invites every youth to get on his feet, stand erect, with eyes forward. [1956C]

The person emerges through interpersonal relationships and stays a person through these continuing relationships. One grows well through some and decreases through others. One becomes stunted if deprived of relationships with persons of merit. Friendly influence is like an atmosphere surrounding persons, and we tend to become molded into the likeness of the lives that come nearest us. They make up the atmosphere we breathe into our character. Cheville once said, "The choice of friends, then, becomes one of the most serious affairs of life, for in it we are selecting the pattern after which we intend to mold our own lives." [1933E]

Jesus is the model friend. That is the relationship the physical Jesus developed with his chosen disciples. Among the 12 were three with whom he seemed to have a closer intimacy. Apparently they understood his mission and felt his personality to a degree the others never did. Only Peter, James, and John were with him on the Mount of Transfiguration. However, as the spiritual Christ, Jesus is the potential friend of all persons. Each person can choose to interact with him, resulting in development toward fullness of character.

A society composed of the family, school, community, church, and government may engender wholesome personhood. What a person is doing for the total good of his or her society indicates the person's worth. Society sanctions the person to the degree that (1) personal potential is discovered, (2) it is developed, (3) it is devoted to the longtime good of all, and (4) it delights in the achievement.

There is nothing static about the self, about personhood. The relationship with person-producing forces keeps going on, bringing changes and requiring continuing adjustment. This simple conclusion stands forth: a person draws on some resources in the universe that enable him or her to become a person. Cheville wrote, "Persons interact to produce personhood, and such interaction can go on and on, but this is hardly enough. There needs to be some reaching into the cosmos itself. In this exploration the Holy Spirit is nominated as resource for producing personhood." [1975A]

Through the ages many people have believed that there is some element of divinity within us all. Cheville merged his religious experience and scientific theory-building to predict where in the scheme of personhood the dynamic of divinity lies, thus setting the stage for further testing and evaluation.

He made a connection between the technical principles he was describing and familiar aspects of religious living of his church:

Recent years have brought contributions to us in the social sciences. They phrase in a technical way the things Amos and Hosea and Jesus of Nazareth were declaring. One of these laws of social psychology affirms that we, born candidates for personalism, become persons through interaction with other persons. Our Zionic endeavor is built upon this law. It affirms that we develop spiritually through mutually helpful associations. This is inherent in the nature of things. [1950AR]

You Have Seen the Father

It is the life and character of Jesus—the great manifestation of God to man. In Jesus we see the qualities of divinity living in actual humanity... John represents Jesus as saying in his final address to his Twelve that, "He that hath seen me hath seen the Father." (John 14:9) For two thousand years the character of Jesus, the Christ has been the chief means for discovering and coming to know God. [1933D]

As Roy Cheville had urged that we read the experiences of biblical persons with divinity in order to learn how divinity works with humans, so he urged that we examine the actions of Jesus in order to learn more about God. Jesus had said that he who had seen him had seen the Father. Cheville did not interpret this to mean that the Father looks like Jesus physically. What Cheville did teach is that the personhood of Jesus is like that of the Father. In the manner and power of interacting with other persons, Jesus and the Father are alike.

The Jews of Jesus' time had been conditioned to look for the Messiah as a new and better version of the Old Testament kings. They were conditioned to seeing persons of power and might sitting on a throne, commanding armies, and showing other physical evidences of that power. When Jesus' contemporaries sensed that he might be something special, they came to hear him to learn if he might lead their army as the Messiah. Instead of a military rallying cry they heard him saying, "blessed are the peacemakers." Many turned aside convinced that he was not the one sent of God.

Many people since Jesus' time have had trouble understanding that the power of divinity can lie in the quality with which one lives. It is easy to decide that the greatness of divinity must lie "out there" somewhere. When

251

Philip asked Jesus at the last supper to "show us the Father," Jesus responded, "Have I been so long time with you, and yet hast thou not known me, Philip?" Cheville noted that there is some sense of weariness in the response of Jesus. Even after so a long a time with him, his disciples still did not understand that divinity was present in the things he did and said—in the quality of life he led. That part of divinity which can interact with human life was in him.

Philip has a great many imitators today—people who look for divinity not in the lives of people, but "out there" somewhere. Many have defaulted by using supernaturalism to explain divinity. Cheville wrote,

> Religion never has as many and as expressive words as it needs to describe its experiences. No man has ever been able to portray to others what he means by the presence of the Holy Spirit. Throughout the centuries men have had to employ this symbol or that figure of speech to suggest their idea of God. First it was King, then Lord, and then Father. The biblical writers had to employ the beliefs and phrases at their convenience. Otherwise their writings and preachings would have had little or no meaning to their contemporaries. [1935D]

If we do not default to supernaturalism, how do we understand God? The word "God" and the word "human" tend to have boundaries around them. Cheville's approach was to take down the boundaries. He urged people to be ready to see divinity working within personality broadly conceived. The disciples of Jesus should have trained their perceptive abilities to recognize the qualities of divinity within Jesus, their friend and their teacher. So should each one of us be tuned to recognize the qualities of divinity within the personhoods of those we are privileged to know.

The Physical Jesus and the Spiritual Christ

> When Jesus was bidding his disciples farewell at the Last Supper, he tried to forewarn them and prepare them for the shock of his crucifixion. They did not understand how he could be the Messiah and be arrested and executed by Jewish priests and Roman rulers. If his kingdom were to be established, he, himself, had to be present and be the ruler. He told them, however, that although he would be leaving them, he would not leave them alone: he would send a "Comforter" to be with them (John 14:16). He was trying to tell them that while his physical presence would not be in their midst, the spiritual power of his personality would be with them. This promise would make him available to all men everywhere... [1933D]

Cheville made a distinction between the physical Jesus and the spiritual Christ. The physical Jesus lived in one place at one time. The spiritual Christ is everliving, with no beginning and no end. In the mature physical Jesus can be seen the aspects of divinity which can be present in human form. The human form is restricting. It can be in only one place at a time. The power that was in Jesus when unrestricted is the spiritual Christ. The spiritual Christ is available everywhere at all times. As such he is the universal friend—with all persons everywhere.

The physical Jesus is the incarnation of spirituality in human form. He is the example for humans. Through his life we can understand that there are spiritual dimensions to personality. Each person can develop in spirituality, as we can develop in other aspects of personality such as our ability to love. As we develop in spirituality we become more Christlike.

It is clear that Cheville did not look forward to the second coming of Christ. He looked back at it. Jesus promised that he would return speedily, and he did. But he returned as the spiritual Christ. He demonstrated his presence on the Day of Pentecost. Though many of Cheville's contemporaries looked forward to a literal second coming of Christ, Cheville never tried to correct them. To do that would be a matter of talking to them about what he did not believe. And Cheville did not talk about what he did not believe. Certainly as early as the 1933 quarterlies, he was explicit about the distinction between the physical Jesus and the spiritual Christ. He made the distinction and established the relevance to scriptures and to contemporary spiritual experience. In that way he set the stage for his students to move forward into what Fred M. Smith had called "the larger light."

In an Easter sermon in Lamoni in 1929, Cheville spoke of the greatness of Jesus in the crucifixion, interpreting that greatness as consisting of the spiritual qualities of sympathy of spirit and conviction of his mission, rather than of physical suffering. This quality of life made it eternal and made him a Son of God indeed.

He wrote in 1935 that the story did not come to an end with the crucifixion of Jesus. The divine personality lived on, now unhampered by local restrictions. He recommended that one reread the story of Saul's conversion as told in Acts 9 to sense the impact of the Christ upon the militant Saul. The young man became charged with this new revelation of God. Impelled by it, he went out to give his life in sacrificial service just as his Lord had done. Jesus had sought to instruct his disciples so that they might tap spiritual resources.

Ten days after Jesus' final departure—on the Day of Pentecost—the disciples came into a full experience of this promised power. This day has often been called the birthday of the church militant. Notice

254

carefully the conditions under which the Holy Spirit was given to the Early Church. There was perfect accord; the disciples were waiting together in prayer. When they were ready, the gift was given them. . . Under this added power the disciples were transformed. Their influence was magnified; their words were with power. The effect of their preaching was miraculous. They had to tell others; they could not keep from witnessing. . . The critical transition from Jesus' immediate influence to that of the less tangible Spirit was passed. [1935C]

Cheville wrote in 1951 that only those who have spiritual qualities in their own natures would be able to detect divine attributes within Jesus. The events of Pentecost assured the believers that their Jesus was still living for they could feel his Spirit. Now he was more than the physical Jesus who had lived with them: he was the spiritual Christ:

He was the Messiah they had been looking for: only they had been mistaken about his mission, about what made him divine. They had to look for a different kind of sign—not what happened before their eyes but what took place inside them. . .[1951B]

He wrote in 1956 that Jesus did not talk very much about his authority. "Rather did he devote his time to developing in his disciples the qualities that would enable them to detect his divinity." [1956B]

255

Prophecy

If anyone is going to speak in my name, he needs more than a license card. He must live with me until he understands my mind and catches my spirit. [1949B]

In Cheville's thought the word *prophecy* did not mean simply foretelling the future, a definition which constitutes only half of the dictionary entry. The other half has to do with uttering that which is divinely inspired. Cheville saw this part as the more important and, indeed, the basis on which foretelling rests. If one is to foretell future events as a result of divine inspiration, that capability assumes that one has established relations with divinity which allow communication to occur.

Prophecy is an important part of the Bible. It is also important in the beliefs and practices of the RLDS Church. Cheville did not shy away from the concept but gave careful consideration to its theory and practice. Prophecy is an integral part of the refined working relations between a person who is spiritually developed and the person of God. It is one of the aspects of inspiration which increases the prophet's insights into the nature of persons, principles, and relationships. Insights into future events grow out of this broad understanding. The defining aspect of prophecy is that one speaks forth in order that the purpose of the divine communication is achieved.

This process is demanding [Cheville would say *exacting*] on the part of the prophet. In the first place one must be in tune with the spiritual processes. That means one has met the personal, moral, and attitudinal criteria to qualify for the divine communication. This includes the kind of moral development that insures that the divine power vested will not be used for any other purpose than the divine intention.

The ability to speak forth directly in response to inspiration requires a significant degree of confident ability to act upon the direction being given. Cheville thought that this was the opposite of "surrendering to God's will" in which one abdicates control and lets God take control of him or her. For him the requisite was that one maintains full control of one's person; one's faculties and one's choice-making abilities. While being all the person one can be, the prophet matches personal will and direction with the divine intention. "Inspiration comes to the active, not to the inert," he said.

Cheville spoke to a student group at Iowa State College at Ames during a "Religion in Life" series about 1956. He said he wanted them to meet a young man who spoke out to his times. This young man was Ezekiel, a Hebrew youth deported to Babylon. In a strange land it would have been easy to be silent. But his God had told him to stand erect and prepare to speak out. God would tell him what to say. Ezekiel was to listen, and he was not to speak until he understood. Cheville went on to tell this college group that they should pay attention to their foundations in order to develop their positive influence. He said,

> As for myself, I will not spend my time stressing what I do not believe. Nor will I surrender to exponents of weak theology. God calls us to stand for and to speak forth—constructively... When we stand to speak we need foundations to stand on. We cannot stand firm on shifting sand, on sliding streets, on nebulous clouds. Some basic conviction, tested and continually being tested in the laboratory of life, must be under our feet. [1956C]

Cheville went on to tell this group that he hoped they got good grades that reflected a true mastery of materials; he hoped they made friends, relationships rooted in spiritual foundations; he hoped they experienced fellowship with those who are co-creators with God. Then he gave them this direct counsel:

> Let us say out of the book of this year: The word of the Lord came unto the student as he lived on this campus, "Son of man, stand upon thy feet and I will speak unto thee. Be not afraid. Speak my words. Son of Man, hear what I say unto thee. Stand up, and speak out!" [1956C]

Cheville told of an encounter with a fervent believer who did not understand the dynamics of prophetic investiture. He wanted the Holy Spirit—right away. He did not consider the value of what he wanted in terms of God's ongoing program. He did not consider his own fitness to receive this Spirit. He did not think of his capacity to "contain" and "use" it. He resolved to fast from three meals, to keep praying, and to make a financial offering. This would persuade God to grant what he wanted. Further conversation disclosed that this man wanted the gift of prophecy so he would be able to stand in the congregation and say, "This is the word of God to you." Cheville was using this example to make the point that divine power in prophecy operates through processes that must be understood and qualities which must be attained if one is to be a prophet.

Cheville described the setting in which the Old Testament prophets worked and spoke out:

> The galaxy of spiritual leaders in ancient Israel whom we call prophets lived in a world that was just as near to them as we are to the social-economic-political affairs of today. They were not recluses or escapists. They noted what was happening in their times. They saw where things would go if they continued in their present direction. They sensed the nature and purpose of God with sweeping perspective. Very deeply they felt their obligation to speak out and

warn and encourage and instruct the people. So they spoke out forthrightly about the will and intent of God. [1956B]

Out of his own experience Cheville wrote about the requirements of the prophet:

Prophecy is an exacting experience. It calls for a long-time self-management that equips the person to see what God has in his mind and in his heart. It is far more than a sudden flash that prompts a man to speak forth. It involves a lifelong development. Who is equipped to speak forth for God? Those who have lived so effectively in communion with God that they can sense what he is and what he is seeking to achieve. This implies that the prophet must be so near to God's universe and to God's people that he can see God at work. [1956B]

He addressed the role of prophecy in a 1963 article on current Mormonism he wrote for *Christian Century*. He noted that the Reorganized Church was experiencing strains of no little consequence. He saw it facing two major questions: (1) the relationship of administrative groups in conducting its affairs, together with the operation of hierarchical and democratic aspects of ecclesiastical government; and (2) identification of basic Latter Day Saint theology. Among the theological issues he noted a pressing concern with the function of prophetic inspiration and the expression of prophetic ministry. He saw the need for personal and general development that would bring about capacity and sensitivity so God can speak significantly. All the saints have a part in accomplishing this objective. [1963O]

He said once that he had heard saints pray simply for God to "speak to them," without having laid an adequate spiritual foundation. He could imagine God saying to those ill-prepared persons, "All right. I'll speak to you. What do you want me to talk about?"

The Hereafter

The saints of a century ago were greatly concerned with questions of doctrine. The nature of the godhead, the millennium, the mode of baptism, the hereafter, church policy, and a score of similar topics engaged their attention. . Doctrine has to touch life if it is to enlist attention today. [1935D]

Roy Cheville did not spend much time thinking, talking, or writing about the hereafter. He did believe that there was a continuity of personhood which was a function of the quality of the life and consequent development of the person. He did not believe that life on earth should be discounted, that the next life was the major reality. He had no use for an "insurance policy" religion which would pay off only after the death of the insured.

He did provide some thoughts on immortality in a 1947 funeral sermon for Bertha Robinson Deskin:

> One day each comes to the terminal city that marks the end of his journey. For centuries this has been visioned as standing on the life-ward bank of a river or sea. This marked sharply the boundary between life and the hereafter. . . There is another picture of this terminal city. It stands not on the edge of water that divides the here from the hereafter, but at the beginning of an isthmus that connects two lands. Such a pattern speaks of the continuity of life. Life moves on across the isthmus; it does not stop at a stream and then start over again. This view squares with the divine process of growth everywhere operative in the universe. In this process one step emerges out of its pre decision and evolves into what comes after. Eternal life becomes a going on existence with continuing unfoldment, not a sudden creation through magical power. [1947E]

He felt that much effort spent on the hereafter was at least useless and frequently destructive of life and energy. He felt that many of the problems the church encountered in Nauvoo were the result of speculation about the nature of the hereafter. Many of those ideas were carried to Utah and institutionalized there. He wanted his church to address the principles of living:

> Many people get concerned about the glories of heaven when they ought to be concerned with building a glorified society here on earth. I confess it irks me when members waste their time speculating about the hereafter when practical jobs are begging for their energies now. I admit how often it bothers me when members who live in the twentieth century think as if they were in the twelfth century. . . We shall center upon Christ as the norm of our achievement, not on any member or group of them. [1951C]

RLDS Distinctives

A movement that has no significant distinctives . . might as well merge into the general run of society and lose its identity. It probably will. [1968B]

A church must have distinctives if it is to survive. [1973C]

Although Cheville had formulated his most important concepts by the middle of his Graceland years, he did not give some of them systematic written expression until later. That includes his views of RLDS distinctives. His mature view was that it took a set of several distinctives together to define the essence of the RLDS church. He worked on expressing that set in 1968 [1968B] and again in 1973 [1973C,D]. Even though he divided them for purposes of explanation and analysis, he saw them functioning holistically, and he made clear that no one distinctive should be emphasized at the expense of the others. He believed the task of church members was to interpret and express these distinctives meaningfully and functionally.

SPIRIT AND ELEMENT ARE ONE

The universe of God is a creation ever in process with the material and the spiritual viewed as phases of a single reality. The Restoration movement advises that "spirit and element" are associated in God's process. Material reality and spiritual reality exist together. There is a *uni*verse. Thus there is no dividing line between humanity and divinity, between mental and spiritual, between natural and supernatural.

GOD IS FRIENDLY

Many religions have focussed on God as a stern and wrathful judge who delivers vengeful retribution on the

263

wicked. There is scriptural support for this idea. But Cheville noted that Jesus spoke to correct this notion. He said that God is more like a caring father. In the parable of the prodigal son the father fits the description Jesus gave of God; he was ready to acknowledge, care for, and teach his son no matter the degree of transgression.

Jesus himself was a more complete example of the friendly and supportive nature of divinity. The physical Jesus walked among the people in friendly regard and acceptance. He used no throne or bodyguard to separate himself from the public. He was aware of human needs in those about him wherever he went. The spiritual Christ, who made that distinctive person's presence felt on the Day of Pentecost, is friendly and supportive. That is a person who is ever present and ever in interaction with those who seek to be in interaction with that one.

THE MISSION OF JESUS CHRIST

To Cheville the mission of Jesus Christ in coming to the earth to live as a human was to teach the way of the good life. He came to teach people that divinity inheres in the quality of the lives they can lead if they choose. Jesus himself lived a life of such eternal quality that death of the physical body had no effect on him. The spiritual Christ, not described by gender, delivers persons from lower expression of their impulses and from evil social factors as they live with Christ. The immediacy of this ministry is expressed in the initial experience of Joseph Smith in the Palmyra grove. The universality of this ministry is expressed in the ministry of Jesus Christ in ancient America as narrated in the Book of Mormon.

THE DOCTRINE OF INSPIRATION

In 1930 Cheville wrote that "a survey of the century leads me to believe that the outstanding achievement of the church has been in the developing interpretation of one of its most characteristic beliefs. This unique doctrine lies at the very heart of the Restoration movement: the doctrine of Inspiration." [1930A] In 1931 "Unk" wrote again about the doctrine of revelation, "If I were to select an outstandingly significant feature of Latter Day Saintism I should name its belief and practice of revelation. . . there was not only a belief but institutions, means, and regulations for revelatory expression. This organic aspect is distinctive." [1931E] In 1933 he wrote that when God reveals his will to his prophets or directs us personally, he does not deal with us as if we were passive stones. He works with us as if we were alert men and women. Inspiration is not an easy method of decision for lazy people. It is direction and assurance for those who seek and search. [1933D]

CHURCH STRUCTURE INSTITUTIONALIZING INSPIRATION

Cheville recognized that other churches and other persons believe in inspiration and work to develop its functions. He described a conversation with a member of another church who also believed in inspiration and was asking about distinctive RLDS beliefs:

> So I answered that a most distinctive feature was that Latter Day Saints not only believed in current revealment but that it affirmed that the church was the agency for manifesting God's will and nature. The church included in its structure the means of receiving and cultivating the gift of revelation . . This organic aspect is distinctive. [1931E]

He saw that many people believe the RLDS Church is audacious in stating that its is guided by revelation and that its church leaders are led by the spirit. These people perceive revelation to be an "all-or-none" process. They believe that revelation makes known the whole mind of God—a rare thing indeed. Cheville described the RLDS belief that all revelation is partial, that "we see through a glass darkly."

THE HOLY SPIRIT

Through most of its life the RLDS Church has been clear in its belief in the function of the Holy Spirit and its procedures which make regular pursuit of contact with divinity. Cheville pointed out that there was a degree of distinctiveness in that, particularly in the willingness to visualize the holy spirit in operational terms leading to possible greater understanding. His view was that the RLDS Church was somewhat alone in that pursuit over the years. In writing about the modern reference to the Holy Spirit, Cheville said,

> Until recent years little has been said about the Holy Spirit. Theologians talked of "grace." The Holy Spirit needs to be interpreted with cosmic significance and in terms of enlightening ministry in persons, in groups; otherwise a generalized "grace" will be talked about, and God will be shut off from fruitful ministry in persons. [1968B]

He called the Holy Spirit "the radiating personal presence of God, affording ministries that encourage in goodness, integrate the person, and enlighten in understanding love." He continued, "This is basic in the Restoration movement (Doctrine and Covenants 10). In right communion with the Holy Spirit, men receive spiritual vitality and vision." [1968B]

THE DEVELOPMENT OF THE INDIVIDUAL

For Cheville the mission of Jesus was to lift the sights of persons to a higher appreciation of what they may become. By following him individuals can incorporate eternal qualities into their living. When individuals face the world with confidence and strength of character, they can become the kind of persons who fulfill the potentials of human nature. Cheville wrote that "The history of our church is a story of a people who have preached and practiced the development of the individual." [1933D]

THE SAINTLY COMMUNITY

We recognize that the qualities of developing person-hoods are influenced by the qualities of persons with whom we interact. Thus it is important to look to the processes of community building. This has long been recognized in the life and work of the church. It has been called Zion, the manifestation of saintly community, of social gospel, here and now. Of this Cheville wrote,

> The Restoration movement affirms an identifiable program of action with a center place as base of operation and satellite communities. This is for the development of Saints and for witnessing in corporate living. Zion provides centers for outreaching evangelistic ministry. Zion functions in a worldwide program. It is a laboratory in saintly living. It looks to a program that includes all phases of balanced, well-rounded living. Men are to live together in mutual support with common allegiance to God. [1968B]

His study of the variables in community building were background for a message given to a conference on zionic community in 1969. That message was reported under the title "Prophetic ministry at institute on Zion." He said in part,

> Ever has the way of Zionic community been in my eternal program. Ever is it designed to bring into realization the quality of person in my design for man... I call you to see the fullness of Zionic community, which included competency in materialistic matters but which rises above mastery of man by material forces. I charge you ...

to bring to realization Zionic living among my Saints. . . that they may help one another in achieving saintly character and expression, that they may reveal the gospel in consociatonal living, that they may afford community into which others may come. . . I call you to expect expanding vision and continuing expression. Remember that Zion is not a finalized achievement but a way of living that is ever in process. Remember that in the work of your God, who is Source for Zionic living, there is no end in creative expression. [1969E]

BEYOND SCRIPTURAL MONOPOLY

One of the clear features of the RLDS Church is that we have more than one canon of scripture. That has been the subject of derision by opponents of the church. Cheville saw it clearly as a strength and asset. He called the scriptures the record of God's relationship with humankind. And, he believed that God speaks and acts as persons permit. Cheville wrote of our multiple scriptures:

The Restoration movement saves God from limitation to the Bible. The Book of Mormon attests the universality of Christ and the largeness of God's purpose and plan. The Doctrine and Covenants affirms the continuing disclosure of God. And there is place for other scripture. Scripture speaks at the level man can comprehend and use.

Scriptures suffer when men consider them final and full. This hems God in and tempts man to use them to legalize rather than to guide. Many religious movements wanting authority interpret the Bible as the "last say-so." [1968B]

BOOK VIII.

Epilogue

BOOK VIII. EPILOGUE
Professor Emeritus

I may have left, but my heart stayed at Graceland. [TWR 7 Oct 77]

Roy Cheville retired from the Graceland faculty in 1959. At the same time Eugene Closson and Gustav Platz retired. Platz had joined the faculty in 1920, Cheville in 1923, and Closson in 1931. The combined faculty service of the three was 103 years.

The 1959 ACACIA was dedicated to Roy Cheville and Eugene Closson. The citation stated, "To two men who have given many years of outstanding and generous service on Graceland's hill, and who have shared many experiences together." The dedication statement for Cheville was:

"Doc," as he is referred to by many, has been one of the great pioneering spirits of Graceland. He has helped to integrate religion into the total life experience of youth; he has been the pioneer and guiding light of the four-year religion curriculum; he has stimulated youth to think for themselves, and has made their growing pains pleasurable as they have sought to grasp new concepts and build a sturdier foundation upon which to grow.

His door always open, "Doc" has been a true friend and bridge back to the fellowship of the living Christ for those whose path may have become obscured; he has been able to get into the soul of a person and help him to blossom out and develop into the sort of person he was capable of becoming; he has lived with Gracelanders through good and bad times.

"Doc" Cheville has always keenly followed the athletic teams and has led the rousing cheers and pep rallies of the campus; he has written many of the songs of Graceland, including the Alma Mater hymn, and has enthusiastically led the singing of a vibrant youth.

A strong and courageous man, Dr. Cheville epitomizes much of what Graceland stands for—the quest for truth, an expanding vision, a sensitiveness to persons, and a deep spiritual insight and integrity.

In the years that followed, Cheville continued to have a close association with the college and community even though in December of 1959 he moved from Lamoni to Independence to a small apartment above the Speaks Funeral Home near the Auditorium. For the fall semester of 1959, "Doc" taught some advanced courses in religion. He preached the funeral sermon for his close friend Roscoe Faunce, long time professor of speech and drama, who died suddenly June 22, 1960.[1] In September 1960 "Doc" returned to the Graceland campus for the first semester to teach advanced religion courses, his last semester there.

In the *Herald* of November 5, 1961, there is a photograph of Cheville, "Presiding Patriarch of the church and instructor at Graceland," leading singing in a crowded Zimmerman Hall at the 1961 Graceland Homecoming. For that occasion Cheville wrote the hymn, "The Hilltop Where," to be sung to the tune Finlandia:

This is my home, the Hilltop where my heart is.
This is the place I come to know as mine.
Here is the tower, that calls me to look upward;
Here is the door that opened to my shrine.
Here is the wealth of memories that linger
And call me on with lifting thoughts sublime.

This is my home, the Hilltop where my heart is,
Where I found friends, who link their hearts with mine,
Where bonds were made that hold across the ocean
With those who walked these paths among the pine.
In memory, I'll come back to this homeland
And feel anew the pull of things divine.

Cheville was in Lamoni June 15–22, 1963, teaching a class on "Basic Considerations in Theology for Today" as a part of the older youth conference on the Graceland campus. On June 10, 1965 he wrote a letter to Bill Higdon, noting that he was happy Bill had become Graceland's president, and voicing some concerns about the religion offerings. Cheville felt strongly that the religious activities on campus should not be separated from the teaching of religion. He had said that each teaching field needs to be tied to its laboratories.

Cheville continued to help individuals from other cultures understand the Christian gospel. In a room in Gunsolley Hall in the summer of 1960, he talked with Hiroshi Matsushita of Tokyo. Hiroshi was telling him of his first contacts with the Church of Jesus Christ in his home city. Though Hiroshi's English was limited, one word kept standing out to him—the word "love." This was new to him for, as a rule, Oriental religions do not have much to say in this vein. This single word kept attracting him. Hiroshi Matsushita was baptized and later ordained. Cheville gave him his patriarchal blessing. Cheville wrote that he "sensed the spiritual quality of this young man to be expressed in the word he first caught when he began attending our meetings in Tokyo. In and through him the love of God is going to be expressed in our Japanese mission. I had a warmer, larger sense of the love of God, of the centrality of this love in the gospel." [1966F]

At the Graceland Homecoming in 1978 there was a SONGFEST WITH ROY CHEVILLE. The songsheet contained 21 songs,

1. Let us sing a world-wide anthem Tune: Nettleton
   [This was the tune Cheville preferred for this hymn]
2. Youth of the Church, arise! Tune: Diademata
3. Afar in old Judea Tune: Webb
4. Still other sheep I have Tune: Boylston

273

5. The light of God awaits our resolution
     Tune: How Great Thou Art
6. We stand erect and hopeful Tune: Webb
7. What a friend we have in Jesus!
     He is steadfast, kind, and sure,
8. Send forth thy light, O Zion!
9. It may be I shall never trace
10. We shall be witnesses for Christ Tune: Ellacombe
11. With brother love we send this word Tune: Evan
12. Shine through our countenances, God Tune: Bethlehem
13. We come, O Lord, to learn of thee Tune: Bethlehem
14. O Lord thy people gathered here Tune: Truro
15. Send me forth, O blessed Master Tune: Cwm Rhondda
16. Master speak! Thy saints are listening Tune: Admonition
17. Redeemer of Israel, our only delight
18. Open my eyes, O Lord
19. Heralds of Christ, stand forth and vow today Tune: National
     Hymn
20. We shall be friends in God's great congregation Tune: Finlandia
21. O come, ye sons of Graceland all (Alma Mater hymn)

Cheville also continued to articulate Graceland's uniqueness to the church. For the *Herald* of May 15, 1962 Cheville summed up his view of the "Way of Graceland:"

1. Graceland is a community. . . A community is a company of people in one place living together with common meanings, common loyalties, common social heritage. Members speak the same language, share in common objectives, join in mutual fortune. . . Graceland maintains this quality of a community. The "Hill" is a symbol of this togetherness. . .

2. Graceland is a laboratory in learning self-management. . .

3. Graceland is an integration center. . . Fields of study tend to speak different languages that do not have speaking acquaintance. One college graduate has put it this way, "College has given me lots of spokes; I need a hub to hold these together."

4. Graceland is a crossroads in our church fellowship. The Graceland flag has two bars of blue that cross, on the field of gold. This crossing symbolizes youth of many places meeting on the campus with the Christian cross the dynamic of their coming to-

gether. Today this is more than a symbol on a flag; it is a reality in youth association. . .

5. Graceland is a company in spiritual exploration. . . Graceland College is to be a company of spiritual explorers.

6. Graceland is an alma mater. "Alma mater" means simply "foster mother." . .

Those who live the life of campus citizenship, of development in self-management, of worldwide friendship, of integrated living, of spiritual exploration can truly sing, "It's a way we have at Graceland!" [1962H]

The college to which he had given so much of himself continued to honor him. At the Graceland Homecoming in 1967, Roy Cheville and United States Senator Milton R. Young were awarded the Graceland College Alumni Distinguished Service Award. Cheville's address was entitled "Graceland College: A Colony in a Changing Culture." The abstract of the paper contained the following ideas:

In this contemporary era of rapid and inclusive social change Graceland College is called to be a colony in the educational life of our church and of our world.

Such a colony is to function within the larger social world of which it is an integral part. College education is related to all other areas of our social living.

The college as a colony is to maintain a distinctiveness that will enable it to have something to contribute to the larger educational world.

The college is to chart a course between (1) isolation which would look to separation from the rest of the world and (2) identification which would make it like all other institutions with little or no reason for existence.

Graceland College has a distinctive mission as a colony in identifying and expressing spiritual values and insights, in exploring in theory, in practice for inclusive approach to reality. These are to permeate the total field of college learning. This entails high competency in academic pursuits.

Such a colony is a community.

Such a mission calls for clarity and soundness in objectives and for competency in operations that are relevant to these objectives.

Such a mission is a stewardship in which colonists on campus and off campus are exploring "together with God."

Graceland's mission is enhanced in such a time as ours.

On May 26, 1968, at the 71st Annual Commencement Roy A. Cheville, in an unprecedented show of respect and affection by Graceland, was awarded the title Emeritus Professor of Graceland College, and he was given the honorary degree Doctor of Divinity.

The Citation for the award of Emeritus Professor read:

In sincere appreciation of the life of service, dedication and love which has touched so many, we salute you

ROY A. CHEVILLE

As an effective leader and revered teacher you have been both eloquent and humble. Your students have been lead and encouraged to develop postures of independence and commitment. In response to your example and your instruction many have achieved distinction in their chosen fields and have rendered significant service to the larger community of men. These students will always admire you and extend themselves in loving service to others because you have influenced their lives.

Now in this moment of official recognition the Board of Trustees of the College does hereby confer upon you the title *Professor Emeritus* with all the rights and privileges and honors appertaining thereto. May God add his blessings now and throughout your life.

The Citation for the Doctor of Divinity degree, written by Velma Ruch, read:

Ralph Waldo Emerson once asserted, "An institution is the lengthened shadow of one man." For Graceland College these words can more truly be applied to Roy Arthur Cheville than to any other person. While there have been many who have dreamed and sacrificed and built and whose imprint this institution bears, Dr. Cheville for 40years as a student and faculty member almost became the embodiment of that which was Graceland. Faculty members and students alike came to depend upon his vision, his fearless inquiry, and his passionate commitment. Through him, many caught fire intellectually and spiritually and learned the art by which man becomes immortal. In him was the intimate welding of passion and knowledge and the commitment "to raise the sights of the people." He held to the dream in the midst of loneliness and misunderstanding and has lived to see the day in which his lonely thoughts have become the thoughts of the many. He conceived of a world church and world education and continues to seek every opportunity to further the brotherhood of man. The mission of the college and the church todays bears the mark, though now anonymous, of the patient teaching of Dr. Cheville and of the hours of searching for the responsive minds of the few who could catch the vision.

As a faculty member Roy Cheville found no area of college, church, or community life too remote from his interest. His unflagging energy and contribution in a multitude of fields have become legendary. He always taught a formidable series of courses, served for many years as Director of Religious Life, gave six years of intensive work to his doctor's degree without a break from his teaching, took a leading role in the activities of Lamoni Stake, organized the Lamoni Community Life Association and otherwise served the community. In the midst of this, he involved himself in all major student activities, never missing a sports event, a lyceum number, or a party. Wherever there was song—frivolous or serious— Dr. Cheville was there, directing and inspiring. In the present *Saints' Hymnal* are 18 hymns of his composition and many college songs were his creation. He always had time to talk to students, to offer them his friendship and counsel, and to correspond with them after they left the college. Few have been able to carry such a daily round of responsibility with more composure and buoyancy of spirit.

Dr. Cheville has been a leader in defining the theology of the church. His central concern has been an exploration of the nature of God and the functioning of the Holy Spirit. He has attempted to interpret the message of the church into meaningful terms for our day and to express those universals of the gospel which have relevance in all cultures. In 1958 he was ordained Presiding Patriarch of the church and has found in that office a further calling to lift the spiritual quality and understanding of the people.

In the "Alma Mater Hymn," Dr. Cheville expressed his dream for a college whose "battlemented tower/ Shall rise to call the youth of lands/ To answer to the hour." In bestowing upon Roy Cheville the degree of Doctor of Divinity, Graceland College not only gives recognition to a great scholar, educator, and man of God but commits itself to further the dream and to become an institution in which the youth of lands shall experience the gospel of hope and expectancy and carry the message in action. The college is proud that in its heritage it has the example of greatness and can today participate in bestowing recognition to leadership so abundantly given.

In the spring of 1977, funds for a new campus chapel had been gathered, and the Board of Trustees sent Cheville a letter asking his permission to name the chapel in his honor. When Cheville received the letter he did not respond immediately. Before answering he talked with the author about what was on his mind. While he appreciated the honor of having a building on campus named for him, he hesitated. Though the chapel would provide a useful place to retreat (he was to use it that way himself), it was not the kind of building which he felt represented what his career at Graceland had meant.

He saw his own work as a Graceland faculty member representing an integration of academic pursuits with religious life. That integration was a deep commitment for him and he pursued it with seemingly boundless energy. The scope of his effort and his range were not suggested at all in the building which would stand apart from the library, the classrooms, and the laboratories. He did not have a plan in mind for the right kind of memorial—he didn't give that kind of thing much thought. He did feel that once a person's name had been used on a building, it was not likely to be used again, even if a more appropriate opportunity opened up.

He felt deeply honored in having the chapel named after him, and he did not want to have any of the people working on his behalf feel that there was any reservation on his part. He finally accepted graciously with the conviction that it was the thing to do. Then he left behind all his discussions and his reservations and honored the building himself by his associations with it.

Roy Cheville died on Sunday April 6, 1986 in Independence. By his pre-arrangement his body was taken to the University of Iowa Medical School for his last laboratory assignment. The day of his death was the first day of World Conference which included the Graceland program in the evening. Graceland's President, Barbara Higdon, opened the program by saying,

> Today Graceland lost a great and good friend. I want to dedicate this program to Roy Cheville. Somehow it does not seem appropriate to show our respect for him by observing a moment of silence. Will you stand and join in three cheers to send him off on his next adventure.

Many people had asked the Patriarch to write his autobiography. He did write a number of autobiographical vignettes. Part of the reason he did not write the full story was that his spiritual experiences were intensely personal. They were like the steel reinforcing rods which bind a cement foundation together (an image buried in the Alma Mater Hymn). He could not have written his story without them, yet he felt that one does not parade one's foundations.

Roy Cheville believed that sin is any action or decision which reduces the amount of good a person can do. Cheville himself should be measured by the amount of good he did in the lives of persons multiplied by the number of those persons. Perhaps, through his writings, the number of persons influenced positively by him will continue grow.

Graceland has changed in many ways since Roy Cheville left to pursue other aspects of his life's work. In this secular time many practices of Graceland are of necessity different from those of Cheville's day. He would undoubtedly disapprove of some of them. However, he would recognize many of the intrinsic characteristics that define Graceland's soul. The spirit-centered, person-centered, community-centered institution of today is a product of his vision and his effort. He would also recognize the continuing effort to integrate the experiences of classroom, chapel, residence hall, disciplinary decisions, and student government. He would recognize these characteristics because he played a major role in their creation. His connection to Graceland lives on.

On some still quiet night on Graceland's campus, one can almost hear the resonant, enthusiastic voice of Roy Cheville singing,

> This is my home, the Hilltop where my heart is,
> Where I found friends, who link their hearts with mine,
> Where bonds were made that hold across the ocean
> With those who walked these paths among the pine.
> In memory, I'll come back to this homeland
> And feel anew the pull of things divine.

Notes

1. Roscoe Faunce was Roy's closest friend during the "Doc" years. When Cheville died he had in his possession Roscoe Faunce's well-marked and well-worn copy of Shakespeare's plays. It is now in the Graceland library.

APPENDIX A.
Books by Roy A. Cheville

The author has assigned a coded designator to each publication of Roy Cheville. The code begins with four digits for the year of publication. Then follows one or more letters to indicate sequence within the year. Thus 1942A is his first publication in the year 1942. When there were more than 26 publications in a given year, two letters may appear after the year.

1939A. *The Bible in Everyday Living*, (Independence, Mo. Herald House, 1939), 343 pages. First printing 1939A. Reprinted 1944A, 1948A, 1951A, 1956A, 1961A. Utilizes material in 1934A, 1935B, 1935C, AND 1935D.

1941A. *The Branch of Today and Tomorrow*, (Independence, Mo. Herald House, 1941), 160 p. Library of Congress listing BX 8671.A1R4 1941.

1941E. *Official Zion's League Handbook*, (Independence, Mo. Herald House, 1941), 285 p. Written by a class in Religious Education under the direction of Roy A. Cheville, edited for publication by Floyd M. McDowell and C. B. Woodstock, 1941.

1942A. Dissertation: *The Role of Religious Education in the Accommodation of a Sect*. Cover title; Religious Education and Sectarian Accommodation. Thesis, University of Chicago, 1942. Library of Congress Number BX8672.C45, typescript, carbon copy. viii, 405 l. 32cm. Chicago, 1942. (University of Chicago Library call number BX 10999.)

1946A. *Through the West Door*, (Independence, Mo. Herald House, 1946), 327 p. A history of Graceland College.

1950G. *The Hymnal for Youth*, (Independence, Mo. Herald House, 1950). Cheville was a member of a committee including Anne Morgan, Aleta Runkle, and Chris B. Hartshorn, which developed the book. The entire hymnal was reprinted in 1951 and 1955.

1951B. *Growing Up in Religion*, (Independence, Mo. Herald House, 1951), 233 p. Library of Congress listing BV 4531.2.C45. Reprinted in 1953.

1954A. *When They Seek Counsel*, (Independence, Mo. Herald House, 1954), 133 p.

1955A. *They Sang of the Restoration*, (Independence, Mo. Herald House, 1955), 267 p. Library of Congress listing BV 420.A1C4.

1955P. *The Latter Day Saints and Family Life*, (Independence, Mo. Herald House, 1955), pp. 108. Reprinted in 1957.

1956B. *By What Authority?* (Independence, Mo. Herald House, 1956), 96 p. Reprinted in 1959. Library of Congress listing BX 8674.C48.

1958A. *Ten Considerations For Family Living*, (Independence, Mo. Herald House, 1958), 150 p. Library of Congress listing BX 8672.C47.

1959B. *The Field of Theology*, (Independence, Mo. Herald House, 1959), 144 p. Library of Congress listing BX 8674.C5. (Univ. of Chicago. listing BX 8671.C517.) Reprinted in 1960.

1960A. *Meet Them in the Scriptures*, (Independence, Mo. Herald House, 1960), 224 p. Library of Congress Listing BS 571.C485.

1962A. *Did the Light Go Out?* (Independence, Mo. Herald House, 1962), 261 p. Library of Congress listing BX 1765.2.C5. Library of Congress Catalog Card No. 62-21344. (University of Chicago Library listing BX 1765.C54.)

1962C. *Spirituality in the Space Age*, (Independence, Mo. Herald House, 1962), 264 p. Library of Congress listing BL 254.C47.

1964A. *Scriptures From Ancient America*, (Independence, Mo. Herald House, 1964), 368 p. Library of Congress listing BX 8628.C5. (Univ. of Chicago Library listing BV 8628.C53)

1966A. *Spiritual Health*, (Independence, Mo. Herald House, 1966), 412 p. Library of Congress listing, BX 8656.C48. (Univ. of Chicago Library listing BV 8656.C52.)

1968A. *When Teen-Agers Talk Theology*, (Independence, Mo. Herald House, 1968), 445 p. Library of Congress listing BX 8643.Y6C5.

1970A. *They Made a Difference*, (Independence, Mo. Herald House, 1970), 350 p. Library of Congress listing BX 8678.A2.

1970E. Chapter, "Charlotte Cheville," pp. 75–80 in Emma M. Phillips, (Ed.), *Dedicated to Serve*. (Independence, Mo. Herald House, 1970), 211 p.

1971A. *The Book of Mormon Speaks For Itself*, (Independence, Mo. Herald House, 1971), 203 p. 21 cm. Library of Congress number BX 8627.C47.

1972A. *Expectations For Endowed Living*, (Independence, Mo. Herald House, 1961), 122 p. Library of Congress listing BX 8656.C47.

1975A. *Spiritual Resources Are Available Today*, (Independence, Mo. Herald House, 1975), 2 volumes. Library of Congress listing BX 8656.C49.

1977A. *Joseph and Emma Smith; Companions For Seventeen and a Half Years, 1827–1844*, (Independence, Mo. Herald House, 1977), 206 p. Library of Congress listing BX 8695.S6C53.

1978A. *Humor in Gospel Living*, (Independence, Mo. Herald House, 1978), 153 p. Library of Congress listing BR 115.H84C47.

APPENDIX B
The Published Hymns of Roy A. Cheville

1921. Hymn, "Song of Entreaty." In Margaret Davis (Ed.) "A Hundred Years of Latter Day Saintism—A most effective pageant, especially adapted for production at Reunions." *Autumn Leaves*, 1921, Vol. 34, No. 5, pp 223,f.

1928D. Hymn, "Sons of Graceland—song" [The Alma Mater Hymn], in *Autumn Leaves*, vol. 41, #9:p. 386, Sept. 1928. Text set to music. First publication of the Graceland Alma Mater Hymn. Republished 1928D, 1933C, 1933J, 1950M, 1955B, 1956Y, 1960AG. Additional verse (humorous) in 1972F. For a description of its writing, see 1955B.

 1933C. Hymn, "Alma Mater Hymn," No. 434 in *Saints' Hymnal*, Herald House, 1933. Text set to music.

 1933J. Hymn, "Alma Mater Hymn," in *Graceland Tower*, March 19, 1933, in text form.

 1950M. Hymn, "O Come Ye Sons of Graceland All," No. 395 in *The Hymnal For Youth*, Herald House 1950. Text set to music.

 1955B. Hymn, "Sons of Graceland," [Alma Mater Hymn], in Cheville 1955A, *They Sang of The Restoration*, Herald House, 1955.

 1956Y. Hymn, "O Come Ye Sons of Graceland," Number 523 in *The Hymnal*, Herald House, 1956. Text set to music.

1960AG. Hymn, "O come, ye sons of Graceland," Number 523 in *The Little Hymnal*, Herald House 1960, in poem form.

1972F. Additional verse to Graceland Alma Mater Hymn. In Edwards, Paul, *The Hilltop Where*, The Venture Foundation, Lamoni, Iowa, 1972.

1930K. Camp song, "We're coming back to you, Dear Old Nauvoo," In article, "The Boys' and Girls' Camp at Nauvoo," *Saints' Herald*, Vol. 77, # 31, p. 859, July 30, 1930. Republished 1930K, 1934B.

1934B. Hymn, "Dear Old Nauvoo," in the *Lamoni Chronicle* of March 8, 1934, p. 1, article entitled "R. A. Cheville addresses audience on Nauvoo."

1932B. Prayer Hymn, "A Youth's Prayer of Thanksgiving." In Cheville 1932A, *What it Means to Be a Latter Day Saint*, p. 46, Herald House, 1932. In poem form. Republished 1938L, 1941I, 1944O, 1946G, 1947N, 1948T, 1949I, 1952F, 1954M, 1955N.

1933F. Hymn, "I Know That My Redeemer Lives," pp. 22f in Cheville 1933E, Quarterly, *Membership Qualifications*, Herald House, 1933. In poem form. Republished 1939O, 1942O, 1945H, 1947K, 1949L, 1956AB, 1959R.

1933G. Poem, "Speak of the Best," pp. 46 in Cheville 1933E, Quarterly, *Membership Qualifications*, Herald House, 1933.

1933I. Hymn, "God Send Us Men," pp. 10 in Cheville 1933H, Quarterly, *The Program of the Church*, Herald House, 1933. In poem form. Republished 1939N, 1942Q.

1939G. Hymn, "Are Ye Able." P. 33 in Pamphlet [1939F] *Youth Shares, A Manual of Review, The Youth Conference, June 10–18, 1939 At Graceland College*, edited by Roy Cheville, Herald House.

1939H. Hymn, "O Lord of Life, of Light and Inspiration." P. 46 in Pamphlet [1939F] *Youth Shares, A Manual of Review, The Youth Conference, June 10–18, 1939 At Graceland College*, edited by Roy Cheville, Herald House. (Written for the convention.)

1939I. Hymn, "Our Homes We Dedicate to Thee." P. 5 in Pamphlet [1939F] *Youth Shares, A Manual of Review, The Youth Conference, June 10–18, 1939 At Graceland College*, edited by Roy Cheville, Herald House.

1941F. Hymn, "The Church of Christ Is Calling." In [1941E] *Official Zion's League Handbook*, Herald House, 1941. In poem form.

1941G. Hymn, "Rise, O Youth," in [1941E] *Official Zion's League Handbook*, Herald House, 285 p. Written by a class in Religious Education under the direction of Roy A. Cheville, edited for publication by Floyd M. McDowell and C. B. Woodstock, 1941.

1941H. Hymn, "Forward," in [1941E] *Official Zion's League Handbook*, Herald House, 285 p. Written by a class in Religious Education under the direction of Roy A. Cheville, edited for publication by Floyd M. McDowell and C. B. Woodstock, 1941.

1941I. Hymn, "Come Up Higher," in [1941E] *Official Zion's League Handbook*, Herald House, 285 p.

1941J. Hymn, "Open My Eyes," in [1941E] *Official Zion's League Handbook*, Herald House, 1941. In poem form. First time published. Republished 1941J, 1950J, 1953L (in German), 1955F, 1956S, 1960AC, 1968L, 1974G, 1975B (in Spanish), 1981N. For a description of its writing see 1955F.

1950J. Hymn, "Open My Eyes, O Lord," Number 365 in *The Hymnal For Youth*. Herald House, 1950. First time set in print with music.

1953L. Hymn, "Open My Eyes, O Lord," translated into German by P. E. Radelow, with the title, "Offne Die Augen Mir," In *Lieder Der Heiligen*, Herald House, 1953.

1955F. Hymn, "Open My Eyes," in Cheville 1955A, *They Sang of the Restoration*. Herald House, 1955. In poem form.

1956S. Hymn, "Open My Eyes, O Lord," Number 355 in *The Hymnal*, Herald House, 1956. Text and tune set in print.

1960AC. Hymn, "Open my eyes, O Lord," Number 355 in *The Little Hymnal*, Herald House 1960, in poem form.

1968L. Hymn, "Open My Eyes, O Lord," No. 355 in *World Conference Hymnal* 1968. Text and tune reprinted from *The Hymnal*, 1956S.

1974G. Hymn, "Open My Eyes, O Lord," No 355 in *World Conference Hymnal* 1974. Text and tune reprinted from *The Hymnal*, 1956S.

1975B. "Open My Eyes" (Abre, Emanuel), translated into Spanish in *Hinario*, Herald House, 1975, 90.

1981N. Hymn, "Open My Eyes, O Lord," no. 454 in *Hymns of the Saints*, Herald House, 1981. Text and tune.

1941K. Hymn, "Prayer of Dedication," in [1941E] *Official Zion's League Handbook*, Herald House, 285 p.

Written by a class in Religious Education under the direction of Roy A. Cheville, edited for publication by Floyd M. McDowell and C. B. Woodstock, 1941.

1944I. Hymn, "Forward Thro' the ages," In article in *Saints' Herald*, "Materials for anniversary on June 27." Vol. 91, #25:p. 790, June 17, 1944. In poem form. [for centennial of Joseph Smith's death]

1944J. Hymn, "We read Thy Word of Promise," in article in *Saints' Herald*, "Materials for anniversary on June 27." Vol. 91, #25:p. 790, June 17, 1944. In poem form. [for centennial of Joseph Smith's death]. Republished 1950T.

> 1950T. Hymn, "We read Thy word of Promise, Lord." p. 378 in *The Hymnal For Youth*, Herald House, 1950.

1944K. Hymn, "For All Those Saints," in article in *Saints' Herald*, "Materials for anniversary on June 27." Vol. 91, #25:p. 790, June 17, 1944. In poem form. [for centennial of Joseph Smith's death]

1950H. Third Stanza of Hymn, "O Jesus the Giver," Number 338 in *The Hymnal For Youth*. Herald House, 1950. Text set to music. Original text by W. W. Phelps. Republished 1950H, 1956I, 1968J, 1974D, 1981E.

1950I. Hymn, "Hast Thou Heard It," Number 354 in *The Hymnal For Youth*, Herald House, 1950. Text set to music. The text in poem form also appears on pp. 365f within an order of worship. The words are somewhat different. Republished 1950I, 1953M (in German), 1955D (altered), 1956U, 1960AD, 1975D (in Spanish), 1981K (altered).

1953M. Hymn, "Hast Thou Heard It, O My Brother," translated into German by P. E. Radelow, with the title, "Hast Du Es Gehort, Mein Bruder," In *Lieder Der Heiligen*, Herald House, 1953. Text set to music.

1955D. Hymn, Hast Thou Heard It, O My Brother, in Cheville 1955A *They Sang of the Restoration*. Book: Herald House, 1955. In poem form.

1956U. Hymn, "Hast Thou Heard It," Number 411 in *The Hymnal*, Herald House, 1956. Text set to music.

Cheville 1960AD. Hymn, "Hast thou heard it?" Number 411 in *The Little Hymnal*, Herald House 1960, in poem form.

1975D. "Hast Thou Heard It?" (Meu Irmao, Tu Ja Ouviste), translated into Spanish in *Hinario*, Herald House, 1975, 131.

1981K. Hymn, "Hast Thou Heard It, O My Brother," no. 390 in *Hymns of the Saints*, Herald House, 1981. Text set to music.

1950K. Hymn, "All Things Are Thine," No. 369 in *The Hymnal For Youth*. Herald House, 1950. Republished 1950K, 1953K (in German), 1955E, 1956V, 1960AE, 1968M, 1974H, 1975C (in Spanish), 1981L (altered).

1953K. Hymn, "All Things Are Thine," translated into German by P. E. Radelow, with the title, "Die Guter Welt Sind Dein." In *Lieder Der Heiligen*, Herald House, 1953.

1955E. Hymn, "All Things Are Thine, O Lord of Life," in Cheville 1955A, *They Sang of the Restoration*, Herald House, 1955. Text in poem form.

1956V. Hymn, "All Things Are Thine," Number 417 in *The Hymnal*, Herald House, 1956. Text set to music.

1960AE. Hymn, "All things are thine." Number 417 in *The Little Hymnal*, Herald House 1960, in poem form.

1968M. Hymn, All Things Are Thine, No. 417 in World Conference Hymnal 1968. Reprinted from *The Hymnal*, 1956V. Text set to music.

1974H. Hymn, All Things Are Thine, No. 417 in *World Conference Hymnal 1974*. Reprinted from The Hymnal, 1956V. Text set to music.

1975C. "All Things Are Thine" (Tudo E De Ti), translated into Spanish in *Hinario*, Herald House, 1975, 126.

1981L. Hymn, "All Things Are Thine," no. 397 in *Hymns of the Saints*, Herald House, 1981. Text set to music.

1950L. Hymn, "Master, Speak! Thy Servant Heareth," no. 370 in *The Hymnal For Youth*. Herald House, 1950. Text set to music. Republished 1950L, 1953J (in German), 1956T, 1981M.

1953J. Hymn, "Master Speak! Thy Servant Heareth," translated into German by P. E. Radelow, with the title, "Meister, Sprich, Dein Diener Horet." In *Lieder Der Heiligen*, Herald House, 1953.

1956T. Hymn, "Master, Speak, Thy Servant Heareth!," Number 367 in *The Hymnal*, Herald House, 1956. Text set to music.

1981M. Hymn, "Master, Speak! Thy Servant Heareth," no. 410 in *Hymns of the Saints*, Herald House, 1981. Text set to music.

1950N. Hymn, "Heaven can be where'er the Lord lifts us from lowly sphere." P. 367 in *The Hymnal For*

Youth, Herald House 1950, reprinted 1951, 1955.

1950P. Hymn, "Commitment Hymn." P. 369 in *The Hymnal For Youth*, published by Herald House in 1950 reprinted 1951, 1955.

1950Q. Hymn, "We honor those, our Father, Whose service honored Thee." P. 370 in *The Hymnal For Youth*, Herald House 1950, reprinted 1951, 1955.

1950R. Hymn adapted from W. G. Tarrant, "Glory to the heroes," P. 373 in *The Hymnal For Youth*, Herald House, 1950, reprinted 1951, 1955.

1950S. Hymn, "Lo, the time is now fulfilled!." P. 374 in *The Hymnal For Youth*, Herald House, 1950, reprinted 1951, 1955.

1950V. Hymn, "Walk Thou with me, O Lord of love." P. 380 in *The Hymnal For Youth*, Herald House, 1950, reprinted 1951, 1955.

1950W. Hymn adapted from Adelaide Proctor, "Softly the shadows fall," P. 380 in *The Hymnal For Youth*, Herald House, 1950, reprinted 1951, 1955.

1950Y. Hymn, "Truth has no single voice." P. 382 in *The Hymnal For Youth*, Herald House, 1950, reprinted 1951, 1955.

1950AA. Hymn. "Sacred books, the Church's treasure." P. 385 in *The Hymnal For Youth*, Herald House, 1950. Reprinted 1950AA, 1956J, 1960B(partial), 1960X.

    1956J. Hymn, "Sacred Books, the Church's Treasure," Number 235 in *The Hymnal*, Herald House, 1956.

    1960B. Hymn, "Thanks to those who sought as prophets." In Cheville 1960A, *Meet Them in the Scriptures*, Herald House, 1960. Library of Congress Listing BS 571.C485. In poem form. Revised from 1950AA, 1956J, 1960B (partial), 1960X.

    1960X. Hymn, "Sacred books, the Church's treasure," Number 235 in *The Little Hymnal*, Herald House 1960, test set to music (St. Asaph). Reprinted 1950AA, 1956J, 1960B(partial), 1960X.

1950AB. Hymn. "Thou, who through all the ages spoke." P. 387 in *The Hymnal For Youth*, Herald House, 1950, reprinted 1951, 1955.

1950AC. Hymn. "O send Thy Spirit, Lord." P. 387 in *The Hymnal For Youth*, Herald House, 1950, reprinted 1951, 1955.

1953D. Hymn, "Conviction." In Article in *Saints' Herald*, "These things I offer you." Vol. 100, #16:p. 372, April 20, 1953. In poem form. Republished 1953D, 1955C, 1962B.

    1955C. Hymn, "Conviction," in Cheville 1955A, *They Sang of the Restoration*, Herald House, 1955. In poem form.

    1962B. Hymn, "It May Be I Shall Never Trace" (CONVICTION). P. 26 in, *Did the Light Go Out?* Herald House, 1962. In poem form.

1955G. Hymn, "The Christ of Every Age" (Afar in Old Judea), in Cheville 1955A, *They Sang of the Restoration*, Herald House, 1955. In poem form. Republished 1955G, 1956P (altered), 1960AB, 1964I (in Spanish), 1974E (altered), 1981F (altered).

    1956P. Hymn, "Afar in Old Judea" , No. 287 in *The Hymnal*, Herald House, 1956. Altered text set to music.

1960AB. Hymn, "Afar in old Judea," Number 287 in *The Little Hymnal*, Herald House 1960, in poem form.

1964I. Hymn, "Alla En Judea Antigua," ("Afar in Old Judea"), translated into Spanish by Clair E. Weldon, No. 89 in *Hinario*, Herald House, 1964.

1974E. Hymn, "Afar in Old Judea," No 287 in *World Conference Hymnal 1974*. Altered text set in music.

1981F. Hymn, "Afar in Old Judea" , No. 296 in *Hymns of the Saints*, Herald House. Text set to music.

1956H. Hymn, "My Soul, Praise the Lord," Altered by Roy A. Cheville, original by William Kethe, Number 12 in *The Hymnal*, Herald House, 1956. (Altered in 1952) Republished 1956H, 1960W, 1981D.

1956K. Hymn, "O Lord, Thy People Gathered Here," No. 240 in *The Hymnal*, Herald House, 1956. Text set to music. Tune: Truro. Republished 1956K, 1960Y, 1981J.

1960Y. Hymn, "O Lord, thy people gathered here," Number 240 in *The Little Hymnal*, Herald House 1960, in poem form.

1981J. Hymn, "O Lord, Thy People Gathered Here," No. 352 in *Hymns of the Saints*, Herald House, 1981. Text set to music.

1956L. Hymn, "Stand, Soldier of the Cross," altered by R. A. Cheville, Number 246 in *The Hymnal*, Herald House, 1956. Original words by Edward H. Bickersteth. Republished 1960Z.

1956M. Hymn, "O Master to All Children Dear," No. 249 in The Hymnal, *Herald House*, 1956. Text set to music. Republished 1956M, 1981I (altered).

1981I. Hymn, "O Master to All Children Dear," No. 347 in *Hymns of the Saints*, Herald House, 1981. Text set to music.

1956N. Hymn, "Friend of the Home," altered by R. A. Cheville, Number 251 in *The Hymnal*, Herald House, 1956. Original words by Howell Elvet Lewis.

1956O. Hymn, "For Bread Before Us Broken," No. 268 in *The Hymnal*, Herald House, 1956. Text set to music. Tune: Ewing. Republished 1956O, 1960AA, 1978C, 1981H.

1960AA. Hymn, "For bread before us broken," Number 268 in *The Little Hymnal*, Herald House 1960, in poem form.

1978C. Hymn, "For Bread Before Us Broken," Printed in the proceedings of the 1978 World Conference Communion Service April 2, 1978. Reprinted from *The Hymnal*, 1956Q. Text set to music.

1981H. Hymn, "For Bread Before Us Broken," No. 340 in *Hymns of the Saints*, Herald House, 1981. Text set to music.

1956Q. Hymn, "Forth in Thy Name," altered by R. A. Cheville, Number 314 in *The Hymnal*, Herald House, 1956. Original words by Charles Wesley. Text set to music. Republished 1956Q, 1968K, 1974K, 1981P.

1956R. Hymn, "Oh, Sometimes the Shadows," altered by R. A. Cheville, Number 354 in *The Hymnal*, Herald House, 1956. Original words by E. Johnson.

1956W. Hymn, "Send Forth Thy Light, O Zion," No. 431 in *The Hymnal*, Herald House, 1956. Text set to music. Republished 1956W, 1960AF, 1968N, 1974I, 1976B, 1978B, 1980A, 1981G, 1992.

1960AF. Hymn, "Send forth thy light, O Zion!" Number 431 in *The Little Hymnal*, Herald House 1960, in poem form.

1968N. Hymn, "Send Forth Thy Light, O Zion," No. 431 in *World Conference Hymnal 1968*. Reprinted from *The Hymnal*, 1956W. Text set to music.

1974I. Hymn, "Send Forth Thy Light, O Zion," No. 431 in *World Conference Hymnal 1974*. Reprinted from *The Hymnal*, 1956W. Text set to music.

1976B. Hymn, "Send Forth Thy Light, O Zion," No. 431 in *World Conference 1976 Business Meeting Hymns*. Reprinted from *The Hymnal*, 1956W. Text set to music

1978B. Hymn, "Send Forth Thy Light, O Zion," No. 431 in *World Conference 1978 Business Meeting Hymns*. Reprinted from The Hymnal, 1956W. Text set to music.

1980A. Hymn, "Send Forth Thy Light, O Zion," No. 431 in *World Conference 1980 Business Meeting Hymns*. Reprinted from The Hymnal, 1956W. Text set to music.

1981G. Hymn, "Send Forth Thy Light, O Zion," No. 317 in *Hymns of the Saints*, Herald House, 1981. Text set to music.

1992. Hymn, "Send Forth Thy Light, O Zion," No. 317 in *1992 World Conference Hymns*, Herald House, 1956. Text set to music.

1956X. Hymn, "Thou Hast Been Our Guide," altered by R. A. Cheville, Number 520 in *The Hymnal*, Herald House, 1956. Original author unknown.

1959O. Hymn, "Speak Thou Today, O Lord," in poem form. In article in *Saints' Herald*, "These are my people." Vol. 106, #52:p. 1235, December 28, 1959.

1968E. Hymn, "Hymn of Zion builders." in poem form. *Saints' Herald*, Vol. 115, p. 359 May 15, 1968.

1979A. Hymn, "Let Us Sing a Worldwide Anthem," No. A-27 in *Sesquicentennial Resource Booklet*, RLDS History Commission, 1979. Republished 1979A, 1980B, 1981O, 1982, 1984B, 1986.

    1980B. Hymn, "Let Us Sing a Worldwide Anthem" No. B in *World Conference 1980 Business Meeting Hymns*.

    1981O. Hymn, "Let Us Sing a Worldwide Anthem," No. 468 in *Hymns of the Saints*, Herald House, 1981.

    1982. Hymn, "Let Us Sing a Worldwide Anthem" No. 468 in *World Conference 1982 Business Meeting Hymns*. Reprinted from *Hymns of the Saints*, 1981O.

    1984B. Hymn, "Let Us Sing a Worldwide Anthem" No. 468 in *World Conference 1984 Business Meeting Hymns*. Reprinted from *Hymns of the Saints*, 1981O.

•   1986. Hymn, "Let Us Sing a Worldwide Anthem," No. 468 in *World Conference 1986 Business Meeting Hymns*. Reprinted from *Hymns of the Saints*, 1981O.

1995A. Hymn, "Here At This Altar," in Ritchie, M.L., *Roy Cheville: The Graceland College Years*, Graceland College, 1995.

1995B. Hymn, "What A Friend We Have in Jesus! He is Steadfast," in Ritchie, M.L., *Roy Cheville: The Graceland College Years*, Graceland College, 1995.

1995C. Hymn, "Home of the Open Heart," in Ritchie, M.L., *Roy Cheville: The Graceland College Years*, Graceland College, 1995.

1995D. Hymn, "This Is My Home," in Ritchie, M.L., *Roy Cheville: The Graceland College Years*, Graceland College, 1995.

APPENDIX C
Pamphlets by Roy A. Cheville

1923. Master's Thesis, "The function of music in Religious Education." University of Chicago, Dept. of Practical Theology, University of Chicago Library call number ML 3999.C54.

1925. D.B. Thesis, "The Junior Church." University of Chicago, Dept. of Practical Theology. University of Chicago Library call number BV 9999.C485.

1929E. Booklet, "Lamoni, The Story of a Town Established Fifty Years Ago, 1879–1929." 40 p. Published September 13, 1929 by the Lamoni Semi-Centennial Committee. The five members of the Booklet committee were, G. N. Briggs, Chairman, Lucy Lysinger, Emma Chasey, Lyda Elefson, and Roy Cheville.

1930J. (Editor) Quarterly, "Education" Gospel Quarterly, Adult April–June 1930, v5 #3, 58 p. (Church History Series). The history and place of education among Latter Day Saints.

1932A. Quarterly, "The Relation of Our Church to Other Churches, Herald House. Gospel Quarterly Senior High," 1932, v41 #1, 56 p. Revised in 1938 as Volume 47, in 1941 as Volume 50, in 1944, 1946, 1947, 1948, 1949, 1952, 1954 and 1955 as Volume 53, and in 1958–1959 as Course A.

1933D. Quarterly, "Beliefs Of Our Church," Herald House. Gospel Quarterly Senior High. 1933, v41, #2, 72 p. Revised in 1939 as Volume 47, in 1942 as Volume 50, in 1945, 1947, 1948, 1949, 1950,

1953, and 1956 as Volume 53, and in 1958–1959 as Course A.

1933E. Quarterly, "Membership Qualifications," Herald House. Gospel Quarterly Senior High. 1933, v41 #3, 71 p. Revised in 1939 as Volume 47, in 1942 as Volume 50, in 1945, 1947, 1948, 1949, 1950, 1953, and 1956 as Volume 53, and in 1958–1959 as Course A.

1933H. Quarterly, "The Program of the Church," Herald House. Gospel Quarterly Senior High, 1933, v41, #4, 61 p. Revised in 1939 as Volume 47, in 1942 as Volume 50, in 1945, 1947, 1948, 1949, 1950, 1953, and 1956 as Volume 53, and in 1959 as Course A.

1934A. Quarterly, "How the Bible Came to Be," Herald House. Gospel Quarterly Older Young People, 1934, v42 #1, 64 p.

1935B. Quarterly, "How to Read the Bible," Herald House. Gospel Quarterly Older Young People, 1935, v42 #2, 64 p.

1935C. Quarterly, "How the Bible Reveals God," Herald House. Gospel Quarterly Older Young People, 1935, v42 #3, 64 p.

1935D. Quarterly, "How Shall We Use the Bible?" Herald House. Gospel Quarterly Older Young People, 1935, v42 #4, 64p.

1936I. Quarterly, "A Journey Into Ancient Times and Places," Gospel Quarterly, Intermediate Grade, Vol. 25, #1, 64 p. Herald House, 1936. Revised in 1942 as vol. 31. Republished as 1936I, 1942E, and 1945A.

1937A. Quarterly, "People Who Lived in Book of Mormon Times," Gospel Quarterly Intermediate. Herald House, 1937, v25 #2, 64 p. (Revised in

1943 as volume 31, 1943G). Republished as 1937A, 1943G.

1937B. Quarterly, "How the Book of Mormon Helps Us Today," Herald House. Gospel Quarterly Intermediate. 1937, v25 #3, 61 p. (Revised in 1943 as volume 31) Revised as 1943H.

1937C. Quarterly, "How the Book of Mormon Helps Us in Everyday Living," Herald House. Gospel Quarterly Intermediate. 1937, v25 #4, 64 p. (Revised in 1943 as volume 31, 1943I)

1939B. Quarterly, "History and Significance of the Family in the Work of the Church," Herald House. Gospel Quarterly Adult, Oct–Dec 1939, v15 #1, 64 p.

1939F. Pamphlet, "Youth Shares, A Manual of Review, The Youth Conference, June 10–18, 1939 at Graceland College, edited by Roy Cheville, Herald House, 92 p.

1940A. Pamphlet, "Youth Shares in Evangelism," Herald House, 1940.

1941J. Quarterly, "The Branch of Today and Tomorrow," Herald House, 1941, 98 p. plus Study Guide, total 119 pages. First published in 1941 as the "Official Report of the Youth Conference of 1941." Revised as 1945J.

1942B. Pamphlet, "The Latter Day Saints and Their Changing Relationship to the Social Order," Herald House in Church School Leadership Series 75p. Library of Congress listing BX 8671.C45. (University of Chicago Library call number BX 8671.C52.)

1943E. Quarterly, "Torchbearers of the Bible," Herald House, 1943. Vol. 51, #2, Senior Young People, 72 p.

1943F. Quarterly, "Torchbearers of the Book of Mormon," Herald House, 1943, Vol. 51, # 3. Senior Young People, 77 p.

1944B. Quarterly, "Overviews of the Book of Mormon," Herald House, 1944, 75p. Gospel Quarterly, Young Adult, v52, 1944 #2. Republished as 1944B, 1945O, 1948R, 1957A.

1944C. Quarterly, "A Journey With the Church," edited by Roy Cheville, Herald House. Units by Georgia Metcalf, Lillian Maxwell, and Jane Ross. Gospel Quarterly, Junior High, 1944–45, v33, #1–4.

1944M. Quarterly, "We Build Loyalty to Christ," Herald House. Gospel Quarterly series, v52 #5, 32 p. 1944.

1945B. Pamphlet, "Does It Make Any Difference?" Herald House 108 p.

1945K. Quarterly, "A Journey Into Ancient America," by Roy Cheville and Charlotte Gould, Herald House. Gospel Quarterly, Junior, 1945 etc. v34 #1. 63 p. (The lessons were originally written by Roy Cheville for the junior high grade and adapted by Charlotte Gould for the junior grade.) Republished as 1945K, 1948K, 1955H.

1945L. Quarterly, "People Who Lived in Book of Mormon Times," by Roy Cheville and Charlotte Gould, Herald House. Gospel Quarterly Junior, 1945 etc. v34 #2. (The lessons were originally written by Roy Cheville for the junior high grade and adapted by Charlotte Gould for the junior grade.) Republished as 1945L, 1946E, 1948L, 1949N, 1954B.

1945M. Quarterly, "A Journey Into Old Testament Times," by Roy Cheville and Charlotte Gould, Herald House. Gospel Quarterly, Junior, 1945 etc. v34 #3. 63 p. (The lessons were originally written by Roy Cheville for the junior high grade and adapted by Charlotte Gould for the junior grade.) Second edition 1948M.

1945N. Quarterly, "People Who Lived in Old Testament Times," by Roy Cheville and Charlotte Gould, Herald House. Gospel Quarterly, Junior, 1945 etc. v34 #4. 63 p. Reissued as 1948N.

1947A. Quarterly, "How Shall We Look at Our World?" Herald House. Gospel Quarterly, Senior High, 1947 etc. v55 #1, 80 pages. First printing 1947, second printing 1950C.

1947B. Quarterly, "What Kind of World Shall We See?" Herald House in 1947, 75p. Gospel Quarterly, Senior High, 1947 etc. v55 #2. First printing 1947, second printing 1950D.

1948O. Quarterly, "What is our Church's Mission to the World?" Herald House, 1948. Gospel Quarterly, Senior High, 1948, v55 #3, 72 p. First printing 1948O, second printing 1951F.

1948P. Quarterly, "How Shall We Equip the Church For Her World Mission?" Herald House, 1948. Gospel Quarterly, Senior High, 1948, v55 #4, 79 p. Second printing 1951G.

1983. Pamphlet, "My Endowing Experiences in Kirtland Temple," Herald House 1983, 68 p.

APPENDIX D

Published Articles by Roy A. Cheville

1920. "Letter to the First Presidency," *Saints' Herald*, Vol. 67, #38, p. 918, September 22, 1920.

1922. "Pride and Porch Paint," *Autumn Leaves*, vol. 36, #3:p. 112–115, March 1922. (A Graceland College Contest Story)

1926A. "The Junior Church, I. Its Purpose and Meaning." *Saints' Herald*, vol. 73, #37:p. 872,873, Sept. 15, 1926. [Derived from Cheville 1925]

1926B. "The Junior Church, II. Its Administration." *Saints' Herald*, vol. 73, #38:p. 897, 898, Sept. 15, 1926. [Derived from Cheville 1925]

1926C. "The Junior Service, III. Activities and Program." *Saints' Herald*, vol. 73, #41: p. 976,977, October 13, 1926. [Derived from Cheville 1925]

1926D. "The Junior Church, IV. The Plan of the Service." *Saints' Herald*, vol. 73, #42: p. 1003, 1004, October 20, 1926. [Derived from Cheville 1925]

1927A. "She came to build," *Autumn Leaves*, vol. 40, #3:p. 135, March 1927. (Story about Mabel Carlile)

1927B. "Religious Life," in the *Report on Graceland College to the RLDS General Conference*, April 6, 1927, Pp. 50–51.

1927C. "Junior church services for the month of December," *RLDS Department's Journal*, vol. 1, #8, November 1927, p. 12.

1927D. "Junior Church services for LDS ordinances," *RLDS Department's Journal*, vol. 1, #9, December 1927, p. 10.

1927E. "The place of music in the church," *Saints' Herald, Conference Daily Edition*, April 16, 1927, pp. 84–86. Partly based on Cheville 1923.

1927F. "Graceland's answer to the College religious problem." *Saints' Herald*, vol. 74, P. 863, July 27, 1927.

1927G. "Loyalties of Life," *Graceland Record*, May 17, 1927.

1928A. "A service for juniors," *RLDS Department's Journal*, vol. 1, # 11, February 1928, p. 26.

1928B. "Lamoni Stake—a description," *Saints' Herald*, vol. 75, #3:p. 957, Aug. 15, 1928.

1928C. "Lamoni Stake—an interpretation," *Saints' Herald*, vol. 75, #34:p. 980, Aug. 22, 1928.

1928E. "Religious Education," in the report on Graceland College, in the *Conference Daily Edition of the Saints' Herald*. October 2, 1928, pp. 9–10.

1928F. "Our College Program in Operation," *Conference Daily Edition of the Saints' Herald*. October 4, 1928, pp. 39–40.

1928G. "Condition and Desires of the Church and Its Membership," Statement by Wilbur E. Prall and Roy A. Cheville in the *Conference Daily Edition of the Saints' Herald*. October 6, 1928, pp. 59–60.

1928H. "At a College Sanctuary." *Saints' Herald*, vol. 75, #41:p. 1171, 1172, October 10, 1928.

1929A. "The Old Man," *Vision*, vol. 42, #1:p. 7, Jan. 1929.

1929B. "Singing A Capella " *Vision*, vol. 42, #5:p. 216, May, 1929.

1929C. "New books in review," *Vision*, vol. 42, #8:p. 365, Aug. 1929. (Review of *Methods of Private Relig-*

ious Living by Henry Nelson Wieman, Macmillan).

1929D. "Good Sabbath," *Vision*, vol. 42, #9:p. 399, Sept. 1929.

1929F. "On discovering details," *Vision*, vol. 42, #10:p. 455, Oct. 1929.

1929G. "A Christmas vesper service," *RLDS Department's Journal*, vol. 3, #9, December 1929, p. 30.

1929H. "The Call of the Old West Door," *Saints' Herald*, vol. 76, # 47, p. 1428, November 20, 1929.

1930A. "What has the church done?" *Vision*, vol. 43, #4:p. 148–149, April, 1930.

1930B. "New books in review." *Vision*, vol. 43, #4:p. 204–205, Apr. 1930. Reviews *The Effective Christian College*, by Laird T. Hites.

1930C. "The intangible influence of a college." *Saints' Herald*, vol. 77, #28:pp. 762f, July 9, 1930.

1930D. "A cross section of Graceland life." *Saints' Herald*, vol. 77, #33:pp. 902–911, Aug. 13, 1930.

1930E. "Graceland makes men of the future." *Saints' Herald*, vol. 77, #37:p. 1011, Sept. 10, 1930.

1930F. "New books in review." *Vision*, vol. 43, #9:p. 491, Sept. 1930. Review of *The Reconstruction of Belief*, by Charles Gore.

1930G. "The graduate." *Vision*, Inside front cover of June 1930 issue.

1930H. "Growing up in religion." *Vision*, vol. 43, #8:pp. 397, 404, Aug. 1930.

1930I. "The positive life." *Vision*, vol. 43, #12:pp. 600f, Dec. 1930.

1931A. "New books in review." *Vision*, vol. 44, #1:p. 27, January 1931. Review of *Religion in the American College*, by Edward Sterling Boyer.

1931B. "The Teacher." *Vision*, vol. 44, #3, inside front cover, March 1931.

1931C. "New books in review." *Vision*, vol. 44, #3:p. 124, Mar. 1931. Review of *The College Student Thinking It Through*, by Jessie A. Charters.

1931D. "Does Graceland offer real preparation?" *Saints' Herald*, vol. 78, #30:pp. 706f, July 29, 1931.

1931E. "Friendly Queries about Revelation." *Zion's Ensign*, vol. 43, No. 34, August 20, 1932, pp. 538, 539. [Similar, but not identical to 1939D]

1931F. "The Function of Theology." *Zion's Ensign*, vol. 43, No. 39, September 24, 1931, pp. 612–614.

1931G. "Acting Your Age in Religion," reported in the *Graceland Tower*, February 17, 1931, under the headline, "Students Discuss Religious Life."

1931H. "The Greatness of Washington And Lincoln." Reported in the *Graceland Tower*, February 24, 1931.

1931I. "Sensing Our Needs," Reported in the *Graceland Tower*, February 24, 1931.

1931J. "Am I Religious?" Reported in the *Graceland Tower*, March 3, 1931.

1933A. "Worship in the young people's program." *Saints' Herald*, vol. 80, #23:p. 714, June. 6, 1933.

1933B. "High Priests in History," *High Priests Bulletin*, vol. 2, #1, October 1933, pp. 4, 5, 20–22.

1933K. "Worship in the young people's program, Reported in the *Graceland Tower* June 24, 1933, under the title, "Young People's Program Given."

1934C. "Report of Graceland College, Religious Life." *Saints' Herald, Conference Daily Edition*, April 7, 1934, pp. 59, 62.

1934D. "Themes of Worship." *Priesthood Journal*, vol. 1, #2:p. 37–41, October 1934.

1934E. "Religious Life," *Saints' Herald, Conference Daily Edition*, of April 7, 1934, p. 59, 62, within the Report of Graceland College.

1935A. "A worship service for young people." *Saints' Herald*, vol. 82, #45:pp. 1548, 1567, Dec. 3, 1935.

1936A. "Re-interpretation of religion for youth." *Saints' Herald*, vol. 83, #2:p. 40, Jan. 14, 1936.

1936B. "The setting for the sermon." *Priesthood Journal*, vol. 2, #3:pp. 28–33, January 1936.

1936C. "The preacher and his bible." *Priesthood Journal*, vol. 2, #3:pp. 68–71, January 1936.

1936D. "The use of songs for prayer meeting." *Priesthood Journal*, vol. 2, #4:pp. 29–33, April 1936.

1936E. "Religious Education," *Saints' Herald, Conference Daily Edition*, April 5–6, 1936, p. 39, in the Report of Graceland College to the RLDS General Conference.

1936F. "The priesthood in the local church school." *Priesthood Journal*, vol. 2, #5:pp. 41–43, July 1936.

1936G. "We start our educational year." *Saints' Herald*, vol. 83, #37:pp. 1159–1160, 1162, Sept. 19, 1936.

1936H. "The place of religion in Graceland." *Saints' Herald*, vol. 83, #47:p. 1482, Nov. 28, 1936.

1937D. "What the religious educator expects of a church building." *Priesthood Journal*, vol. 3, #2:p. 26–31, Apr. 1937.

1937E. "Foundations of worship." *Priesthood Journal*, vol. 3, #4:pp. 4–10, Oct. 1937.

1938A. "A tempered community," *Saints' Herald*, vol. 85, #13:p. 393–396, Mar. 26, 1938.

1938B. "From the book of experience." *Saints' Herald*, vol. 85, #25:p. 779, 789, June. 18, 1938.

1938C. "Guidance in religious thinking." *Priesthood Journal*, vol. 4, #3:p. 5–16, July 1938.

1938D. "The Christian philosophy of the home." *Priesthood Journal*, vol. 4, #4:pp. 7–12, October 1938.

1938E. "Teaching Values in Church History—Monday Class Study With Roy A. Cheville." (Reported by G. Wyatt) From *Saints' Herald Conference Daily Edition*, April 6, 1938, p. 67–68.

1938F. "Teaching Values in Church History," Reported in *Saints' Herald Conference Daily Edition*, April 7, 1938, p. 80.

1938G. "Teaching Values in Church History." Reported in *Saints' Herald Conference Daily Edition*, April 7, 1938, p. 88.

1938H. "Teaching Values in Church History." Reported in *Saints' Herald Conference Daily Edition*, April 10, 1938, p. 100.

1938I. "Teaching Values in Church History." Reported in *Saints' Herald Conference Daily Edition*, April 10, 1938, p. 104.

1938J. "Teaching Values in Church History." Reported in *Saints' Herald Conference Daily Edition*, April 11, 1938, p. 120.

1938M. "Survey of Reasons Why Families Come to Lamoni to Make Their Home." *Lamoni Chronicle*, August 11, 1938, p. 5.

1939C. "God's purpose for his chosen people." *Saints' Herald*, vol. 86, #4: pp. 107f, January 28, 1939.

1939D. "Friendly queries about revelation." *Priesthood Journal*, vol. 5, #2:pp. 30, 31, April 1939. [similar, but not identical to 1931E.]

1939E. "I met Nauvoo." *Saints' Herald*, vol. 86, #18:pp. 549, 542, May 6, 1939.

1939J. "Our branch plans." *Saints' Herald*, vol. 86, #44:pp. 1383f, November 4, 1939.

1940B. "The three delegates," *Saints' Herald*, vol. 87, #9:p. 267, March 2, 1940.

1940C. "Selection according to the circumstances and conditions," *Priesthood Journal*, vol. 6: #4:pp. 15–19, October 1940.

1940D. "Salvation of the people, the church and society," *Priesthood Journal*, vol. 6: #4:p. 61–62, October 1940.

1940E. "Guest Editorial," *Graceland Tower*, vol 20: #13, p. 2, May 31, 1940.

1941B. "These things are planned," *Saints' Herald*, vol. 88, #34:p. 1068, August 23, 1941.

1941C. "Religious education and life," *Saints' Herald*, vol. 88, #42:p. 1323–1324, 1333, October 18, 1941.

1941D. "A test in church loyalties," *Saints' Herald*, vol. 88, #42:p. 1326, October 18, 1941.

1942F. "From the book of experience—The Three Delegates," *Saints' Herald*, vol. 89, #5:p. 141, January 31, 1942.

1942G. "Latter Day Saint policy and procedure," *Saints' Herald*, vol. 89, #9:pp. 270–271, 278, February 28, 1942. [Continued in 1942H]

1942H. "Latter Day Saint policy and procedure," *Saints' Herald*, vol. 89, #11:pp. 331, 332, March 14, 1942. [Continued from 1942G]

1942I. "Religious Life," *Saints' Herald, Conference Daily Edition*, April 7, 1942, in Graceland College report to the Conference, p. 50–51.

1942J. "Freedom and vision," *Saints' Herald*, vol. 89, #28:p. 871–873, 888, July 11, 1942.

1942K. "From the book of experience," *Saints' Herald*, vol. 89, #20:p. 1238, September 26, 1942.

1942L. "This church school has an assembly period," *Guidelines to Leadership*, vol. 1, #1, pp. 10, 11, Oct. Nov. Dec. 1942.

1942R. "How is it at Graceland?," *Graceland Tower* (Supplement) December 4, 1942, p. 7.

1943A. "What of the church as a hobby?" *Saints' Herald*, vol. 90, #4:p. 109, January 23, 1943.

1943B. "The church's wartime ministry to family life," *Priesthood Journal*, vol. 9, #1:p. 24–29, January 1943.

1943C. "What of special days?" *Guidelines to Leadership*, vol. 1, #3, pp. 5–8, Apr.–June. 1943.

1943D. "We make covenant," *Saints' Herald*, vol. 90, #42:p. 1317, October 16, 1943.

1943J. "Democracy's place in a lasting peace," *Graceland Tower*, March 26, 1943, under the title, "Doctor Cheville Speaks On Peace for G.F.T.A."

1944D. "Is Latter Day Saint Education Christian?" *Guidelines to Leadership*, vol. 2, #2, pp. 4–6, Jan.–Mar. 1944.

1944E. "Shall we utilize these days?" *Guidelines to Leadership*, vol. 2, #2, pp. 20–21, Jan.–Mar. 1944.

1944F. "What kind of church home do children need?" *Guidelines to Leadership*, vol. 2, #3, pp. 3–4, Apr.–June. 1944.

1944G. "Junior highs, are they intermediates?" *Guidelines to Leadership*, vol. 2, #3, pp. 22–23, Apr.–June. 1944.

1944H. "Materials for anniversary on June 27." *Saints' Herald*, vol. 91, #25:p. 790, June 17, 1944.

1944L. "We are victorious through praying." *Guidelines*

to Leadership, vol. 2, #4, pp. 3–4,32, July.–September. 1944.

1945C. "How to build a better vocabulary." *Saints' Herald*, vol. 92, #14:p. 315, 335, April 7, 1945.

1945D [probably written by Roy Cheville]. "Music, the Church, and Graceland College," *Saints' Herald*, vol. 92, #16:p. 367, April 21, 1945.

1945E. "Camping objectives," *Guidelines to Leadership*, vol. 3, #4, pp. 3–4, July.–September. 1945.

1945P. "New Words come with new experiences says Dr. Cheville," *Graceland Tower*, 12 Jan 45, p. 2.

1946B. "How much education?" *Saints' Herald*, vol. 93, #1:p. 7, 15, January 5, 1946.

1946C. "Shall holidays be holy days?" *Guidelines to Leadership*, vol. 5, #1, pp. 12,20–21, Oct–Dec. 1946.

1946D. "This year the league plans a balanced program," *Guidelines to Leadership*, vol. 5, #1, p. 17, Oct.– Dec. 1946.

1947E. "Over the Isthmus, thoughts on immortality," *Saints' Herald*, vol. 94, #6:p. 101, 102, 110, February 8, 1947.

1947F. "One world and the church," *Saints' Herald*, vol. 94, #26:p. 597, 598, June 28, 1947.

1947G. "How can I help my friend?" *Saints' Herald*, vol. 94, #34:p. 791, August 23, 1947.

1947H. "Dads are parents, too," *Saints' Herald*, vol. 94, #38:p. 845, 846, 870, September 20, 1947.

1948B. "Our college and missions abroad," *Saints' Herald*, vol. 95, #5:p. 111, January 31, 1948.

1948C. "What about pacifism?" *Saints' Herald*, vol. 95, #11:p, 261, March 13, 1948.

1948D. "Shall there be prayer meetings?" *Saints' Herald*, vol. 95, #21:p. 485, 486, 502, May 22, 1948.

1948E. "Suggestions in planning young people's worship services at reunion," *Guidelines to Leadership*, vol. 6, #4, p. 7, July.–September. 1948.

1948F. "Graceland Futuramic," *Graceland College Bulletin (Alumni Magazine)* September 1948.

1948G. "What is a woman's place?" *Saints' Herald*, vol. 95, #48:p. 1148, November 27, 1948.

1948Q. "Religious education at Graceland College," *Guidelines to Leadership*, vol. 7, #1, pp. 51–54, Oct.–Dec. 1948.

1949A. "Conducting discussion in the adult church school," *Guidelines to Leadership*, vol. 7, #2, pp. 29–30, Jan.–Mar. 1949.

1949B. "An authorized church," *Saints' Herald*, vol. 96, #17:pp. 392,f, April 23, 1949.

1949C. "We shall still sing together," *Saints' Herald*, vol. 96, #23:p. 538, June 6, 1949.

1949D. "I wanted to go to Europe," *Saints' Herald*, vol. 96, #44:p. 1039, 1054, October 31, 1949.

1949E. "I visited the Rotterdam branch," *Saints' Herald*, vol. 96, #46:p. 1090, November 14, 1949.

1949F. "I lived with saints in Germany," *Saints' Herald*, vol. 96, #47:p. 1114, 1115, 1118, 1119, November 21, 1949.

1949G. "I was at home in the British mission," *Saints' Herald*, vol. 96, #49:p. 1161–1163, December 5, 1949.

1950A. "Letters worth sharing," *Saints' Herald*, vol. 97, #18:pp. 424,f, May 1, 1950.

1950B. "The church on the move," *Saints' Herald*, vol. 97, #33:pp. 784,f, August 14, 1950.

1950AR. "The Financial Law and social responsibility, in *The Report of the Conference of High Priests*, held at Kirtland Temple, October 5–8, 1950, pp. 48–50.

1951C. "Religion on trial," *Saints' Herald*, vol. 98, #19:pp. 452–454, May 7, 1951.

1951D. "They come from many lands," *Saints' Herald*, vol. 98, #32:pp. 751, 758, August 6, 1951.

1951E. "The Graceland spirit," *Saints' Herald*, vol. 98, #42:p. 993, October 15, 1951. [From 1946A "Through the West Door"]

1951H. "The Book of Mormon in the life of the church." In *Book of Mormon Institute Outlines*, Independence, Herald Publishing House, 1951, pp. 29–32.

1952A. "Graceland inaugurates agriculture curricula," *Saints' Herald*, vol. 99, #23:p. 548, June 9, 1952.

1952B. "And gladly teach," *Saints' Herald*, vol. 99, #23:pp. 944–946, 950, June 9, 1952.

1952C. "Campus ministry calls us," *Saints' Herald*, vol. 99, #44:pp. 1039,f, November 3, 1952.

1952D. "How shall I make ready for a Patriarchal Blessing?" *Saints' Herald*, vol. 99, #50:pp. 1196–1198, December 15, 1952.

1953B. "An enduring heritage," *Saints' Herald*, vol. 100, #4:pp. 79–81, January 26, 1953.

1953C. "These things I offer you," *Saints' Herald*, vol. 100, #16:p. 372, April 20, 1953.

1953E. "Be not afraid," *Saints' Herald*, vol. 100, #25:pp. 584,f, June 22, 1953.

1953F. "In church life after Graceland," *Guidelines to Leadership*, vol. 11, #6, pp. 20–24, Summer, 1953.

1953G. "We make things come true," *Saints' Herald*, vol. 100, #42:p. 1000, October 19, 1953.

1953H. "Our curriculum research moves on," *Guidelines to Leadership*, vol. 11, #9, pp. 1–5, Nov., 1953.

1953I. "The kind of Christmas we need this year," *Saints' Herald*, vol. 100, #51:pp. 1205–1207, 1220, December 21, 1953.

1954C. "Young ministers at Graceland," *Guidelines to Leadership*, vol. 12, #1, pp. 21–22, Jan. 1954.

1954D. "Just population or persons," *Guidelines to Leadership*, vol. 12, #2, p. 40, Feb. 1954.

1954E. "When they seek counsel," *Guidelines to Leadership*, vol. 12, #4, pp. 16–18, April 1954.

1954F. "Faith for modern life." *Saints' Herald*, vol. 101, #8:pp. 174–176, February 22, 1954.

1954G. "She exalted common things," *Saints' Herald*, vol. 101, #10:pp. 224, 225, March 8, 1954.

1954H. Review of the book, "Face your life with confidence," by William E. Hulme, in *Saints' Herald*, vol. 101, #14:p. 329, April 5, 1954.

1954I. "My father's world," *Saints' Herald*, vol. 101, #27:p. 641, July 5, 1954.

1954J. "These things shall happen in us," *Saints' Herald*, vol. 101, #44:pp. 1049–1052, November 1, 1954.

1954K. "Remembering," *Saints' Herald*, vol. 101, #50:p. 1205, December 13, 1954.

1955I. "Youth and problem-solving," *Saints' Herald*, vol. 102, #2:pp. 38, 39, 45, January 10, 1955.

1955J. "That we be revived," *Reminder*, vol. 7, #2, pp. 1, 4, June 1955.

1955K. "Our people are singing," *Saints' Herald*, vol. 102, #42:p. 996, October 17, 1955.

1955L. "Let it be a rising sun," *Saints' Herald*, vol. 102, #44:pp. 1041–1043, 1052–1053, October 31, 1955.

1956C. "Stand up! Speak out!" *Saints' Herald*, vol. 103, #2:pp. 29–31, 45, January 9, 1956.

1956D. "Benedictory prayer of blessing," *Saints' Herald*, vol. 103, #16:p. 373, April 16, 1956.

1956E. "Radiant impression in great teaching," *Saints' Herald*, vol. 103, #34:pp. 809–812, August 20, 1956.

1956F. "Conference summary (Science conference at Graceland)," *University Bulletin*, vol. 9, #1:pp. 28–32, September 1956.

1956G. "Third in four," *Stride*, vol. 1, #1:pp. 21–24, October 1956.

1957B. "Interpreting morals," *Guidelines to Leadership*, vol. 15, #2, p. 7, Feb. 1957. (paragraph filler)

1957C. "Under scrutiny," *Guidelines to Leadership*, vol. 15, #2, p. 17, Feb. 1957. (paragraph filler)

1957D. "The highest good," *Guidelines to Leadership*, vol. 15, #3, p. 18, Feb. 1957. (paragraph filler)

1957E. "How are we looking at Japan and Korea?" *Saints' Herald*, vol. 104, #10:pp. 221–223, March 11, 1957.

1957F. "A greeting to Australia," *Saints' Herald*, vol. 104, #41:p. 974, October 14, 1957.

1957G. "An exploration on social planning," *University Bulletin*, vol. 10, #1:pp. 8–13, Fall 1957.

1957H. "Lesson I've learned," *Stride*, vol. 1, #14: pp. 38–41, November 1957.

1958B. "Women testify through active membership," *Saints' Herald*, vol. 105, #1:p. 12, 13, 16, January 6, 1958.

1958C. "What kind of a date?" *Stride*, vol. 2, #10:p. 30, October 1958.

1959C. "In high expectancy," *Reminder*, vol. 11: #1, pp. 1, 2, March 1959.

1959D. "Ten considerations for family living," *Guidelines to Leadership*, vol. 17, #5, p. 29–32, May 1959.

1959E. "These are my people," *Saints' Herald*, vol. 106, #33:p. 780,781, August 17, 1959. [first in series?] "I single out the company of the Saints, and I say as I walk with them, These are my people!"

1959F. "These are my people," *Saints' Herald*, vol. 106, #35:p. 828, August 31, 1959.

1959G. "Don't Wait—Serve Now!" *Stride*, vol. 3, #9, p. 2–5, September.

1959H. "These are my people," *Saints' Herald*, vol. 106, #41:p. 967,978, October 12, 1959.

1959I. "An inspired message given through the Presiding Patriarch at the 1959 Kirtland Conference of High Priests." *Saints' Herald*, vol. 106, #43: October 26, 1959.

1959J. "The branch as our laboratory." *Guidelines to Leadership*, vol. 17, #9, p. 1, Nov. 1959.

1959K. "These are my people." *Saints' Herald*, vol. 106, #48:pp. 1136–7, November 30, 1959.

1959L. "Bethlehem Potential." *Stride*, vol. 3, #12, p. 2, December.

1959M. "These are my people." *Saints' Herald*, vol. 106, #50:p. 1185, 1199, December 14, 1959.

1959N. "These are my people." *Saints' Herald*, vol. 106, #52:p. 1235, December 28, 1959.

1959T. "Inspired Message Through the Presiding Evangelist," pp. 73–74 in *The Report of the Conference of High Priests, Kirtland Temple, October 8–11, 1959*.

1959U. "Action in Lamoni." In *Iowa Community Life*, Iowa Council for Community Improvement. (Cited in Lamoni Chronicle 30 Apr 59)

1960C. "Funeral Sermon for Steven V. Carter," pp. 47–51 *Congressional Record, 86TH Congress, Second Session.*

1960D. "These are my people." *Saints' Herald*, vol. 107, #7:p. 160, February 15, 1960.

1960E. "These are my people." *Saints' Herald*, vol. 107, #8:p. 185, February 22, 1960.

1960F. "These are my people." *Saints' Herald*, vol. 107, #10:pp. 211, 222, February 29, 1960.

1960G. "These are my people." *Saints' Herald*, vol. 107, #10:p. 233, March 7, 1960.

1960H. "It shall be Bethel." *Saints' Herald*, vol. 107, #12:p. 279, 290, 291, March 21, 1960.

1960I. "These are my people." *Saints' Herald*, vol. 107, #20:p. 474, May 16, 1960. 5 weeks in Hawaii. Describes.

1960J. "These are my people." *Saints' Herald*, vol. 107, #22:p. 524, 525, May 30, 1960. More about Hawaii, then Berkeley Provo, St. Louis.

1960K. "These are my people." *Saints' Herald*, vol. 107, #24:p. 567, June 19, 1960. Indiana.

1960L. "Letter to Orman Salisbury." In, Salisbury, Orman. "Memoirs of Patriarch Orman Salisbury, Part IX." *Saints' Herald*, vol. 107, #12, June 27, Pp. 620, 621.

1960M. "Winds and Tides on God's Ocean." *Saints' Herald*, vol. 107, #30:p. 709–712, July 25, 1960.

1960N. "These are my people." *Saints' Herald*, vol. 107, #31:p. 743, August 1, 1960.

1960O. "These are my people." *Saints' Herald*, vol. 107, #33:p. 784, August 15, 1960.

1960P. "Hawaiian saints were singing." *Saints' Herald*, vol. 107, #36:p. 863, 864, September 5, 1960.

1960Q. "Universals of the gospel in 1960." *Saints' Herald*, vol. 107, #38:p. 900–902, September 19, 1960.

1960R. "These are my people." *Saints' Herald*, vol. 107, #41:p. 984–985, October 10, 1960.

1960S. "These are my people." *Saints' Herald*, vol. 107, #42:p. 1006, October 17, 1960. [Source of title "These are my People."]

1960T. "These are my people." *Saints' Herald*, vol. 107, #48:p. 1154, November 28, 1960.

1960V. "Report of the Order of Patriarchs," *General Conference Bulletin*, April 3, 1960, pp. 6–7.

1961B. "These are my people." *Saints' Herald*,108, #1:p. 9. Joe Baldwin. Belleville, IL. Liahona in Iowa City. Walnut Park. St. Louis.

1961C. "The common man is a philosopher." *Priesthood and Leader's Journal*, vol. 1, #1, pp. 2–4, January 1961. Subtitle: "Men and life's meaning: A study of philosophy."

1961D. "These are my people." *Saints' Herald*, vol. 108, #7:p. 155, February 13, 1961.

1961E. "Socrates: He turned to man himself." *Priesthood and Leader's Journal*, vol. 1, #2:pp. 64–67, February 1961.

1961F. "Plato: He sought the enduring." *Priesthood and Leader's Journal*, vol. 1, #3:pp. 112–115, March 1961.

1961G. "Four scenes out of the story of inspiration." *Saints' Herald*, vol. 108, #12:p. 268–270, March 20, 1961.

1961H. Article in Reminder, "Sharing the good news with our neighbors," vol. 13: #1, , p. 1, March 1961.

1961I. "These are my people." *Saints' Herald*, vol. 108, #17:p. 395, April 24, 1961.

1961J. "Augustine: He sought for the unchanging amid change." *Priesthood and Leader's Journal*, vol. 1, #4:pp. 141–145, April 1961.

1961K. "Aquinas: He sought to bring reason and faith together." *Priesthood and Leader's Journal*, vol. 1, #5:pp. 174–177, May 1961.

1961L. "Descartes: He dared to think and thought a dualism." *Priesthood and Leader's Journal*, vol. 1, #6:pp. 223–226, Summer 1961.

1961M. "These are my people." *Saints' Herald*, vol. 108, #25:p. 584–585, 591, June 19, 1961.

1961N. "These are my people." *Saints' Herald*, vol. 108, #26:p. 611, 618, June 26, 1961.

1961O. "These are my people." *Saints' Herald*, vol. 108, #36:p. 853–854, September 4, 1961.

1961P. "Kant: He stayed at home and saw a world view." *Priesthood and Leader's Journal*, vol. 1, #7:pp. 302–305, September 1961.

1961Q. "Nietzsche: He took apart and did not put together." *Priesthood and Leader's Journal*, vol. 1, #8:pp. 326–330, October 1961.

1961R. "The thrill of theology." *Saints' Herald*, vol. 108, #41:p. 964–965, 973, 978, October 9, 1961.

1961S. "14 questions people ask about Patriarchal Blessings." *Saints' Herald*, vol. 108, #42:p. 990, October 16, 1961.

1961T. "These are my people." *Saints' Herald*, vol. 108, #47:p. 1116, 1120, November 20, 1961.

1961U. "William James: He affirmed the right to believe." *Priesthood and Leader's Journal*, vol. 1, #9, pp. 373–377, November 1961.

1961V. "Here's your answer to administrative procedures." *Priesthood and Leader's Journal*, vol. 1, #9:p. 377, November 1961.

1961W. "Henry Bergson: He perceived something vital in the Universe." *Priesthood and Leader's Journal*, vol. 1, #10:pp. 405–407, 411, December 1961.

1962D. "Is the Restoration relevant in 1962?" *Stride*, v.6–#1:p.2–5, 13, January.

1962E. "Alfred North Whitehead: He perceived a Universe of process." *Priesthood and Leader's Journal*, vol. 2, #1:pp. 36–38, January.

1962F. "Karl Jaspers: He asks whether man will continue." *Priesthood and Leader's Journal*, vol. 2, #2:pp. 63–65, February.

1962G. "A time for philosophy." *Priesthood and Leader's Journal*, vol. 2, #3:pp. 106–109, 112, March.

1962H. "The way of Graceland." *Saints' Herald*, vol. 109, #10:p. 352–354, May 15.

1962I. "Are they intermediates?" *Priesthood and Leader's Journal*, vol. 2, #6:pp. 239, 240, 244 Summer.

1962J. "Sons of the saints." *Saints' Herald*, vol. 109, #18:p. 644, 645, September 15.

1962K. "The witness came to me." *Saints' Herald*, vol. 109, #20:, p. 714, 715, October 15. [The story of Rhodes and his coming into the church]

1962L. Article in *Reminder*, "Four persons in four places." v.14:#4, p. 2, December.

1962M. "The Order of Evangelists," *1962 World Conference Reports*, pp. 19–21.

1963A. "Theology—believing that makes a difference." *Stride*, 7–1:2–5, January.

1963B. "God—sustaining the universe." *Stride*, 7-2:24–28, February.

1963C. "The Restoration is a Message of Good Cheer." *Restoration Witness*, v.2, pp. 6, 7, 10, February 1963.

1963D. "Man relating himself to God." *Stride*, 7-3:6–10, March.

1963E. "Jesus Christ revealing and redeeming." *Stride*, 7-4:16–19, April.

1963F. "The Holy Spirit, enlightening, enlivening, harmonizing." *Stride*, 7-5:8–13, 15, May.

1963G. "Introducing the Work of the Patriarch." *Restoration Witness*, May, 1963, p. 16.

1963H. Abstract, "Basic Considerations in Theology for Today," in Saints' Herald article "Older Youth Conference." *Saints' Herald*, vol. 110, #9:p. 306, May 1.

1963I. "The church functioning as fellowship." *Stride*, 7-6:16–19, June.

1963J. "Scriptures guiding in purposive living." *Stride*, 7-7:14–17, July.

1963K. "Priesthood ministering with authority." *Stride*, 7-8:7–11, August.

1963L. "Basic considerations in theology for today." *Stride*, 7-9:12–14, September. (Reported by Bob Gunderson and Margaret McKevit.)

1963M. "Stewardship, expressing responsible relationships." *Stride*, 7-9:40–43, September.

1963N. "Zion-Providing Spiritual Nucleus." *Stride*, 7-10:16–19, October.

1963O. Article in *Christian Century* for October 30, 1963, "Mormonism on the Move," pp. 1328–30. Reprinted in *Saints' Herald, Saints' Herald*, January 1964.

1963P. "Needed saintly sharing not superselling." *Saints' Herald*, vol. 110, #22:p. 770, November 15. Editorial.

1963Q. "History, Disclosing God's purpose and plan." *Stride*, 7-11:12–15, November.

1963R. "Eschatology—indicating the outcome." *Stride*, 7-12:18–21,35, December.

1964B. "Mormonism on the move." *Saints' Herald*, vol. 111, #1:p. 10–12, January 1. Reprinted from *Christian Century* of October 31, 1963.

1964C. "Our times and our theology." *Saints' Herald*, vol. 111, #2:p. 44, 45, 51, January 15.

1964D. "Lights along the way—Book lists." *Priesthood and Leader's Journal*, vol. 4, #1:p. 31, January.

1964E. "The patriarch needs to see and sense the program." *Priesthood and Leader's Journal*, vol. 4, #1:p. 52, 53, February.

1964F. "Prayer for guidance." (offered at World Conference) *Saints' Herald*, vol. 111, #8:p. 254, 274, April 15.

1964G. "Our spiritual brotherhood in Christ." *Saints' Herald*, vol. 111, #23:p. 796–798, 806, 807, December 1.

1964H. [An article entitled "One Hundred and Forty Years of the Latter Day Saint Movement" was given to and printed in the conference report of the American Theological Library Association in Kansas City. On November 20, 1964 Cheville gave reprint permission to Calvin L. Porter, Associate Editor of *Encounter*, Christian Theological Seminary, Box 88267, Indianapolis, Indiana, 46208.]

1964J. "The Order of Evangelists," in *1964 World Conference Reports*, pp. 81–84.

1965A. "How did you get into this church?" *Restoration Witness*, January 1965, pp. 8–9, 11–12.

1965B. "What's your concept of God?" *Restoration Witness*, February 1965, pp. 8–9, 13–14.

1965C. "On narrating experiences." *Saints' Herald*, vol. 112, #3:p. 80, February 1, 1965.

1965D. "Are Latter Day Saints Christian?" *Restoration Witness*, March 1965, pp. 8–9, 14–15.

1965E. "Was another church needed?" *Restoration Witness*, April 1965, pp. 8–9, 11–12.

1965F. "The revelation in the crucifixion." *Stride*, vol. 9, p. 126–128, 130, April 1965.

1965G. "Was the Book of Mormon a public stunt?" *Restoration Witness*, May 1965, pp. 8–9,14–15.

1965H. "What's that other book of yours?" *Restoration Witness*, June 1965, pp. 8–9, 11, 13.

1965I. "Do you feel the spirit?" *Restoration Witness*, July 1965, pp. 8–11, 13.

1965J. "Words of adventuring faith." *Saints' Herald*, vol. 112, #14:p. 475, July 15.

1965K. "Words of expanding faith." *Saints' Herald*, vol. 112, #15:p. 511, August 1.

1965L. "Words of foundationing faith." *Saints' Herald*, vol. 112, #16:p. 547, August 15.

1965M. "Did you have your baby baptized?" *Restoration Witness*, August 1965, pp. 8–9, 14–15.

1965N. "How did you become a minister?" *Restoration Witness*, September 1965, pp. 8–9, 11, 13–14.

1965O. "Do you pay income tax to your church?" *Restoration Witness*, October 1965, pp. 8–9, 14–15.

1965P. "Do you think you're ready for baptism?" *Restoration Witness*, November 1965, pp. 8–9,11–13.

1965Q. "These are my people." *Saints' Herald*, vol. 112, #21:p. 734, November 1.

1965R. "These are my people." *Saints' Herald*, vol. 112, #24:p. 841, December 15.

1965S. "Has God had anything to do with my finding the church?" *Restoration Witness*, December 1965, pp. 8–10.

1965T. "The High Priest As Servant," in *The Report of the Conference of High Priests*, Kirtland Temple, October 7–10, 1965, pp. 25–27.

1966B. "How detailed in direction." *Saints' Herald*, vol. 113, p. 10, January 1, 1966.

1966C. "Our church polity in conference operation." *Saints' Herald*, vol. 113, p. 114, 115, February 15, 1966.

1966D. "1966—Conference Year." *Saints' Herald*, vol 113, p. 149, March 1, 1966.

1966E. "Are they let out?" *Saints' Herald*, vol. 113, p. 221, April 1, 1966.

1966F. "These are my people." *Saints' Herald*, vol. 113, p. 447, July 1, 1966.

1966G. "Glorying in martyrdom." *Saints' Herald*, vol. 113, p. 582, September 1, 1966.

1966H. "These are my people." *Saints' Herald*, vol. 113, p. 742, November 1, 1966.

1966I. "What about Wednesday evening?" *Priesthood and Leader's Journal*, vol. 6, #10:pp. 406–408, December, 1966.

1966J. "The Order of Evangelists," *1966 World Conference Reports*, pp. 73–75.

1967A. "In our church by 1977." *Saints' Herald*, vol. 114, pp. 78–80, 95. February 1, 1967.

1967B. "Patriarchs in the congregational program." *Priesthood and Leader's Journal*, vol. 7, pp. 89–92, March 1967.

1967C. "A youth meets God in a grove." *Restoration Witness*, vol. 4, pp. 2, 11, 12 April, 1967.

1967D. "These are my people." *Saints' Herald*, vol, 114, p. 269, April 15, 1967.

1967E. "Why have patriarchs—Roy A. Cheville." *Saints' Herald*, vol. 114, pp. 402–404, June 15, 1967.

1967F. "In a north country." *Saints' Herald*, vol. 114, pp. 590–592, September 1, 1967.

1967G. "These are my people." *Saints' Herald*, vol. 114, pp. 700–710, October 15, 1967.

1968B. "What distinctives count today." *Saints' Herald*, vol. 115, pp. 8–10, 25 January 1, 1968.

1968C. "Living evangelism! Reaching out wisely and caringly." *Saints' Herald*, 115:119 February 15.

1968D. "These are my people." *Saints' Herald*, vol. 115, pp. 237–239, April 1, 1968.

1968E. "Hymn of Zion builders." (poem) *Saints' Herald*, vol. 115, p. 359 May 15, 1968.

1968F. "Beyond scriptural monopoly." *Saints' Herald*, vol. 115, pp. 440–441 July 1, 1968.

1968G. "These are my people." *Saints' Herald*, vol. 115, pp, 562–563 August 15, 1968.

1968H. "Twelve pointers for pastors when requesting ministry from patriarchs." *Priesthood and Leader's Journal*, vol. 8, p. 265 August 1968.

1968I. "The Patriarchs," *1968 World Conference Reports*, pp. 73–75.

1969A. "These are my people." *Saints' Herald*, vol. 116, pp. 13,21 February 1969.

1969B. "The temple in today's church life, part 1." *Saints' Herald*, vol. 116, pp. 5–7 March, 1969.

1969C. "The temple in today's church life, part 2." *Saints' Herald*, vol. 116, pp. 20, 21, 22, 29 April 1969.

1969D. "My favorite scripture." *Restoration Witness*, vol. 4, pp. 12–13 April 1969.

1969E. "Prophetic ministry at institute on Zion." *Saints' Herald*, vol. 116, pp. 4, 5, 14 November 1969.

1969F. "These are my people." *Saints' Herald*, vol. 116, pp. 33, 34 December 1969.

1970B. "Helpers in healing." *Saints' Herald*, vol. 117 #1 pp. 28, 29 January.

1970C. "In Palmyra grove today (Excerpts from 1970 conference sermon." *Saints' Herald*, vol. 117, pp. 10, 11, 12, 16 August 1970.

1970D. "These are my people." *Saints' Herald*, vol. 117, pp. 17, 18 September 1970.

1970F. "The Patriarchs," *World Conference Reports 1970*, pp. 36–37.

1971B. "These are my people." *Saints' Herald*, vol. 118, pp. 21, 34 February 1971.

1971C. "These are my people." *Saints' Herald*, vol. 118, pp. 25–36 June 1971.

1971D. "20 questions people are asking about patriarchal blessings, part 1." *Saints' Herald*, vol. 118, pp. 10–12, 62 October, 1971.

1971E. "20 questions people are asking about patriarchal blessings, part 2." *Saints' Herald*, vol. 118, pp. 16, 17, 34 November.

1971F. "These are my people." *Saints' Herald*, vol. 118, pp. 27, 28 December 1971.

1972B. "Out of inquiring and investing." *Restoration Witness*, 3/72:4 March.

1972C. "These are my people." *Saints' Herald*, vol. 119, pp. 35, 36 May 1972.

1972D. "Endowment for witnessing (Excerpts from conference sermon)" *Saints' Herald*, vol. 119, pp. 10–13, 38 September.

1972E. "These are my people." *Saints' Herald*, vol. 119, pp. 25, 26 October 1972.

1972G. "Patriarchs," in *World Conference 1972 Report*, pp. 40–41.

1972H. "A Conference Calls for Conferring," In *Courage: A Journal of History, Thought and Action*, Winter 1972, pp. 387–389.

1973A. "What kind of a God should the preacher play?" *Saints' Herald*, vol. 120, pp. 10–12, 49 February 1973.

1973B. "These are my people." *Saints' Herald*, vol. 120, pp. 30, 53 March 1973.

1973C. "Living distinctives, part 1." *Saints' Herald*, vol. 120, pp. 10, 11, 17 September 1973.

1973D. "Living distinctives, part 2." *Saints' Herald*, vol. 120, pp. 19, 20, 36 October 1973.

1973E. "These are my people." *Saints' Herald*, vol. 120, pp. 19, 52 December.

1974A. "Enthusiasm in living Zionically today, part 1." *Saints' Herald*, vol. 121, pp. 418–420, 425 July.

1974B. "Enthusiasm in living Zionically today, part 2." *Saints' Herald*, vol. 121, pp. 494, 495, 513, 514 August.

1974C. "Order of Patriarchs," *World Conference 1974 Reports*.

1976A. "The book of Revelation can speak to us today." *Saints' Herald*, vol. 123, pp. 238f(44f) April 1976.

1977B. "Priorities in Patriarchal Ministry-Part 1." *Saints' Herald*, vol. 124, pp. 46f January 1977.

1977C. "Priorities in Patriarchal Ministry-Part 2." *Saints' Herald*, vol. 124, pp. 112f February 1977.

1978D. "On Patriarchal Ministry," in Reed M. Holmes, *The Patriarchs*, Independence, MO: Herald House, 1978, 110–113 .

1981A. "A trilogy of memories." *Saints' Herald*, vol. 128, pp. 114–116 March 1981. Villy Lundin, George Ventura, Mariko Saito.

1981B. "A letter and a prayer." *Restoration Witness*, vol. 3, pp. 23–25 March 1981.

1981C. "Insight and foresight: Experiences in discernment." *Restoration Witness*, vol. 10, pp. 14–25 October 1981.

1984A. "God provides for continuing enlightenment." *Saints' Herald*, vol. 131, p. 410(26) September.

APPENDIX E

Selections from
Roy Cheville's Diary of 1921–1922

June 20. Arrived in Chicago and came out to University. Met a young man and came to room with him—Chas. Baker at 5511 Drexel. Registered. Courses: Elementary. Greek, Intro. to Phil., and Religion of Israel before Amos. Place is beautiful. However felt tired and a little lonesome for Graceland.

June 21. Met first classes. Convocation, etc. Greek appears hard.

June 24. Classes. Went for boat ride on Lake in evening.

June 25. Excursion to Field Museum. Also went to Art Institute. Wonderful places. Spent day downtown. In afternoon went to beach and tried to swim.

June 26. Went to First Chicago Branch. Very sociable group. Spent pleasant day at McCaig's. Church again in the evening.

June 27. Studies as usual. Philosophy is great.

June 28. Classes. Went to beach in afternoon. Have been attending 4:30 lectures.

June 29. Classes etc. Am feeling more at home.

July 1. Classes. Wrote philosophy paper. Attended concert by Emmanuel Choir of La Grange in evening.

July 2. Spent day with Lawrence Campbell who was passing thru on way to his mission. Visited beach etc. Studied in evening.

July 3. Went to So. Side Branch. Spent day at Keir's. Miss Whiting was there. Enjoyable time. Saints very friendly.

July 4. S.S. picnic at Elmhurst. Enjoyable, quiet Fourth. Judged a debate.

July 6. Classes. Beach again in afternoon. More at home at University.

July 8. Classes. Spent afternoon on philosophy. Very enjoyable work. Heard Prof. Dodd lecture on "The South."

July 9. Went to Greek class. Studied in park. Received letter from Bro. Tordoff in Isle of Pines wanting me to go there—a real Macedonian call.

July 10. Spoke at First Chicago Branch—on Zion etc. Good liberty. Much appreciated by Saints. Attended priesthood meeting at South Side in the afternoon. Supper at Keir's. Church at night.

July 14. Heard Lorado Taft, sculptor lecture on European sculpturing. Prof. Dodd on "Wilson, League and Present Situation" in the evening. High tribute to Wilson. Said the presidents Lincoln and Washington had gone out with hostility.

July 15. Classes. Beach in PM after studies. Waves high. My first wave riding. Heard Lorado Taft in afternoon on St. Gauden's.

July 16. Studied sermon etc. at Washington Park Boat House in morning. Studied and wrote letters in afternoon.

July 17. Spoke at South Side Church in morning. Same theme as previous Sunday. Appreciated. Dinner at Keir's. Sacrament service in the afternoon. Assisted. Charge of service in evening. Bro. Jowett spoke.

July 18. Classes. Spent most of morning on Philosophy. Received letter from Gunsolley and good one from Crum.

July 19. Classes. Sr. Keir and I went to Northwestern and Miss Whiting conducted us over campus. Large but not as beautiful as Chicago Univ. Dinner at Evanston. Went to Ravinia to Open Air Grand Opera—"Aida." Thus one desire of many years was realized. Home about one o'clock.

July 20. Classes. Answered letters in afternoon. Went in Univ. pool for first time.

July 21. Classes. Saw Dean Boynton about courses. Swam in pool.

July 22. Classes. Worked on sermon and other lessons at Wash. Park. Went to Tivoli Theater in evening. Beautiful music and wonderful architecture. Didn't care much for pictures.

July 23. Studied in morning on Phil. with Miss Bennett and Mr. Olsen. In afternoon studied in room. Walked thru park and worked on sermon in the evening.

July 24. Spent day at West Pullman. Service in hall. Spoke in morning. Blessed two babies. Dinner with family of saints. Staid for evening service. Good group of saints—need leader.

July 27. Exams. Went to Keir's in evening and, to prayer meeting. Then back to Keir's. Good time.

July 28. Started second term. Continued Greek. Took American Phil. under Tufts. Enrolled for Epistle to Hebrews under Goodspeed. Appeared to be a language course and didn't think much of instructor so changed to Hebrew Ethics under Smith.

July 29. Getting started in new courses well. At 7:30 went to hear reading of Shaw's "Back to Methuselah." Not much impressed by it.

July 30. Excursion to Sears, Roebuck with Univ. students. Luncheon at Sears R & Co. Mr. Ivers and I were together. Watched parade of Pageant of Progress for over an hour. Fine affair. Spent evening studying on sermon, etc.

July 31. Spent day at West Side. F. M. Cooper spoke in morning. At Bone's for dinner and day. Spoke in evening on Jesus Visit to Nazareth, etc. Good crowd and attention.

Aug. 1. Monday. Spent most of day digging into philosophy. Problems arise that I do not know how to meet. Have faith though.

Aug. 2. Classes. Am pondering over scriptural interpretation and criticism of Old Testament.

Aug. 3. Classes. Went to prayer meeting on South Side. Had charge of meeting. Received strength.

Aug. 4. Classes. Swim every day in pool.

Aug. 5. Classes. Lecture on Aztec Mexico in PM. Choir practice in evening.

Aug. 6. Excursion to Ghetto and Hull House. Impressed with big need of social work as never before at seeing dirt and filth of Maxwell St. market. Ate lunch at Coffee House of Hull House. Made new determinations for a clean life.

Aug. 7. Attended Church at South Side. Taught S.S. class, assisted at Sacrament meeting. Spent enjoyable day at Keir's. Spoke in evening, speaker having not filled appointment.

Aug. 10. Classes. Dinner at Keir's and evening before Miss Whiting leaves for home. Prayer service. Enjoyable time singing etc.

Aug. 11. Classes etc. Went to Y.M.C.A. Sing in evening. Desired in a way to get back to congregational song leading.

Aug. 12. Classes. Lecture on Mexico by Prof. Fred. Starr, Professor of Anthropology. He stated hope of Mexico lay in Indians. From them her great men had come.

Aug. 13. Excursion to Union Stock Yards. Went through Armour's big plant. Studied in the afternoon.

Aug. 14. Attended service at University. Sermon by Rev. Penyilly of Flint. Touched on present social conditions. Said morals, society etc. was nearly bankrupt. Fine sermon. In afternoon went to Lincoln Park. Saw zoo etc. Most beautiful thing was the Lincoln Statue. Attended the Moody Institute in the evening. Big crowd. Sermon on catastrophes coming on earth etc. Very dramatic though shallow. Man inquired if I was saved etc. Had a long talk together in aisle.

Aug. 19. Usual school work. Went to Elmhurst Reunion in evening. *Rained.* Led a congregational sing during rain.

Aug. 20. Assisted at prayer meeting. Sang solo at S.S. institute. Good time with saints. Floyd McDowell there. Played volley ball.

Aug. 21. Got up early for young people's prayer service. Ushered at prayer service, led music at S.S. Sang solo and solo in anthem at afternoon service. Solo was "In The Garden" by request. In afternoon, F. M. McDowell and mother, Paul Hanson and I went for a ride in the country with

Dr. Schwartz thru beautiful rural land. Came home. Got in about one o'clock.

Aug. 22. Somewhat tired from Reunion. Worked on term paper.

Aug. 23. Classes. Heard lecture by Professor Hayden, Professor of Comparative Religion on "What is Religion."

Aug. 25. Classes. Lecture by Professor Hayden. Lecture at YMCA by Dr. Tittle, pastor of Evanston Methodist Church on "My Conception of God."

Aug. 26. Classes. Went out to Elmhurst Reunion in evening. Musical Program—good.

Aug. 27. Attended Young Peoples and Senior Prayer Meetings. Studied Greek. Played volley ball. Tore knee out of trousers in game. Sermon by Bro Whipper. Wiener Roast and Program on Floyd McDowell in evening. Led community sing. Gave toast on McDowell on "What Would Graceland Do Without Him?" Game of "Run Sheep Run."

Aug. 28. Young People and Adults Prayer Service. Sermon by Bishop Becker. Sang solos in Anthem in PM. Came home in afternoon.

Sept. 2. Exams. Received philosophy paper back—on James' conception of truth—subject "What Is Truth?" Defined truth as in D.C. 90:4–5.—This subject as well as History of Hebrew Ethics caused me to wonder at many things as to origin and existence of the Universe. Will await fuller understanding before forming opinions. Finished work of Summer Quarter. Registered for Correspondence Work in Greek. Hurried to get off for home. Dinner at Keir's. Led sing at Religio.

Elected president of Central Religio. Left at 7:30 on Northwestern via Cedar Rapids—to transfer to Chicago Minneapolis and St. Paul.

Sept. 3. Arrived home. Bro. Dowker and Smith holding services in tent.

Sept. 4. Sunday—services in tent. Asa Smith down for dinner. Led singing in evening. Sang "Hold Thou My Hand."

Sept. 7. At home. Services. Went to Baxter with Hickman's after Church. Leona also went.

Sept. 8. Spent day with Hickman's. Came home in afternoon for evening services. Sang solo, "When Peace—"

Sept. 9. Dowker was at Boone. Spoke on "Baptism of Holy Spirit." Boy's Chorus Sang. Enjoyed good liberty.

Sept. 10. At home. Went to Perry in evening. Staid at Taylors.

Sept. 11. Profitable day with Perry Saints. Spoke morning and evening on Zion and Revelation respectively. Good crowds.

Sept. 12. Staid in Perry for funeral of a Dave Wasson. Held at house in the afternoon. Spoke on rewards of life hereafter.

Sept. 13. Returned to Rhodes in morning. At home. Services at night. Began correspondence studies in Greek, books having come.

Sept. 14. At home. Lights off at night, but interesting services in tent.

Sept. 15. At home. Studies Greek. Dowker and Asa for dinner in evening.

Sept. 18. Services in tent. Dinner at Pitchers. Spoke in evening on Church Organization.

Sept. 25. Folks drove to Nevada for church. Spoke in the morning. Spirit present. Good to meet the saints with whom I had labored. Home in the evening for services.

Sept. 26. Entertained the Rhodes Choir at home. Day was busy with studies and preparations for the evening. Jolly games, musical contests and recital.

Sept. 29. Bro. Dowker and I at Baxter, came back for services.

Sept. 30. Finished studies. Spent day at Klutts's. No church. Went to Carnival at the School house. Kept time at Basket ball game.

Oct. 1. Came to Chicago via the Milwaukee. Enjoyed the trip and scenery. Felt a little out of place at first and wished for Graceland chums and home.

Oct. 2. At Church. Took charge of sacrament service, young peoples service and preached in the evening. Speaker being absent.

Oct. 3. School began. Registration lines, etc. Started four courses. Greek 3, Sociology, Beginnings of Christianity, and Beginnings of Old Testament History, also swimming.

Oct. 4. Classes begin. Also begin work in the Commons. Life is evident in university.

Oct. 7. Religio. Gave social for their new president. The work of directing the Chicago Religio starts out favorably.

Oct. 8. Spent forenoon in study. Afternoon—the Chicago Purdue football game. Thrilling. My first big game. 9-0 for Chicago.

Oct. 9. At church. Lectured to the Priesthood in PM on "Religion." Was well received.

Oct. 14. Religio. Small attendance. Organized Glee Club.

Oct. 16. Church. Spend day at Lester's. Sacrament service at West Side in PM. Played for church at South Side in evening.

Oct. 20. Classes. Sociology Club in evening. Heard lecture by Professor Burgess on Sociology of the Criminal.

Oct. 22. Studied. Worked at Commons. Wrote letters. Received word that Chicago Defeated Princeton 9-0.

Oct. 23. Began teaching young ladies class at S.S. Spoke at morning service on "Revelation." Dinner at Jean Keir's. Began practice on Religio Glee Club in the afternoon. Took charge of Young People's prayer service in evening.

Oct. 25. Studies. Attended Gavel Club. Undecided about entering debating.

Oct. 26. Studies. Heard Sherwood Eddy on Character Foundations etc. Was masterful discourse. Prayer meeting.

Oct. 29. Studied at library, worked at Commons. Chicago—Colorado game 35-0. At home in evening.

Oct. 30. At Church. Took charge of service. At Bell's for the day. Glee Club in the afternoon. Took charge of Y. P. Prayer Service. A native Babylonian spoke in the evening of his conversion to Christianity and his experiences. Was very good. Was going back as a missionary.

Oct. 31. Classes. Went to Halloween party of Religio in the evening.

Nov. 2. Classes. Heard lecture by Stephen Langdon, Professor of Assyriology at Oxford on Origin and

Development of Babylonian Temple Worship. Prayer meeting.

Nov. 4. Classes. Religio. Good session. Glee Club practice.

Nov. 5. Went down town. Bought overcoat and trousers. In afternoon went to Ohio State vs Chicago game. Ohio won 7-0. Big game over 30,000. Best game I ever saw. Fine bands. Studied on sermon in evening. Wrote letters.

Nov. 6. Took charge of sacrament service at Central. Dinner at Lesters. Glee Club practice. Spoke in evening on "The Basis of Religion." My first effort at this theme. Got along quite well. Rode home in an auto.

Nov. 11. Classes. Heard lecture by Professor McLaughlin on Disarmament. He pictured the terrible conditions of world today, the awful terrors of another war, the expense of armament and the necessity for disarmament. Brother Murray gave pictures of Paris at Religio.

Nov. 12. Wrote paper on "The Relation of Genesis 1–11 and Babylonian Tradition." for Old Testament History. Tired but glad to get it finished. Went down to LaSalle Hotel to register for Convocation of Colleges on Disarmament as Graceland's delegate. Chicago defeats Illinois 14-6. Wrote letters. Am glad to know of Fred's baptism last Sunday.

Nov. 13. Spoke at colored mission in the morning—my first experience with the sons of Ham. Brother Lester accompanied me. Spoke on church organization. Enjoyed it. I understood the difficulties under which they meet. Dinner at Keir's. In the afternoon attended session of Convocation of colleges on Limitation of armaments at the Colonial Theater. Addresses by Sherwood Eddy, Charles Tindley (Negro preacher of Philadelphia) and Dr. Boynton of N.Y. A chorus of over 150 sang choruses from The Messiah. Went to church in evening. Took charge.

Nov. 14. Attended the Convocation at the Hotel LaSalle. Business session. Represented Graceland in organization of a national organization of colleges for limitation of armaments. Studied in the afternoon.

Nov. 15. Classes etc. Mr. Byron, instructor in Sociology has asked me to make term report on L.D.S. people.

Nov. 19. Studied in morning. Wisconsin—Chicago game in afternoon 3-0 in Chicago's favor. Last game of season. Average 30,000 at game.

Nov. 20. Spoke at Colored Mission on Restoration. Realized the handicap of the black people and the problems of sociology in Zion. Their great need is leadership and training. Glee Club in P.M. Y.P Prayer Service and took charge of service in evening.

Nov. 21–23. Classes & Studies. Prayer Service Wednesday Evening. Received a long letter from Leonard L. about problems troubling him. Am perplexed over many of them.

Nov. 24. Thanksgiving. Attended prayer service. Had dinner at the Commons and worked there. Studied in P.M. about 7 hours.

Nov. 25. School. Exam in New Testament. Relgio in the evening. Good session.

Nov. 26. Studied at library. Had picture taken for Cap and Gown & for photos. Studied again. Wrote letters.

Nov. 27. Preached at West Pullman in morning on Zion. Glee Club in P.M. Keir's for supper. Had charge of Y.P. service and evening service.

Nov. 30. Studies. Heard Jane Addams on Russian famine.

Dec. 3. Studies. Am working on a sociology report on L.D.S. Church. Is a big task.

Dec. 4. Assisted in sacrament service. Glee Club at Bells. Spoke in evening on "The Four Ships of Zion."

Dec. 8. Studies. Received word from Graceland about finances. Rather perplexed. All will turn out.

Dec. 11. At church. Dinner at Sherman's. Glee Club. Priesthood meeting. Supper at Keirs. Didn't stay for church.

Dec. 15. Classes etc. Received fine box of eats from home. Practiced glee club in the evening. Final practice.

Dec. 16. Classes. Glee Club Concert. Rainy. Good crowd considering. Margaret Wickes played and gave readings. Young people at their best. Audience appreciative. Felt repaid for work.

Dec. 17. Finished writing paper on Samuel. Went down town after pictures. Sent some home. Studied in library.

Dec. 18. At church. Went to Keir's for dinner. Brother Greene was there. Had good visit. Had charge of music at evening service. Glee Club sang. Brother Greene delivered an uplifting sermon.

Dec. 21. Sociology exam. Reviewed for exams. Long and hard hours.

Dec. 22. New Testament and Old Testament exams. Tired. Reviewed Greek.

Dec. 23. Greek exam. Quarter ended. Relaxed. Began work to finish up correspondence course. Xmas program in evening. Sang solo. Late. Brother Sly and I went to administer. Later learned it was attended with blessing.

Dec. 24. Worked on correspondence work all day. Went over to Keir's in evening to spend Sunday. Tent to theater—movies. Visited late.

Dec. 25. A group of young people rose early and went Christmas caroling. Was beautiful. Returned to Keirs and had breakfast. Preached a Christmas sermon at the Negro mission. Fine Xmas dinner at Keir's. Pleasant day. Had charge of Young people's prayer service. Sang solo at church— from the Messiah.

Dec. 26. Staid at Keir's. Brother Keir and I had charge of a funeral of a babe of outsiders. Preached the sermon. Met the young people at Keir's in the evening to arrange for trip around world.

Dec. 28. Worked on Correspondence Lessons. Had charge of prayer service.

Dec. 30. Studied. In afternoon went over to church and prepared for social. The Religio gave the social "trip around the world." Young people staged a parody on Grand Opera.

Dec. 31 Studied. In evening went over to Keir's. Watched Old Year out. Staid all night.

Summary of Ministerial Work for 1921. Sermons 28. In Charge 35. Assisted 10. Other 281. Total 354.

Baptized 1. Blessed 5. Confirmed 2. Assisted to Confirmation 2. Administered 20. Assisted to Administration 10.

Jan. 1, 1922. Early priesthood prayer service, S.S, Sacrament service. Dinner at Keirs. Went to West Side. Spoke. Good Liberty. Spoke on Personality of Christ. The new year opens. Perplexed as to finances, but glad to be in college.

Jan. 3. School Opens. Am enrolled in New Testament Literature, Ethics, Old Testament History and Literature, and History of Religion. Am working at Commons. Glad to be back in school.

SAINTS' HERALD, January 4, 1922, p. 22, Central Chicago Branch. On Christmas morning the sermon was by Brother Philemon Pement. In the evening, Brother Ward L. Christy occupied the pulpit, and his opening remarks were in remembrance of his pleasant awakening in the morning to the sweet strains of the Christmas carol sung by our young folks under the leadership of Brother Cheville at every Latter Day Saint home near enough to be reached by them.

Jan. 7. Went down town to Post Office and cashed in W.S.S. Bought few articles at fair from Branch Xmas gift. Tried to get opera ticket but could not. Came back to University, paid tuition. Studied in P.M. Went to Chicago—Ohio Basketball in the evening. 25-13 in favor of Chicago.

Jan. 8. S.S. and Church. Dinner at Christy's. Attended Priesthood meeting on West Side. Young Peoples, Church,—

Jan. 11. Classes. Met Briggs at the university. Held consultation. The outcome is that I'm to stay at the University another year and secure my Masters degree in place of returning to Graceland. Glad of the opportunity—don't know where finances are coming from.

Jan. 15. S.S. and Church. Series of services began at South Side. Sacrament service in P.M. Church at night. Brother Pement spoke.

Jan. 21. Studied. Went to Northwestern vs Chicago Track Meet. Chicago won.

Jan. 22. At church. Read paper at S.S. on Israel's religion. Spent day at Keir's. Church at night. Ad 4. Am perplexed—yet have faith—as to many things of the Church.

Jan. 24. Classes. Attended lecture by Lorado Taft in evening—wonderful. He did modeling work.

Jan. 25. Classes. Am perplexed as how to enroll for future work. Wrote to Briggs about the 2 year course.

Jan. 28. Studies. Went to Swimming meet with Milwaukee Athletic Association in evening with Wham, Keir. Water Basket Ball Game. Chicago won.

Jan. 29. Spoke at colored mission. At Keir's. Charge of Young Peoples Prayer Service and Preaching service.

Jan. 31. Studies and classes. Tea at Dr. Goodspeed for his New Testament class and members of Divinity faculty—my first fashionable tea. Beautiful home. Music. Tea etc. Enjoy such functions much.

Feb. 4. Studies. Basket ball—Illinois and Chicago—favor of latter—a thrilling game.

Feb. 5. Priesthood prayer Service, S.S., Sacrament Service. At Keir's. Prepared Religio program at Bells. Y.P. Prayer Service, Preaching. Problems, perplexities, doubts as to the gospel, L.D.S. harass on every hand. I long for solution—may I have faith.

Feb. 11. Studied on Comparative Religion. Am making a report on Karma. Iowa vs Chicago Basket Ball. Punk game in Iowa's favor 27-17. Chicago didn't play.

Feb. 12. Preached at Central Church on Personality of Christ—good liberty. At Keir's. Young People's. Church at night. Priesthood lecture in afternoon.

Feb. 13. Studied. Wrote out application for scholarship in the divinity school.

SAINTS' HERALD, February 15, 1922, p. 173, Central Chicago.

Recently a very successful musical program was given by the Religio Glee Club with Roy Cheville as director and Sister Margaret Wickes as pianist and reader.

Though Brother Cheville is with us for only a short time, he is doing a splendid work.

Feb. 18. Studied on Ethics paper on Kant, Mill, and Dewey.

Feb. 19. At church. At Keir's for dinner. Attended a baptismal service at church in the afternoon. Had charge of the Young Peoples Service at night. Played for Church.

Feb. 21. Classes and Studies. Went to choir practice in evening. Had charge of the choir.

Feb. 22. Washington's Birthday. Studied. Went over and

talked on Ethics with Meier. He is a fine young man. Studied.

SAINTS' HERALD, February 22, 1922, p. 196, Central Chicago. Religio under Superintendent Roy Cheville is proving both interesting and instructive.

Feb. 24. Studies and classes. Religio. Bluebird program. Felt the jar of big quarry explosion while at Religio.

Feb. 25. Worked on Studies. Finished Ethics paper on "Moral Theories of Kant, Mill, and Dewey. In evening attended the Minnesota—Chicago Basket Ball game. Rough and lively. In Chicago's favor.

Feb. 26. At church. Now have charge of the Young Ladies S.S. class. At Keirs. Went to baptismal service in afternoon. Practiced His Uncle John—a good start.

Feb. 27. Worked on term paper on History of Religion— "The Development of the Karma Doctrine in Religions of India."

Feb. 28. Classes. Received most favorable comment on exam paper in Ethics class. Interviewed Dean Matthews. he assured me of scholarship in the Divinity School next year. Received check of $200 loan from Father. Dean Matthews received me most cordially. Am not yet certain as to my course yet.

Mar. 1. Classes etc. Instructor commented most favorably on my Ethics paper.

Mar. 5. At church. Most edifying and spiritual service. Prophecy thru Brother Keir. Peace prevailed. Dinner at Keirs. Practiced in the afternoon. Fine Young People's Service. Led music at night.

Mar. 7. Classes. Went to choir practice and led the choir.

Mar. 10. Classes etc. Religio in the evening. Program on Current events.

Mar. 11. Worked at Library and at home on papers in Ethics and Old Testament. Went to Wisconsin— Chicago Basket Ball Game. Chicago defeated but was a good game. Came home and studied on sermon.

Mar. 12. At S.S. Preached in the morning on Our World View. Dinner at Keirs. Practiced in the afternoon. Had charge of Young Peoples. Effected an organization for Young Peoples Day. Had charge of music in the evening.

Mar. 14. Classes etc. Being tired in the evening I went to choir practice and teacher's meeting.

Mar. 16. Studies and classes. In evening I attended the Blackfriar musical program given by the band, orchestra and glee club.

Mar. 17. Classes and Studies. Religio in evening. Program by Orioles. Practiced the Religio Play, His Uncle John.

Mar. 19. At church. Practiced in P.M. Dinner at Sherman's. Led music at night.

Mar. 20. Studied. Surprise in the afternoon when Dad came in having come with some shipping association stock. We went thru the university and around, went to movie. He stayed with me over night.

Mar. 21. Dad left for home. Last classes of the quarter.

Mar. 25. Spent the day on Greek for a correspondence course.

Mar. 26. Spoke at the mission. Dinner at Keirs. Committee meeting. Went to flower show at Ogden Park. Young Peoples Meeting. Church at night.

Mar. 27. Worked on Greek Correspondence Course. Went to church early to begin on stage for the play. Practiced.

Mar. 31. Studied in the morning. In afternoon got stage ready for Religio Play. Rainy and snowy weather. Play went off a success, good acting, footlights etc.

Apr. 1. When came home last night I found that Max Carmichael and Cyril Wight had called. So went down to the Congress Hotel to the National Meeting of Religious Education and saw them Studied in evening and afternoon.

Apr. 2. All day service at the church. Cyril and Leslie Wight came out and I had a good visit with them. At afternoon service Jean Keir, Art, S. and C. Oliver were ordained. Led song service. A happy day. Cyril spoke in the evening.

Apr. 3. Spring quarter begins. Enrolled in Social Psychology—Faris; Teachings of Jesus—Burton; and Old Testament History—J.M.P. Smith. Transferred to work in School of Education cafeteria at noons, Commons in morning. Met one class.

Apr. 5. Am getting settled in school work. Look forward to commencement.

Apr. 7. Classes. Secured work in the divinity library. Glad of this. Worked 2 hours. Religio.

Apr. 8. Spent morning working at commons and at the library.

Apr. 9. Spoke in church on "The Beauty of Holiness." The service was worshipful. Spent the day with the McNicol's. Y.P. Prayer Service and Preaching.

Apr. 10. Rose early to get school work ready. Am working in the library 2 hours daily or more.

Apr. 14. Classes. Spent 3 hours in the library of Religion. Good orchestra program.

Apr. 15. Spent morning at Commons Library. Tired. Studied in afternoon and evening.

Apr. 16. Easter. Sang a solo at S.S. Exercises. Dinner at Keir's. Practiced Young People's Chorus in the afternoon. Took a walk with several of the young people—fine time. Jean Keir and I had charge of Young Peoples.

Apr. 18. Studies and Classes. Attended the concert by the "A Capella" Choir of Northwestern. Beautiful tonal effects. Music was unaccompanied. Revived ideals of our music possibilities.

Apr. 22. Worked at library a little. Studied on Social Psychology.

Apr. 23. At church. Dinner at Jean Keir's. Jean and I walked to Marquette Park in the afternoon. Church in the evening.

Apr. 25. Studies, classes etc. My daily program. Work at Commons 7:15–8:45. Social Psychology 9:00–10:00. Work in Library 10–11:00. New Testament Course 11:00–12:00. School of Ed. Cafeteria 12:00–1:00. Old Testament History, Literature 1:30–2:30. Library work 2:30–3:30. Conducted practice of Young People's chorus Tuesday evening.

Apr. 28. Classes, Work, etc. Religio in the evening, service given by the young people—a symposium on church history with appropriate old hymns. Was well carried out.

Apr. 29. Worked at library. Studies in P.M. Young people's social at church. Cleaned church afterward. Daylight savings time ushered in. Little sleep.

Apr. 30. Young Peoples Day at Central Chicago Branch. Early Prayer Meeting 8:30. Jean and I in charge. Conducted music and had charge of 11:15 service. Talks on "The Work of the Church As Seen by Youth." Pastoral, Economic, and missionary. Concert and address in evening by H. P. W. Keir. The day did not nearly meet my expectations but accomplished much.

May 5. Sent Fred a ring as commencement gift. Religio.

May 7. Sacrament service—assisted. Attended early morning priesthood service. Practiced "Tale of Hot." Took walk with George and Alf. Supper at Lester's. Charge of Young People's. Led music at church.

May 9. Looked up for term paper. Am working on a committee of 5 on report on Immigrant Attitudes in Social Psychology under Faris. Am chairman of committee. Hurried over to choir practice. Staid long enough to practice male quartet.

May 12. Did not go to class. Worked on Sociology paper all morning. Met again in afternoon. Left at 7:30. Late to Religio. Good session.

May 14. Mother's Day. Sang solo and in male quartet. At Keirs. Went to West Side to Priesthood meeting. Jean and I stayed for Religio. Small crowd.

Read "Aunt Mary" (Riley). Their Religio needs pep. Jean and I had a good visit.

May 17. Stopped off at All University Sing for little while in the evening.

SAINTS' HERALD, May 17, 1922, p. 466, Central Chicago. The auto race which has been in progress for some time, was won by young ladies' senior class; Roy Cheville, teacher.

May 18. Handed in paper on Sabbath and Kindred Institutions. Quarter draws to a close. Very busy.

May 21. At colored mission. Sherman's for dinner. Began practice on "Tale of Hot" in the afternoon. In charge of service at night.

May 22. Wrote examination for correspondence course, Greek 2 in the morning. Studied in afternoon.

May 23,4,5. Classes etc. as usual. Busy days. Received preliminary announcements about graduation as if I were going to be graduated. Hope so.

May 26. Studies etc. Went to Religio early to clean off the back yard.

May 27. Worked on Old Testament paper in morning. In the afternoon I spent some time at the Interscholastic Track Meet. Worked at banquet in the evening. Tired.

May 28. Spoke at church on "Problem of Suffering." At Keir's. Practiced "Tale of Hot." Young People's Meeting and Church.

May 29. Worked in library the usual time. Worked on paper for Old Testament.

May 31. Exam in Social Psychology. Worked as usual. In evening went to Graduating Concert of Columbia School of Music at Orchestra Hall as guest of

Brother Christy. Enjoyed it though long and heavy.

June 1. Spending time on Old Testament paper, hurrying to get it finished. Worked a little while at School of Education luncheon.
June 2. As usual. Good Religio session in evening. Radio program—not much success. Practiced "Tale of Hot."
June 3. Spent most of day copying paper on Old Testament. Tired.
June 4. Went to the Mission to take charge of the Sacrament service. At Keir's for dinner. Practiced "Tale of Hot" in afternoon. Had charge of Music at evening service.
June 5. Finished writing Old Testament paper. Practiced "Tale of Hot" in evening. Ray Hurst was baptized. Confirmed him. Beautiful spirit pervaded. He was brought into the church by reading its literature. Not very well satisfied with operetta.

Ministerial work to June 5. Sermons 7. In Charge 33. Assisted 2. Other activities 81. Total 123.

"Graduation from the University of Chicago, June 1922, with the degree Ph. B., after four quarters of 'heavy schedule.' Continuation in the University of Chicago, in the Divinity School, the summer of 1922. Briggs advised me to stay on for the Master's degree."

APPENDIX F
Chicago Divinity Faculty
1927–1942

The Divinity Faculty during the periods Cheville was in attendance as a doctoral candidate, 1927–1942, were:

Joseph M. Artman, Associate Professor of Religious Education. 1922

Edwin E. Aubrey, Christian Theology and Ethics, 1930–42

Archibald G. Baker, Missions, 1922–41

Fredric Mason Blanchard, Assistant Professor of Public Speaking. 1922

William C. Bower, Religious Education, 1927–42

Raymond A. Bowman, Oriental Languages, 1936–42

Ernest D. Burton, Professor of New Testament Literature and Interpretation. 1922

Shirley Jackson Case, History of Early Christianity, 1927–38, Dean 1933–38

Ernest J. Chave, Religious Education, 1927–42

Ernest C. Colwell, New Testament Literature, 1936–42

Davis Edwards, Public Speaking, 1927–38

Winfred E. Garrison, Church History, 1927–42

Charles W. Gilkey, Preaching, 1927–42

Edgar J. Goodspeed, Biblical and Patristic Greek, 1936–37

William C. Graham, Old Testament Language and Literature, 1936–39

Albert E. Hayden, Comparative Religion, 1936–42

Charles Hartshorne, Philosophy, 1939–42

Charles T. Holman, Pastoral Duties, 1927–42

Arthur E. Holt, Social Ethics, 1927–42

William A. Irwin, Old Testament Literature, 1937–42

John Knox, Preaching, 1939–42

Shailer Mathews, Historical Theology, 1922–33, Dean to 1933

Andrew C. McLaughlin, Church History, 1922–42

John T. McNeill, History of European Christianity, 1927–42

Peter G. Mode, Assistant Professor of Church History. 1922

John W. Moncreif, Christian History, 1922–29

Alonzo K. Parker, Modern Missions, 1922–29

Wilhelm Pauck, Historical Theology, 1939–42

Donald W. Riddle, New Testament, 1936–42

Massey, H. Shepherd, Music, 1937–41

Cecil M. Smith, Music, 1929–41

Gerald B. Smith, Christian Theology, 1922–30

Theodore G. Soares, Religious Education, 1922–31

Matthew Spinka, Church History, 1939–42

Martin Sprengling, Semitic Languages, 1936–39

William W. Sweet, History of American Christianity, 1927–42

Harris R. Vail, Music, 1927–29

Henry N. Wieman, Christian Theology, 1927–42

Harold R. Willoughby, New Testament Literature, 1936–42

John A. Wilson, Egyptology, 1939–42